The decadence and depravity of the ancient
place of serious history, popular novels and
book is concerned not with the question of h
Romans were but why the literature they pro
with immorality. The modern image of imme ......c derives from
ancient accounts which are largely critical rather than celebratory.
Upper-class Romans habitually accused one another of the most lurid
sexual and sumptuary improprieties. Historians and moralists
lamented the vices of their contemporaries and mourned for the virtues
of a vanished age. Far from being empty commonplaces these assertions constituted a powerful discourse through which Romans negotiated conflicts and tensions in their social and political order. This
study proceeds by a detailed examination of a wide range of ancient
texts (all of which are translated) exploring the dynamics of their
rhetoric, as well as the ends to which they were deployed. Roman
moralising discourse, the author suggests, may be seen as especially
concerned with the articulation of anxieties about gender, social status
and political power. Individual chapters focus on adultery, effeminacy, the immorality of the Roman theatre, luxurious buildings and
the dangers of pleasure.

This book should appeal to students and teachers of classical
literature and ancient history. It will also attract anthropologists and
social and cultural historians.

THE POLITICS OF IMMORALITY IN ANCIENT ROME

The Politics of Immorality
in ancient Rome

CATHARINE EDWARDS

Lecturer in Classics and Ancient History
University of Bristol

CAMBRIDGE
UNIVERSITY PRESS

PUBLISHED BY THE PRESS SYNDICATE OF THE UNIVERSITY OF CAMBRIDGE
The Pitt Building, Trumpington Street, Cambridge, United Kingdom

CAMBRIDGE UNIVERSITY PRESS
The Edinburgh Building, Cambridge CB2 2RU, UK
40 West 20th Street, New York NY 10011–4211, USA
477 Williamstown Road, Port Melbourne, VIC 3207, Australia
Ruiz de Alarcón 13, 28014 Madrid, Spain
Dock House, The Waterfront, Cape Town 8001, South Africa

http://www.cambridge.org

First published 1993
First paperback edition 2002

A catalogue record for this book is available from the British Library

Library of Congress Cataloguing in Publication data
Edwards, Catharine.
The politics of immorality in ancient Rome / Catharine Edwards.
p.   cm.
Includes bibliographical references and index.
ISBN 0 521 40083 X
1. Latin literature – History and criticism.   2. Moral conditions
in literature.   3. Politics and literature – Rome.   4. Literature and
society – Rome.   5. Rome – Moral conditions.   6. Ethics in literature.
7. Rome in literature.   8. Sex in literature.   I. Title.
PA6029.M67E38   1993
870.9′353–dc20   92-12933   CIP

ISBN 0 521 40083 X   hardback
ISBN 0 521 89389 5   paperback

For my parents

Contents

Preface

Numerous debts, which it is a pleasure to acknowledge, have been incurred in writing both this book and the Ph.D thesis on which it is largely based. Keith Hopkins supervised the inception and completion of the thesis with his customary incisiveness; if this book can lay any claim to clarity or elegance, it is largely due to him. As part of the Cambridge regime of musical supervisors, Mary Beard and John Henderson, in their different but equally stimulating ways, also directed my research for a time. I am grateful, too, to John Crook, Peter Garnsey, Fergus Millar, Paul Millet and Andrew Wallace-Hadrill for their comments and criticisms. Friends from other disciplines, David Feldman, James Laidlaw and Paul Taylor, in particular, have also been generous with their time and helped me to negotiate a number of theoretical problems. My sister Elisabeth kindly read and commented on a draft as well.

Over the last two years, my colleagues in the Department of Classics and Archaeology at the University of Bristol have provided me with a challenging and supportive environment in which to think and write. Particular thanks go to Denis Feeney, Duncan Kennedy, Charles Martindale and Thomas Wiedemann, who read and commented on draft versions of the book. I cannot claim to have succeeded in answering all the criticisms offered but know I have learnt a great deal from the attempt.

Introduction

In an attack on luxury, Seneca praises the frugality of the elder Cato:

> M. Cato Censorius, quem tam e republica fuit nasci quam Scipionem, alter enim cum hostibus nostris bellum, alter cum moribus gessit . . .
>
> *Marcus Cato the Censor, whose life was of as much benefit to the state as that of Scipio, for while Scipio waged war on our enemies, Cato waged war on our morals . . .*

(Sen. Ep. 87.9)[1]

Romans laid claim to a particular preeminence in the spheres of both fighting and morality. Seneca presents the activities of the guardian of morals as parallel to those of the general; each has made a vital contribution to the *res publica*. As a Stoic, Seneca was committed to the notion that the ties which bind all human beings to one another transcend those which bind the individual to any particular state, and yet for Romans there was only one *res publica*, Rome itself.[2] By using the traditional vocabulary of Roman moralists, by taking as examples the figures of Scipio and Cato, Seneca situated his text in a long line of Roman moralising. Seneca wrote his moral and philosophical works over two hundred years after the time of the elder Cato, who lived in the second century BCE; Cato's writings in turn referred back to the virtues of still earlier Romans, *maiores nostri* ('our ancestors').[3] The highpoint of Roman moral virtue was always already situated in an idealised past.

Just as Scipio waged war on Rome's enemies, hostile peoples who

---

[1] Translations are my own except where otherwise indicated.
[2] Elsewhere Seneca himself refers to the dual allegiance of the Stoic to his or her particular state and also to a commonwealth which includes all gods and all human beings (*De otio* 4). On Stoic cosmopolitanism, see Malcolm Schofield *The Stoic idea of the city* (Cambridge 1991).   [3] E.g. Cato, frags. 18, 58, 144 Malcovati.

(in theory at least) threatened the security of the *res publica*, so Cato fought the enemy within, *moribus [sc. nostris]* ('our morals'), according to Seneca's picture. While Romans fought foreigners on the margins of their empire to determine its physical boundaries, they also attacked their fellow citizens at the empire's centre, in disputes over the bounds of *Romanitas* ('Romanness') itself. As in most civil wars, allegiances in this conflict were unclear, the meanings of words contested. Roman claims to preeminence in defending morality were paradoxical; a crusade against corruption could only be seen as heroic when corruption was a serious threat. If Romans wished to claim distinction in fighting bad morals, they implicitly admitted their own preeminence in immorality.

Conceptions of immorality were central to the way elite Romans (the only ones whose views survive) thought about themselves, both as a people in relation to those who were not Romans and as individuals in relation to the state and to one another. The criticism of immorality was constructed by Romans themselves as a characteristically Roman activity; satire, a kind of poetry particularly concerned with the criticism of immorality, of transgression and excess, was regarded in antiquity as the only literary genre invented by the Romans.[4]

The project of this book is to explore the tradition of moralising which runs through so much of surviving Roman literature. My focus is the culture of the Roman elite from the time of Cicero in the mid first century BCE to the time of Tacitus in the early second century CE, though the figure of the elder Cato (who flourished a century before Cicero) hovers sternly in the background. The moralising tone of much Roman literature was found a source of edification in the nineteenth and early twentieth centuries but has not been so viewed in more recent decades. Scholars now tend to be embarrassed by Roman moralising, which they dismiss as rhetorical and repetitive, a curious accretion to be ignored by those in pursuit of the real matter in Roman texts. I want to argue that moralising rhetoric permeated the habits of thought of those who wrote virtually all the texts which today constitute the principal remains of Roman culture. An appreciation of the dynamics of Roman moralising rhetoric is crucial to any understanding of these texts and their context. The topic is a large one

---

[4] Cf. Quint. *Inst.* 10.1.93–5.

and my discussion does not aim to be comprehensive. This general introductory chapter is intended to set the scene for the particular studies which follow.

The moral prescriptions of Roman writers were for several centuries appropriated by western educationalists in the service of elite socialisation. Future public servants were encouraged to follow the advice dispensed by Cicero and to draw inspiration from the *exempla* set out in Livy's history.[5] The following chapters concentrate on aspects of Roman moralistic discourse which do not so easily lend themselves to elision with current moralities. Thomas Kuhn, referring to the study of Aristotle and other early scientific thinkers, sets out succinctly the hermeneutic advantages of focusing on the alien:

> When reading the works of an important thinker, look first for the apparent absurdities in the text and ask yourself how a sensible person could have written them. When you find an answer . . . when those passages make sense, then you may find that the more central passages, ones you previously thought you understood, have changed their meaning.[6]

The same argument can be applied to the study of cultures. By focusing on and attempting to understand apparently bizarre features of ancient Roman thought, we may find that we have acquired a new and strange perspective on what once seemed a familiar landscape.

DEFINING IMMORALITY

'Immorality' is a term for which there is no close Roman equivalent (though it conveniently suggests a number of the related notions with which this book is concerned). *Mos* (frequently in its plural form,

---

[5] On the role of classical education in elite socialistion, see F.M. Turner *The Greek heritage in Victorian Britain* (New Haven 1981), in particular pp. 8–9 on the elision of Greek concerns with those of nineteenth-century Britain. In nineteenth-century public schools, the study of Latin and Greek regularly occupied ¾ or even ⅘ of the timetable (see Jonathan Gaythorne-Hardy *The public school phenomenon* (London 1977) 137). While in the nineteenth century the literature of ancient Greece was accorded a more prestigious position in universities and grander schools, educationalists and others continued to view the stories told by Livy, for instance, and the moral outlook of Cicero as useful and improving for youthful members of Britain's governing class. Norman Vance of the University of Sussex has kindly drawn my attention to various nineteenth-century school texts which emphasise the morally improving content of Latin literature, such as G.M. Edwards ed. *Horatius and other stories. Adapted from Livy with notes and vocabulary* (London 1875) and E.StJ. Parry *'Origines Romae', or, tales of early Rome . . . for the use of schools* (London 1862).

[6] Thomas S. Kuhn *The essential tension* (Chicago 1977) xii.

3

INTRODUCTION

mores) is often used in Roman texts to designate both customs and morals. When not qualified by *maiorum* ('of our ancestors') it is fairly neutral in its associations; the *mores* against which Seneca represents Cato as crusading are implicitly bad morals. *Mores maiorum*, however, are sanctioned by their antiquity and by their Romanness. Roman texts regularly contrast the alleged constancy of *mores maiorum* with cultural and moral changes, which are thereby characterised as changes for the worse.

Roman categories rarely map straightforwardly onto modern ones. Recent studies have drawn attention to the ways in which the categories of the political and the religious, usually seen as quite separate in modern western culture, overlap in Roman discourses.[7] The political and the moral were also overlapping categories.[8] Issues which for many in the present day might be 'political' or 'economic' were moral ones for Roman writers, in that they linked them to the failure of individuals to control themselves. It was the weakness or perversity of individuals, their lack of self-control, on this view, which caused undesirable events. Problems could be solved only if individuals embraced virtue. Thus what now might be seen as, for instance, political problems were explained in terms of the ambition of individuals, economic ones in terms of their greed.

This 'moral' view of human behaviour has implications which are political in the broad sense of the modern term. The discourses of morality in Rome were profoundly implicated in structures of power. This relationship is one of the principal preoccupations of my book. Attacks on immorality were used by the Roman elite to exercise control over its own members and to justify its privileged position. Roman moral norms can be seen as constituting a 'cultural arbitrary' in the sense in which Pierre Bourdieu uses that term.[9] That is to say, they were norms which were not deduced from any universal principle but which were, to a certain degree, internalised by members of the society which used them. And they were rarely subject to overt challenge, since their arbitrary nature was largely misrecognised.

[7] See Alan Wardman *Religion and statecraft among the Romans* (London 1982), Mary Beard and Michael Crawford *Rome in the late republic* (London 1985) 25–39.
[8] Cf. Donald Earl *The moral and political tradition of Rome* (London 1967) 11–43.
[9] Cf. e.g. Pierre Bourdieu and Jean Claude Passeron *Reproduction in education, society and culture*, tr. Richard Nice (London 1977). On Bourdieu's notion of the 'cultural arbitrary', see John B. Thompson *Studies in the theory of ideology* (Oxford 1984) 57.

4

INTRODUCTION

The vices on which this book concentrates might at first seem a rather disparate collection. The first chapter looks at adultery, the second at *mollitia* (effeminacy), the third at the association of the theatre with both sexual immorality and luxury; the fourth chapter explores Roman attacks on luxurious building, while the final chapter examines the association Romans perceived between prodigality and pleasure. All the vices discussed here can be seen as manifestations of what Roman moralists sometimes termed *incontinentia*, 'self-indulgence', 'lack of self-control' (though they by no means exhaust this category).[10] As will become increasingly clear, Roman moralists did not draw a sharp distinction between sexual immorality, on the one hand, and sumptuary excesses, on the other. Again and again, *licentia* (licentiousness) and *luxuria* (luxury) are associated in narratives of the history of the Roman people and in attacks on particular individuals. The historian Sallust, for instance, speaks of the *luxuria* and *licentia* which began to infect Roman citizens in the time of Sulla (*Cat.* 11–13), while Livy, in the preface to his history, tells of the *luxus* and *libido* (luxury and lust), which new prosperity aroused in previously virtuous Romans (1.*pr.* 12). From among prominent individuals attacked for their *incontinentia*, one might select for special mention Mark Antony (to whom Cicero and other writers attribute an astonishing list of excesses) and the emperor Nero (whose self-indulgence is described in luxuriant detail by Suetonius and Tacitus).

For Romans, luxury and lust were cognate vices; those susceptible to sexual temptation, it was felt, were also prone to indulge to excess their appetites for food, drink and material possessions. Attacks on these vices were articulated in similar terms: the skirmishes between Roman moralists and alleged voluptuaries took place on the conceptual borders between masculine and feminine, public and private, Roman and alien. The parallels between the arguments adduced by Roman moralists regarding different aspects of *incontinentia* allowed these arguments to reinforce one another. The present work, in juxtaposing studies of diverse aspects of Roman immorality, could itself be seen as proceeding by somewhat similar means, though to a rather different end.

---

[10] On *incontinentia* as a rubric in biography and encomium see A. Wallace-Hadrill *Suetonius* (London 1983) 157–8, 171–4.

INTRODUCTION

APPROACHES TO 'IMMORALITY'

The nineteenth century saw the publication of numerous works concerned with the history of morals – an interest which should perhaps be related to eighteenth- and nineteenth-century Protestant attempts to privilege morality over revelation as the essence of Christian religion.[11] William Lecky's work, *A history of European morals from Augustus to Charlemagne* (1869), begins by referring to the 'relative importance that in different ages has been attached to different virtues' – a statement which seems to imply that the essential meaning of a particular virtue, such as chastity (whatever word is used to refer to it), remains constant through the ages, even if it is held in higher esteem at some times than at others. This unwillingness to examine the particularity of moral notions in their historical context has continued to be a feature of modern works concerned with Roman morality. More recently, Donald Earl, Andrew Lintott and others have looked at Roman accounts of decadence with the apparent purpose of plotting the progress of this alleged decline.[12] These studies, while they acknowledge the importance of the moral pre-occupations of Roman writers, concern themselves with the question of whether they were right or wrong, rather than examining their concepts of moral decline. Earl, for instance, observes of Sallust that: 'his basic notion that the failure of the Roman republic was connected with a failure in the ideal of *virtus* was not without merit.'[13]

Those who have studied Roman moralising texts have usually been preoccupied with the real behaviour felt to lie behind them rather than the way the texts themselves are articulated. Luxury and sexual immorality are closely associated in the writings of Roman moralists, as I have emphasised. However, since in modern moral schemes luxury and sexual immorality are not so closely associated, scholars have tended to treat them as separate fields of study. Roman attacks on luxury have been viewed primarily as documents of the extent of

---

[11] Thereby defending Christianity from rationalist attacks on the notion of revelation. See Mary Douglas *Purity and danger* (London 1966) 25–31 for a discussion of the effects of this development on the study of magic and 'primitive' religion in the works of, for instance, Robertson Smith.

[12] For instance, Earl 1967; A.W. Lintott 'Imperial expansion and moral decline in the Roman empire' *Historia* 31 (1972) 626–38. For an earlier example of a study in a similar vein, see Henry W. Litchfield 'National *exempla virtutis* in Roman literature' *HSPh* 25 (1914) 1–71.

[13] Earl 1967: 55

Roman wealth. On the basis of such texts, early modern scholars of ancient Rome represented Roman luxury as both unparalleled and reprehensible.[14] By the late eighteenth century, some took a more favourable view. Although Edward Gibbon traced a connection between the prosperity of the Roman empire and the gradual eclipse of freedom and genius,[15] he also observed: 'Luxury, though it may proceed from vice or folly, seems to be the only means that can correct the unequal distribution of property.'[16] Ludwig Friedländer's *Darstellungen aus der Sittengeschichte Roms* (1862) expresses a liberal approval of the economic effects of 'luxury' quite close to that of Gibbon.[17] He criticises in previous scholars 'the habit of assenting unreservedly to the condemnation by Roman writers of certain forms of luxury, whereas an unprejudiced examination would have shown them innocent and sensible, even welcome symptoms of advance in civilisation and prosperity.'[18] The traditional view of the ancient Romans as immoral and extravagant to an unparalleled degree he attributes to the asceticism of those authors (in particular, Varro, the elder Pliny and the younger Seneca) who are the main authorities for Roman luxury. They were, he argues, mistaken.

Friedländer's magisterial work sets out to discover from Roman discussions of immoral behaviour how Romans actually behaved. So

[14] This is the view taken by e.g. Johannes Meursius' treatise of 1605, *De luxu Romanorum* (The Hague). Similar views are to be found expressed by some scholars of the eighteenth and nineteenth centuries, for instance: C.G. Zumpt *Über den Stand der Bevölkerung und die Volksmehrung in Altertum* (Berlin 1841) 70–5. Friedländer presents this as the orthodoxy against which he argues.

[15] Edward Gibbon *The history of the decline and fall of the Roman empire* (first full octavo edition London 1788). Pages numbers here refer to the edition of J.B. Bury (London 1909).

[16] Gibbon goes on to suggest, however, that luxury became a problem when it led to an imbalance of trade between the Roman empire and other states (1909 I: 59). On Gibbon's attitude to economic questions, see J.G.A. Pocock *Virtue, commerce and history* (Cambridge 1985) 143–56.

[17] Ludwig Friedländer *Darstellungen aus der Sittengeschichte Roms: in der Zeit von Augustus bis zum Ausgang der Antonine* (1st edn. Königsberg 1862, 10th Stuttgart 1964, later editions ed. Georg Wissowa). There is an English translation from the seventh edition: *Roman life and manners under the early empire* tr. J.H. Freese and Leonard A. Magnus (London 1908–28). This unfortunately abridges Friedländer's footnotes. An approach similar to that of Friedländer is adopted by Wilhelm Kroll in his study of the republic, *Die Kultur der Ciceronischen Zeit* (Leipzig 1933).

[18] Friedländer 1964 II: 280 (= II: 141 in Eng. tr.). Cf. 'Luxury in food . . . improved the standard of living and so helped to spread and promote civilisation' (1964 II: 307 = II: 165 in Eng. tr.). As support for his argument, Friedländer points to the greater prosperity and higher degree of civilisation among northern Europeans of his day in comparison with the inhabitants of southern European countries (1964 II: 285 = II: 146 in Eng. tr.).

that his readers may see Roman habits in perspective, he devotes a great deal of space to comparisons between the behaviour of the Roman elite and that of various European aristocracies in more recent centuries, in terms of the absolute value of the goods they purchased. Friedländer concludes that, in most respects, members of the Roman elite were relatively modest in their expenditure on luxury goods, houses and exotic foods.[19] But deciding whether the term 'luxury' can reasonably be applied to the habits of the ancient Romans is not simply a question of measuring their expenditure. Rather than denying Seneca's assertions that it is luxurious to drink before dinner or to keep indoor plants (*Ep.* 122.6, 8), we might consider what lay behind these claims. What did *luxuria* mean for Roman writers?

Friedländer warns his readers against extrapolating from the behaviour attributed to Nero or Caligula the customs of the majority of the Roman elite.[20] However, he assumes, like many other scholars, that Roman accounts of how Nero or Caligula behaved were in themselves accurate (there are good reasons for scepticism here which will be discussed below). More recent scholars have shared Friedländer's preoccupation with the realities of Roman luxury.[21] Recent interest in the ancient economy, for instance, has prompted some scholars to use moralising texts as a means of recovering patterns of trade and consumption in the ancient world.[22] The scholar's common sense is invoked as the test for differentiating 'rhetorical exaggeration' from the 'kernel of truth' which is felt to lurk in, for instance, the elder Pliny's description of Scaurus' temporary theatre building (which will be discussed in chapter four, below).

Roman sexual morality is usually considered quite separately from discussions of luxury. While this was not a subject with which nineteenth-century scholars often concerned themselves (publicly, at any rate), some scholars of the early twentieth century, in line with the concerns of an intellectual world transformed by the work of Freud, produced psychological studies of Roman attitudes to sex, often

---

[19] See 1964 esp. II, ch. 2.   [20] Friedländer 1964 II: 269 (= II: 132 in Eng. tr.)

[21] Though a small number of studies published in the last few years have focused rather on the terms in which luxury was attacked by Roman moralists and the nature of its associations. See, for instance, Jasper Griffin *Latin poets and Roman life* (London 1985) esp. ch. 1; Andrew Wallace-Hadrill 'Pliny the elder and man's unnatural history' *G&R* 37 (1990) 80–96.

[22] Filippo Coarelli, for instance, attempts to work out the cost of pillars from the figures given by the elder Pliny ('Il commercio delle opere d'arte in età tardo repubblicana' *DArch* 1 (1983) 45–53).

suggesting links with the alleged Roman love of cruelty.[23] Over the last decade, the sexual *mores* of the ancient world have become a fashionable subject of study, partly as a result of Michel Foucault's work in this field.[24] Greek sexuality has a particular resonance in the context of Foucault's project[25] and many of these highly sophisticated recent studies have concentrated on ancient Greece.[26] Despite the concern of these studies with attitudes rather than real behaviour in the ancient world, they have offered relatively little exploration of the relationship between discussions of sexual immorality and those concerning other vices, areas which are intimately connected in ancient literature (as I hope to show, with respect to Latin moralising texts). David Halperin, for instance, in his book on homosexuality in ancient Greece, somewhat paradoxically observes that sexuality needs to be decentred from studies of ancient sexual experience, while apparently organising his book around precisely this topic.[27]

RHETORIC AND REALITY

The relationship between moralising and 'social reality' is by no means so straightforward as many of those who have studied Roman moralising texts have implied. This problem is highlighted by the claims sometimes made by Roman poets. A poem of Catullus includes the following assertion:

nam castum esse decet pium poetam
ipsum, versiculos nihil necesse est;

[23] For instance, Otto Kiefer *Kulturgeschichte Roms unter besonderer Berücksichtigung der römischen Sitten* (Berlin 1933). For an illuminating discussion of Hans Licht's study (in a similar vein) of Greek sexual *mores*, see the introduction to D.M. Halperin, J.J. Winkler and F.I. Zeitlin eds. *Before sexuality: the construction of erotic experience in the ancient Greek world* (Princeton 1990).

[24] For a full bibliography on this subject, see chapter two below. The second and third volumes of Foucault's *History of sexuality* are concerned with ancient Greece and the Roman empire respectively: vol. II *The use of pleasure* (London 1986); vol. III *The care of the self* (London 1988).

[25] See the discussion by Mark Poster, 'Foucault and the tyranny of Greece', in David Couzens Hoy ed. *Foucault: a critical reader* (Oxford 1986) 205–20.

[26] There have, however, been a few studies of Roman material, in particular: Paul Veyne 'La famille et l'amour à Rome sous le haut-empire romain' *Annales ESC* 33.1 (1978) (= Paul Veyne *La Société romaine* (Paris 1991) 88–130); 'Homosexuality in ancient Rome' in Philippe Ariès and André Béjin eds. *Western sexuality* (Oxford 1983) 26–35; 'The Roman empire' in Paul Veyne ed. *A history of private life* I (Cambridge, Mass. 1987); Amy Richlin *The garden of Priapus* (New Haven 1983).

[27] D.M. Halperin *One hundred years of homosexuality* (New York 1990) 38.

qui tum denique habent salem ac leporem,
si sunt molliculi et parum pudici.

*For a serious poet should himself be pure but his verses need not be so.
Indeed, they possess wit and charm only when a little soft and not
altogether modest.*

(Cat. 16.5–8)

Catullus appears to contrast the 'immoral' subjects of his poetry with
the purity of his own life.[28] Assertions about the sexual behaviour of
the poet and of others, too, need not be read at face value (though, in
drawing attention to the unreliability of poetic texts, Catullus' poem
at the same time problematises its own status).[29] The sexual content
of epigram (and other genres of Latin literature) can be seen as an
elaborate literary game – a game in which protestations of sexual
purity have their own place.[30]

Such problems do not only apply to the interpretation of poetry.
Rhetorical invective is full of assertions about the immorality, sexual
and sumptuary, of prominent individuals. R.G.M. Nisbet, in his
commentary on Cicero's *In Pisonem*, points out that many of the vices
of which the ex-consul Piso is accused are elsewhere attributed to
Cicero himself. In Cicero's case we are happy to dismiss these lurid
allegations of adultery, gluttony, luxury and avarice as false or
exaggerated. We should be equally suspicious of what Cicero himself
alleges about Piso, argues Nisbet.[31] Neither should we assume that
those who listened to the speeches of Cicero and other Roman orators
were persuaded of the literal truth of the claims they made about their
opponents' behaviour. Such claims functioned as vivid and highly
entertaining assertions about the general character of their victims.
They also served to display the orator's mastery of the traditional
vocabulary of invective.[32] Rhetorical treatises emphasise the importance of *inventio*, 'elaboration', in all branches of the orator's art.[33] In

[28] The association of the term *mollis* will be discussed in detail in chapter two. For similar
protestations see Martial 1.4; 11.15 and Pliny, *Ep.* 4.14.
[29] For the paradoxical nature of the claim, cf. Griffin 1985: 18.
[30] Richlin 1983: 2–13; Duncan Kennedy *The arts of love* (Cambridge 1992).
[31] R.G.M. Nisbet ed. *Cicero In Pisonem* (Oxford 1961) appendix 6. Cf. Richlin 1983: 96–104
and Judith P. Hallett '*Perusinae glandes* and the changing image of Augustus' *AJAH* 2 (1977)
151–71.
[32] Quintilian's discussion of encomium and invective allows the orator a great deal of
imaginative licence (*Inst.* 3.7).
[33] Cf. e.g. *Ad Her.* 1.2; Cic. *De inv.* 1.7.9; Quint. *Inst.* 12.10.36. See too Quint. *Inst.* 2.17.27–9,
justifying the orator's use of fictions in a good cause. Cf. Barton (forthcoming b).

invective, this might manifest itself in the skilful deployment of innuendo (for instance, Cicero's repeated hints about an incestuous relationship between Publius Clodius and his sister)[34] or else in the detailed description of what might be entirely imaginary scenes.[35] Insults exchanged in the courtroom or on the *rostra* are profoundly unreliable as guides to the actual behaviour of their victims. But to claim they were not taken literally is not to say that they were empty or meaningless.[36] This kind of abuse was a major element in the arsenal deployed in the agonistic rituals of Roman political life.

Texts generally classified as 'history' are equally problematic. The assertions they contain about the morals of prominent figures are often, in Amy Richlin's words, a 'fossilised version' of contemporary political invective.[37] Anecdotes (such as those told by Suetonius about Roman emperors) are also untrustworthy as a guide to what really happened – though they can give fascinating insights into what was thought typical of, for instance, a tyrannical emperor. Richard Saller has drawn attention to the suspicious frequency with which similar anecdotes are told about different subjects.[38] Whether these incidents actually happened or not is impossible to ascertain and considerably less important (for the present discussion) than the fact that people told the stories and their reasons for doing so. Such tales were told not to give later historians an accurate picture of patterns of behaviour in ancient Rome but in the service of more urgent ends, to express hostility, contempt, envy, to make sense of the world the teller lived in.

We cannot use these texts, these fragments of a vanished and largely alien world, to reconstruct the behaviour of particular individuals or to explore personal idiosyncrasies. Yet neither can we see them as entirely independent of the material world which produced them. While it is not possible to determine the motives of individual

---

[34] Innuendos concerning Clodius: Cic. *De domo sua* 92, *De har.resp.* 9, 38, *Pro Sestio* 16–17.

[35] Quintilian praises Cicero's skill in describing the extraordinary luxury of Antony's slaves in order to hint at the still greater luxury of their master. 'Cicero could hardly have imagined such luxury in Antony himself' (*Inst.* 8.4.25). Quintilian, interested in the passage as evidence of Cicero's rhetorical skills, takes his exaggeration for granted.

[36] Cf. Jeanne Favret-Saada's anthropological study of accusations of witchcraft in the Bocage in western France (*Deadly words: witchcraft in the Bocage* (Cambridge 1980)). She demonstrates that accusations of witchcraft are part of a complex power game in which no-one ever admits to being a witch. Indeed, it seems no-one in this society believes himself or herself to be a witch. But the accusations are nonetheless heart-felt and serious for all that.

[37] Richlin 1983: 86.

[38] Richard Saller 'Anecdotes as historical evidence for the principate' *G&R* 27 (1980) 69–83.

Romans, even of those about whom we are best informed, such as Cicero or the younger Pliny, we can, I think, speak of the interests of a social group or sub-group. A central premise of my book is that accusations and descriptions of immorality were implicated in defining what it meant to be a member of the Roman elite, in excluding outsiders from this powerful and privileged group and in controlling insiders. This is not an idea which can be derived from any ancient text, but we cannot negotiate a relationship with the past except in terms of our own concepts. The most we can do is to acknowledge the historical specificity of those concepts. If, then, we begin by assuming the politically interested nature of Roman moralistic discourse, what sense can we make of Roman moralising texts? We cannot get any closer to the ancient Romans than to the texts we read; we need to recognise that, for us, these highly rhetorical texts are Roman reality. Rather than trying to see through them, we can choose to look at them – an enterprise which can prove entertaining as well as enlightening.

DEFINING THE ELITE

Roman moralistic discourse, I have suggested, played an important role in defining the Roman elite. Who constituted this elite? Roman social hierarchy might at first sight seem quite clear-cut: senators forming the highest class, the next highest composed of equestrians, with the rest of the citizens beneath them. But how were these classes marked off from one another? And how was relative social status determined within these orders? The following discussion refers to the upper classes of both late republic and principate, indicating where qualifications for membership of the elite were different at different times.

Members of the Roman senate and their families were by and large seen as occupying the highest level of the social hierarchy.[39] Senators held public office, commanded Rome's armies and governed the provinces of the empire. The number of senators at any one time varied between 300 before Sulla (who doubled it to 600, in 81 BCE), rising briefly to 1,200 under Julius Caesar, before settling at around

[39] Though under the principate an individual's membership of the senate became a less crucial determinant of his status, provided his father or grandfather had been a senator. On the structure of the senatorial elite under both republic and principate, see Keith Hopkins *Death and renewal* (Cambridge 1983) 31–200 (with Graham Burton).

600 under Augustus. By the later republic, higher magistrates automatically became senators for life (though they might be expelled by the censors for particularly grievous misdemeanours). Under the republic, such magistrates gained their posts by popular election (the voting assemblies gave disproportionately great influence to the wealthy).[40] From the time of the emperor Tiberius, however, voting assemblies were reduced to rubber-stamping the selection of candidates already determined by the emperor and senate.[41] Wealth was, throughout the period studied here, a prerequisite for election to high office. Under the republic, a senator needed a fortune of at least 400,000 sesterces; the emperor Augustus raised the senatorial census to 1,000,000 sesterces, thereby emphasising the distinction between the two orders. Although many senators came from families with a tradition of membership of the senate, by no means all did. Similarly, a significant number of families failed to maintain representation in the senate over the generations.[42] Thus, although it was clear who was a senator, it was not so clear who would or should attain this prestigious position. Hence, in part, the significance of debates as to the relative importance of wealth, birth and virtue in determining a man's worth.

The equestrians made up the second order of Roman citizens. In the early Roman republic, equestrians were those who formed the cavalry of the Roman army. Later there was still an inner core of 1,800 men who were known as holders of the public horse but the nature of their role remains unclear.[43] Under the principate, equestrians were increasingly to be found in senior administrative posts (for instance, as financial officials or governors of minor provinces).[44] But the equestrian order is rather more difficult to define than the senatorial.[45]

---

[40] On the voting assemblies for higher magistrates, see Claude Nicolet *The world of the citizen in republican Rome* (London 1980) 219–24, 246–67; Lily Ross Taylor *Roman voting assemblies from the Hannibalic war to the time of Caesar* (Ann Arbor 1966) 84–106.

[41] On this procedure and other aspects of the functioning of the senate under the principate, see R.J.A. Talbert *The senate of imperial Rome* (Princeton 1984).

[42] Cf. T.P. Wiseman *New men in the Roman senate, 139 BC–AD 14* (Oxford 1971); P.A. Brunt 'Nobilitas and novitas' *JRS* 72 (1982) 1–17; Hopkins 1983: 39–200.

[43] On this, see P.A. Brunt 'The *equites* in the late republic' in Robin Seager ed. *The Crisis of the Roman republic: studies in political and social history* (Cambridge 1969) 83–115 (= Brunt *The fall of the Roman republic* (Oxford 1988) 144–93) and T.P. Wiseman 'The definition of the *eques Romanus* in the late republic and early empire' *Historia* 19 (1970) 67–83.

[44] On this development see P.A. Brunt '*Princeps and equites*' *JRS* 73 (1983) 42–75.

[45] Emphasised by Peter Garnsey and Richard Saller *The Roman empire, economy, society and culture* (London 1987) 112–14.

There were several thousand men in the Roman empire who could claim to be *equites*. Wealth was a prerequisite for membership of the equestrian order: to qualify, it was necessary to have a fortune of 400,000 sesterces. Under Tiberius, the free birth of one's parents and grandparents also became a necessary qualification (Pliny, *NH* 33.32). But it is not clear whether equestrian status was automatically attained by all who fulfilled these requirements or whether it was acquired by imperial grant.[46]

Some equestrians were far grander than others. On the one hand, the distinction between senators and the most illustrious equestrians was almost entirely a juridical one. Senatorial and equestrian families socialised together, intermarried and shared many political and economic concerns; indeed, many senators came from equestrian families. Other equestrians led rather less glamorous lives, far from the centre of Roman elite society.[47] Similarly not all senators were equal and, in some respects, (particularly under the principate) a non-senator, if he was especially rich, aristocratic or congenial, might enjoy a higher level of social prestige than some senators.[48]

The attainment of high status in Rome depended on a number of factors: ancestry, wealth, achievements and culture. Although these qualifications did not always neatly coincide, they are often to some extent elided in Roman texts. The term *nobilis*, for instance, was ambiguous, suggesting distinguished birth (specifically that one's family had included at least one *consul*)[49] but also preeminence in personal qualities.[50] Nevertheless, a distinctive feature of the social and political elite in Rome in the period covered by this study is that prestigious ancestry played a relatively minor part in determining its structure (by comparison with, for example, aristocracies of early

---

[46] For the former view, see Fergus Millar *The emperor in the Roman world* (London 1977) 280; for the latter, Wiseman 1970.

[47] Cf. Garnsey and Saller 1987: 114. On the wide variation in economic circumstances among equestrians under the republic, see Claude Nicolet *L'Ordre équestre à l'époque républicaine* (Paris 1966) 285–456.

[48] Hopkins emphasises the dangers in seeing political office as the only or even the dominant determinant of social status, especially under the principate (1983: 110). He argues for the existence of different social 'sets' within the senate, contrasting those of humbler background whose status depended heavily on the attainment of high office with those whose status was more a consequence of their family background and social connections (1983: 171–5).

[49] On the technical use of this term, see Brunt 1982.

[50] Cf. Ernest Gellner 'Concepts and society' in *Cause and meaning in the social sciences* (London 1973) 18–46. Gellner explores the ambiguities of an imaginary term 'boble' which closely corresponds to the English term 'noble'.

modern Europe).[51] The elder Seneca puts the following words in an orator's mouth:

quemcumque volueris revolve nobilem: ad humilitatem pervenies.
quid recenseo singulos, cum hanc urbem possim tibi ostendere? nudi
<hi> stetere colles, interque tam effusa moenia nihil est humili casa
nobilius . . . potes obiurgare Romanos quod humilitatem suam cum
obscurare possint ostendunt, et haec non putant magna nisi apparuerit
ex parvis surrexisse?

*Unroll the family tree of any nobleman you like: you will arrive at low
birth if you go back far enough. Why should I list individuals? I could use
the whole city as my example. Once these hills stood bare and within the
extensive confines of our walls there is nothing more distinguished than a
lowly hut [that of Romulus the legendary founder of Rome] . . . Can you
reproach the Romans? They could conceal their humble beginnings but
instead they make a display of them and do not regard all this as great
unless it is made obvious that it rose from a small beginning.*

(Sen. *Contr.* 1.6.4)

The humble origins of both the city and the families of its leading citizens could be seen as a source of pride.[52] In a speech delivered to the Roman senate, Cicero attacked Piso for having secured election to the consulship on the basis of his illustrious family background rather than his personal qualities (*In Pis.* 1). Juvenal's eighth satire is concerned with asserting the unimportance of noble birth in comparison with virtue (8.1–55) (though of course the insistence in these texts on the unimportance of noble birth at the same time suggests that others might view ancestry as an important factor).[53]

But neither noble birth nor virtue was sufficient qualification for high status; a degree of wealth was a prerequisite for membership of the senatorial and equestrian orders, as we have seen, and these minimum requirements were far exceeded by at least some individuals.[54]

---

[51] Cf. Hopkins 1983: 45.
[52] Cf. Sall. *Jug.* 85.17 *ex virtute nobilitas coepit*, 'Nobility has its source in *virtus*.'
[53] Cf. Sall. *Jug.* 85.38–9, where Marius is made to complain of those who have inherited riches and portrait busts (i.e. an illustrious family background) but have no virtue (this is discussed by Earl 1967: 48–53). For other instances and further discussion, see J. Hellegouarc'h *Le Vocabulaire des relations et des partis politiques sous la république* (2nd edn., Paris 1972) 474–83.
[54] See Israel Shatzman on the scale of senatorial fortunes under the republic, *Senatorial wealth and Roman politics* (Brussels 1975). On senatorial wealth under the principate, see Richard Duncan-Jones *The economy of the Roman empire* (2nd edn., Cambridge 1982) 17–32.

As the profits of empire flowed into Rome in the last centuries of the republic, status was increasingly maintained by conspicuous consumption. There was fierce competition for access to wealth (in the form of provincial governorships and army commands).[55] Those who had the opportunity used their wealth to acquire greater power and status. Why should Roman generals be outdone by the grandeur and sophistication of the Hellenistic princes they conquered?

Some members of the elite felt themselves to be relatively poor and wished to play down the importance of wealth as an agent of social distinction.[56] Those who merely had money, moralists asserted, were not qualified to be part of the elite; they had no link with the virtuous past.[57] Attacks on the social pretensions of imperial freedmen focus on their 'misuse' of money. However rich the imaginary freedman Trimalchio became, he could never be more than a parody of a real Roman noble.[58] Moralising may be seen as, in part, a strategy for controlling the spending of the rich. For upper-class Romans, wealth was an ambiguous criterion – useful for distinguishing between the elite and the rest of society, but dangerous if invoked to underpin distinctions within the elite. The satirist Juvenal relentlessly attacked his contemporaries' obsession with wealth. He represents himself as wishing only for a modest sufficiency, 400,000 sesterces – just enough to qualify for equestrian status (14.323).

Thus, although the term 'elite' will recur throughout this study, it must be understood as a category whose definition was subject to constant renegotiation, a process in which moralising rhetoric was intimately concerned. Social status depended not only on satisfying relatively objective criteria, such as census requirements, but, more importantly, on securing the recognition of one's peers and superiors (and to a lesser extent, those of lower social status). Roman moralising

---

[55] On the increased competition of the late republic, see Keith Hopkins *Conquerors and slaves* (Cambridge 1978) 25–56.

[56] Cf. David Daube's discussion of the function of the sumptuary legislation of the second century BCE which he suggests was aimed at 'the protection of the non-tipper' (*Aspects of Roman law* (Edinburgh 1969) 117–28). On sumptuary laws, see also Ingo Sauerwein *Die leges sumptuariae als römische Massnahme gegen den Sittenverfall* (Hamburg 1970); Ernst Baltrusch *Regimen morum: die Reglementierung des Privatlebens der Senatoren und Ritter in der römischen Republik und frühen Kaiserzeit* (Munich 1989) 40–131; G. Clemente 'Le leggi sul lusso e la società romana tra III e II secolo AC' in Andrea Giardina and Aldo Schiavone eds. *Società romana e produzione schiavistica* III (Rome 1981) 1–14.

[57] A slave in one of Plautus' plays is mocked for appealing to *mores maiorum*. A slave had no ancestors (*Trin.* 1028–32).

[58] On Petronius' depiction of Trimalchio, see Paul Veyne 'La vie de Trimalchion' *Annales ESC* 16.1 (1961) 213–47 (= Veyne 1991: 13–56).

texts are concerned with the recommendation of codes of behaviour appropriate to educated, freeborn, wealthy, male Roman citizens. These codes of behaviour were heavily implicated in marking off the elite from the rest of society, as well as in structuring relationships within the elite. Moralising writing in Rome was a weapon in a continuing battle over how the elite was to be defined.

MORALISTS AND THEIR AUDIENCE

It is perhaps not surprising, then, that the moralising literature which will be examined in this book was in general produced by writers whose claims to being authentic members of the Roman elite might be in some way open to question. The elder Cato, the archetypal Roman moralist, was a 'new man', the first in his family to become a senator.[59] Cicero, too, was the first man in his family to reach the senate.[60] As in the case of Cato, his family was not Roman but Italian.[61] The poet Horace was the son of a freedman. The Senecas, father and son, originally came from Spain.[62] The Plinys, uncle and nephew, came from Comum in a region of Italy (Transpadane Gaul) that had only become fully Roman under Julius Caesar.[63] The family of Tacitus, it seems, came from Gaul.[64] These men were not part of the old Roman aristocracy. They did not even come from Rome and yet they, above all, have come to be seen as the voices of Rome.

Voice may not have counted for everything (and we perhaps overvalue the role of words, since these have survived better than much of the rest of the ancient Roman world); in certain contexts, ancestry or wealth may have been more eloquent. But these voices were listened to. Whom did they persuade in their insistence on the supremacy of *virtus*? While it was mainly the rich who bought these texts (and in some cases commissioned them),[65] we can conjecture that some of

[59] On the origins of the elder Cato, see A.E. Astin *Cato the censor* (Oxford 1978) 1–10.

[60] On Cicero's background, see E. Rawson *Cicero, a portrait* (London 1975) 1–28.

[61] On the Italian rather than Roman origin of many authors in the late republic, see T.P. Wiseman 'Domi nobiles and the Roman cultural elite' in *Les 'bourgeoisies' municipales italiennes aux IIe et Ier siècles av. J.C.* (Naples 1983) 299–307.

[62] See M. Griffin *Seneca: a philosopher in politics* (Oxford 1976) 29–34.

[63] Ronald Syme *Tacitus* (Oxford 1958) 60, 75–85.

[64] See Syme 1958: 59–74, 611–24.

[65] On literary patronage, see Barbara Gold *Literary patronage in Greece and Rome* (Chapel Hill 1987). While Roman elite women were, it seems, sometimes well-educated and, to a certain degree, financially independent, there are very few examples of female literary patrons (for a possible exception, see R.G.M. Nisbet '*Felicitas* at Surrentum (Statius *Silvae* 2.2)' *JRS* 68 (1978) 1–11).

them at least were attended to by a wider audience. Before the reign of the emperor Tiberius, the public speeches of politicians aimed to persuade all potential voters, for the votes even of the poorest might prove crucial. But it is impossible to gauge what value poorer Romans may have placed on displays of impeccable morals, as compared with military successes, for instance, or the liberal provision of games.[66]

Some writers were more ambivalent in their use of Roman moralistic traditions. Petronius, for instance, in the *Satyricon*, puts moralising speeches into the mouths of low characters, drawing attention to their incongruity.[67] A passage from Ovid's *Ars amatoria* (an appropriation of the usually respectable didactic genre for the art of love) rejects the more rugged ideals attributed to the Romans of earlier days and admired by some of Ovid's contemporaries, in favour of the sophistication of his own time:

> prisca iuvent alios: ego me nunc denique natum
> gratulor; haec aetas moribus apta meis.
> non quia nunc terrae lentum subducitur aurum,
> lectaque diverso litore concha venit:
> nec quia decrescunt effosso marmore montes,
> nec quia caeruleae mole fugantur aquae:
> sed quia cultus adest, nec nostros mansit in annos
> rusticitas, priscis illa superstes avis.

Let ancient times delight others: I am glad I was not born till now; this age suits my mores *well. Not because stubborn gold is now drawn from out of the earth, and pearls come gathered from far-flung shores, nor because mountains shrink as the marble is dug from them, nor because masonry puts to flight the dark blue waters; but because we have culture, and rusticity, though it survived until our grandfathers, has not lasted to our days.*

(Ovid, *Ars.* 3.121–8)

The details of attacks on luxury of the kind parodied here will be examined more closely in chapter four, below. But for the time being

---

[66] Inscriptions and graffiti perhaps give us the views of somewhat less privileged groups than the wealthy Romans on whom my study focuses. However, there do not seem to be marked differences between the sorts of insults found here and those recorded in literary texts such as Suetonius' lives. On moralising graffiti, see Richlin 1983: 81–3; Paul Veyne 'Le folklore à Rome et les droits de la conscience publique sur la conduite individuelle' *Latomus* 42 (1983) 3–30 (= Veyne 1991: 57–87).

[67] E.g. Pet. *Sat.* 55 where Trimalchio quotes part of a poem which includes numerous topoi of moralising rhetoric. Cf. too the attack on decadence put in the mouth of the debauched philosopher Eumolpus (88).

INTRODUCTION

we should note in particular Ovid's appropriation of the term *mores* ('morals'), here qualified not by the term *antiqui* ('ancient') – indeed Ovid explicitly distances himself from the coarseness of ancestral custom – but by the term *mei* ('mine'). The seductive power of Ovid's text derives at least in part from his subversion of the vocabulary of traditional Roman moralising. Some Romans, in some contexts, were ready to mock the moralist's gravity. Yet that too is an indication of the central place of moralising in Roman culture.

THE INFINITE CITY

The city of Rome was a crucial reference point for Roman moralists. Its physical aspect was an ever-present, concrete reminder of past generations of Romans. Much of the discourse of Roman moralising is articulated in terms of the relationship between the present and the past. The elder Seneca (in a passage quoted above) drew a parallel between Romans' attitude to the physical traces of their past (in the form of the alleged hut of Romulus, the founder of Rome) and the attitude they should adopt to the humble origins of now illustrious families. The monuments of the city, the organisation of space within it, had strong moral resonances (some of which will be explored in chapters three and four, below). In particular, the emperor Augustus' remodelling of the monumental centre of Rome had moral as well as political significance.[68]

But Rome could not be unproblematically identified with the city itself. For the Roman state had exceeded its bounds. Ovid writes:

> gentibus est aliis tellus data limite certo:
> Romanae spatium est urbis et orbis idem.

> *Other nations have fixed boundaries to their lands; the limits of our city are the limits of the world.*

(Ovid, *Fasti* 2.683–4)

This was an uncomfortable paradox (though perhaps not so paradoxical after all for the poet who finished this poem on the rough edge of

---

[68] Paul Zanker's magisterial work has established the vital importance of monuments to the foundation of the principate (*The power of images in the age of Augustus* (Ann Arbor 1988)). On the Augustan transformation of the way space was conceptualised in Rome, see Claude Nicolet *Space, geography and politics in the early Roman empire* (Ann Arbor 1991).

Roman territory, to which he had been exiled by Augustus). A state that shared its boundaries with those of the entire world effectively had none. The city was full of people whose families had not long lived in Rome; Roman citizens dwelt all over the known world. To be Roman no longer meant to be an inhabitant of the city of Rome. What then could it mean?

ROMAN VIRTUE

Moribus antiquis res stat Romana virisque, 'The Roman state is built on ancient *mores* and on men'. Cicero opens the fifth book of his treatise on the ideal state (*De republica*) with this quotation from Ennius, whose epic poem, the first to be written in Latin, was composed in the early second century BCE.[69] This line of verse, plainly a resonant one for Cicero's purposes, is made up of a conjunction of value-laden terms which together could be seen as summing up the preoccupations which are the subject of this book. *Viris*, 'men' (a term which, unlike *homines*, never includes women but rather distinguishes male from female) is cognate with the word *virtus*.[70] *Virtus*, which may be translated as 'virtue', 'courage' or 'manliness', is a term heavy with moral significance for Roman writers. Roman men and ancient Roman custom, *mores* ('morals' or 'customs'), are presented as together forming the foundations of the *res Romana* ('the Roman state', or perhaps 'Romanness'). Morality and manliness are constructed here as the distinguishing features of Rome.

Many Roman authors represented Roman national identity in terms of the moral superiority of Romans in comparison with other peoples.[71] The elder Pliny (writing in the mid first century CE) observes:

> gentium in toto orbe praestantissima una omnium virtute haud dubie Romana exstitit. felicitas cui praecipua fuerit homini non est humani iudicii, cum prosperitatem ipsam alius alio modo et suopte ingenio quisque determinet.

---

[69] Ennius, *Annales* 156 Skutsch (= 500 Vahlen). The line is extensively discussed by O. Skutsch in his commentary on Ennius' *Annals*.

[70] Roman texts regularly play on the etymological link between *vir* and *virtus*; thus emphasising the conceptual association (e.g. Cic. *Pro Sest.* 93; Virgil, *Aen.* 1.566–7). For a comprehensive collection of Roman discussions of *virtus*, see Werner Eisenhut *Virtus Romana: ihre Stellung im römischen Wertsystem* (Munich 1973). [71] See Earl 1967: 36–9.

INTRODUCTION

Of all the peoples in the world, the Roman nation is unquestionably the one most outstanding in virtue. Mankind is not fit to judge what human being has had the greatest happiness, since different people define prosperity in different ways and each according to his own character.

(Pliny, NH 7.130)

For Pliny, the definition of happiness is open to interpretation – but not the definition of *virtus*. The conviction that one's own race is morally superior is hardly a rare one – particularly not among nations who rule empires. But Roman historians and moralists seem unusually preoccupied with Roman virtue. Livy's history begins with the observation that:

> nulla umquam res publica nec maior nec sanctior nec bonis exemplis ditior, nec in quam civitatem tam serae avaritia luxuriaque inmigraverint, nec ubi tantus ac tam diu paupertati ac parsimoniae honos fuerit.

> *No country has ever been greater or purer than our own, or better endowed with noble precedents. Nor has any country managed for so long to keep itself free from avarice and luxury. Nowhere has the simple life of frugality been held in such honour until recently.*

(Livy 1 pr. 11)

Other authors too emphasise Roman preeminence in *virtus*.[72] Roman moral superiority was a guarantee of the divine favour which assured Roman military successes.[73] This was the basis on which the empire was built.

Roman expositions of virtuous behaviour do not differ very substantially from Greek.[74] But the Platonic canon of virtues – courage, wisdom, justice, temperance – is only exceptionally set up as an ideal in Roman texts. Roman authors generally refer to figures from the mythologised past of their own city as models for behaviour rather than to the theoretical writings of Greek philosophers.[75] Idealised

---

[72] E.g. Nepos, *Han.* 1.1.

[73] Cf. e.g. Hor. *Carm.* 3.6. For the connection Romans constructed between divine favour and military success, see Nathan S. Rosenstein '*Imperatores victi': military defeat and aristocratic competition in the middle and late republic* (Berkeley 1990) 54–91.

[74] Theoretical expositions of virtue were in many cases heavily influenced by earlier Greek writings. See Eisenhut on the difference between the uses of *virtus* in Cicero's speeches and in his philosophical works (1973: 57–76).

[75] Quintilian contrasts the Greek practice of looking to *praecepta*, 'precepts' for instruction with the Roman reliance on *exempla*, 'examples' or 'precedents' (*Inst.* 12.2.29–30). Cf. Val. Max. 2.1.10. On the Roman practice of making collections of *exempla*, often for use by orators, see G. Maslakov 'Valerius Maximus and Roman historiography: a study in the *exempla* tradition' *ANRW* II 32.1 (Berlin 1984) 437–96.

INTRODUCTION

Roman forefathers gave authority to the moral precepts enjoined on their descendents. Indeed, philosophical theory could be seen as a hindrance rather than a help: Cicero observes in the *Pro Caelio*, that, although the Greeks achieved honour and brilliance in their speech and writing, they fell short of this in their actions – unlike the Romans (40–1).[76] The picture became more complicated as many Romans (including Cicero himself) immersed themselves in the writings of Greek philosophers, such as the Stoics Chrysippus and Posidonius, yet even in the works of the Roman Stoic Seneca, as we have seen, Cato and Scipio might be set up as models for the behaviour of later Romans.

HELLENISATION

Contact with Greece was seen by Roman moralists as a factor of particular importance in the changes which characterised Roman culture in the later republic.[77] Rome had always been subject to Greek influences.[78] But in the last two centuries BCE, as Roman military expansion brought individual Romans into more frequent and intense contact with the cultures of the eastern Mediterranean, the place of Greek and Asiatic goods and practices in Roman life seems to have acquired a new importance, as Romans came to entertain more extensive cultural ambitions, ambitions which they now had the resources to pursue.[79] At the same time, the influence of eastern cultures on Roman life became the object of new anxieties.[80]

The physical aspect of Rome bore witness to the depth of penetration of Greek culture.[81] Wealthy Romans became collectors of

---

[76] Cf. Cic. *De orat.* 3.56–7.

[77] The Hellenisation of Rome has been the subject of several recent studies. Some of the nuances of the problem are set out by Clara Gallini 'Che cosa intendere per ellenizzazione' *DArch* 7.2–3 (1973) 175–91. See too E.S. Gruen *Studies in Greek culture and Roman policy* (Leiden 1990).   [78] See Arnaldo Momigliano *CAH* VII (1989) 52–112.

[79] On this development, see Beard and Crawford 1985: 12–24. See also Alan Wardman *Rome's debt to Greece* (London 1976).

[80] T.P. Wiseman stresses Greek influences even in the earliest phases of Rome's development but suggests Romans themselves were not as preoccupied with the polarity between Roman and Greek as they were later to become ('Roman legend and oral tradition' *JRS* (1989) 129–37). Already in the plays of Plautus (the earliest substantial pieces of Roman literature to survive) the contrast between the Greek and the Roman carries a moral significance (on this see Erich Segal *Roman laughter* (2nd edn., Oxford 1987) 42–69).

[81] On the impact of Greek architectural styles, see Pierre Gros 'Les premières générations d'architectes hellénistiques à Rome' in *Mélanges Huergon* (Rome 1976) 387–410; Paul Zanker ed. *Hellenismus in Mittelitalien* (Göttingen 1975).

Greek works of art.[82] No Roman could claim to be educated unless he was at least passingly familiar with Greek literature (or so at least claimed the literary elite whose works we now read).[83] The elite marked themselves off from the rest of society in part by their education and manners. Greece was associated with sophistication and philosophy.[84] But for Romans these associations aroused feelings of cultural inferiority which did not arise when they came into contact with 'barbarians'.[85] The elder Cato was indignant that Greeks called the Romans themselves *barbari* (Pliny, *NH* 29.14).

Members of the Roman elite had to be cultured – but not too cultured. Tacitus' military hero Agricola was tempted by philosophy in his youth but did not altogether succumb to its charms (*Agr.* 4).[86] Tacitus praises him for taking the right course. Romans represented themselves as a morally superior people who, unlike the Greeks, had a sense of proportion when it came to dealing with that dangerous commodity, culture.[87] A life devoted to literature and contemplation was often elided with a life devoted to pleasure.[88] Neither was appropriate for an honourable Roman who should view his duties to the state as paramount.

Some elite Romans were far more Hellenised than others (though even the elder Cato was, it seems, familiar with the language and literature of Greece – indeed how else could he have recognised the Hellenising excesses of his contemporaries?)[89] This was another arena in which members of the Roman elite strove to outdo one another, but lack of aptitude or interest, as well as a sense of duty, might limit a wealthy Roman's familiarity with Greek culture –

[82] See J.J. Pollitt *The art of Rome* (Englewood Cliffs, New Jersey 1966).

[83] On the Hellenisation of Roman education and literary culture, see Elizabeth Rawson *Intellectual life in the late republic* (London 1985).

[84] In the later republic, it became fairly common for wealthy young men to spend some years in Athens or other intellectual centres of the Greek world to complete their formal education. On this, see L.W. Daly 'Roman study abroad' *AJPh* 71 (1950) 40–58; Rawson 1985a: 3–18.

[85] On Roman attitudes to the Greeks and other peoples, see A.N. Sherwin-White *Racial prejudice in imperial Rome* (Cambridge 1967); Nicholas Petrochilos *Roman attitudes to the Greeks* (Athens 1974); J.P.V.D. Balsdon *Romans and aliens* (London 1979).

[86] On Roman attitudes to philosophy, see Miriam Griffin 'Philosophy, politics and politicians at Rome' in Jonathan Barnes and Miriam Griffin eds. *Philosophia togata* (Oxford 1989) 1–37.

[87] Cf. Cic. *De rep.* 1.30. Sallust contrasts Greek literary achievements with Roman deeds (*Cat.* 8.5).

[88] Cf. e.g. Tac. *Hist.* 4.5. On this elision see J.-M. André *L'otium dans la vie morale et intellectuelle* (Paris 1966). Brian Vickers' discussion of attitudes to leisure in the Renaissance includes extensive treatment of some Roman texts, 'Leisure and idleness in the Renaissance: the ambivalence of *otium*' Part I *Renaissance Studies* 4.1 (1990) 1–37.

[89] On this see Astin 1978: 157–81.

hence, in part, the concern felt by some to depreciate Hellenic sophistication.[90] We could see conflicts over acceptable degrees of Hellenisation as parallel to conflicts over acceptable levels of spending. Just as some Romans sought to play down the importance of their rivals' economic capital, others were concerned to devalue the 'cultural capital' enjoyed by some among their peers.[91]

MORALITY AND POLITICS

A striking feature of Roman discussions of immoral behaviour (and one not generally remarked on by modern historians) is that they are concerned overwhelmingly with the behaviour of the upper classes. Roman moralists of the late republic and early principate seem to have found the vices of the poor uninteresting. The urban poor of their own day they considered naturally lacking in virtue.[92] This is an oversimplification, of course, but even Juvenal's criticism of the *plebs* for being obsessed with bread and circuses implies that their social betters were to blame (10.77–81). The elite had the duty of setting the rest of society an example.[93] It was their behaviour that mattered.

Roman preoccupations with the morality of the elite form a marked contrast with later European discussions of immorality. In the eighteenth century, for instance, according to John Sekora's study of the term 'luxury', this word was used to describe the excesses particularly of poorer sections of society.[94] Some nineteenth-century scholars claimed that 'immorality' in Rome spread upwards from 'oriental' slaves.[95] That claim is not made by any Roman writer (though Juvenal and others object to the upward mobility of those of servile origins). This contrast should be related to the different ends

---

[90] Beard and Crawford stress the role of the Roman elite ethos of competition in the Hellenisation of Roman culture in the late republic (1985: 14).

[91] The term 'cultural capital' is taken from the work of Pierre Bourdieu. Cf. in particular *Distinction: a social critique of the judgement of taste* (London 1984).

[92] The rural poor, however, especially if associated with the mythologised past, could be seen as especially virtuous. On representations of the poor in ancient Rome, see C.R. Whittaker 'Il povero' in Andrea Giardina ed. *L'uomo romano* (Rome 1989) 299–333.

[93] Cf. e.g. Cic. *De leg.* 3.30–1.

[94] John Sekora *Luxury: the concept in western thought from Eden to Smollet* (London 1977). Henry Fielding, for instance, in an essay published in 1751 on the reasons for what was perceived to have been an increase in the rate of robberies, sees as partly responsible 'the vast torrent of Luxury which of late years has poured itself into this Nation'. This has, he suggests, 'almost totally changed the manners, customs and habits of the people, especially of the lower sort' (Sekora 1977: 5).   [95] See e.g. Lecky 1869: 263.

to which conceptions of immorality are deployed in different cultures. Later European elites might be seen as using accusations of immoral behaviour primarily to emphasise the difference between themselves and those they exploited. What ends did Roman moralising serve?

In a sense, the rhetoric of moralising did play a key role in marking off the Roman elite (or at least male members of the elite) from the rest of society. The elite justified their privileged position by pointing to their superior morals. Their capacity for self-control legitimated the control they exercised over others who were, it was implied, unable to control themselves. Augustus' defeated rival, Mark Antony, was accused of the worst excesses of luxury:

> ... Antonium triumvirum aureis usum vasis in omnibus obscenis desideriis, pudendo crimine etiam Cleopatrae. summa apud exteros licentiae fuerat ... Antonius solus contumelia naturae vilitatem auro fecit.

> *The triumvir Antony used golden vessels in satisfying all his baser needs, an outrage even Cleopatra would have been ashamed of. Till then, foreigners had held the record in extravagance ... but Antony alone insulted nature by staining gold in this manner.*

> (Pliny, *NH* 33.50)

Pliny emphasises the enormity of Antony's behaviour by stressing that his luxury outdid the proverbial extravagance of women and eastern tyrants. Such behaviour was marked as undesirable by its association with the feminine and the foreign.

These associations of vice with the 'other' implicitly justify the dominant position of elite male Romans. Yet most of the accusations of immorality examined here were aimed not at women, slaves or foreigners but at precisely those who claimed to be honourable Roman men. Cicero accuses his opponents of a wide range of vices which appear to bear little relation to the question ostensibly at issue in a particular dispute. Similar exchanges of insults also seem to have been typical of propaganda campaigns Roman political leaders conducted through issuing edicts. During the period between the assassination of Caesar and the battle of Actium, Antony and Octavian relentlessly accused one another of adultery, bribery and luxury, in their struggles for preeminence in Rome.[96] Those who could not govern themselves, whose desires were uncontrollable, such accusations implied, were not fit to control the state. The *Institutio oratoria* of Quintilian suggests that the practice of impugning one's opponents for alleged sexual and sumptuary excesses continued under the principate.

Scholars have tended to see the frequency of accusations of immoral behaviour in ancient Rome as one of the 'faits autonomes' of a society (in the words of Veyne) which have no necessary relation with other social practices.[97] Accusations of immoral behaviour, it is often implied, were not really taken seriously by Romans.[98] Cicero writes of the hypocrisy of Appius, when the latter, as censor, concerned himself with the sexual misbehaviour and luxurious possessions of his fellow senators (*Ad fam.* 97).[99] This kind of assertion is often seen as evidence that all Roman moralising was hypocritical.[100] But Cicero's claim should not be taken as an indication that morality was not a real issue in disputes between members of the Roman elite. Leading Romans habitually accused one another of luxury and sexual immorality and were in turn accused of hypocrisy. Accusations of immorality were a fundamental part of the political vocabulary of the elite in ancient Rome. We cannot separate the substance, the 'real' issues, of the disputes from the language through which they were articulated.

Just as a man might boast of his wealth, his military achievements or his ancestry in his attempts to secure power and influence, so too he might parade his moral rectitude as a form of 'symbolic capital'.[101] On a more general level, moralising was a strategy for controlling individuals within the elite and preventing them from pursuing their own ends to the detriment of others within their class. But this picture is in some ways an oversimplification. Roman moral norms could

---

[96] For discussions of the use of moralising invective in political disputes, see Kenneth Scott 'The political propaganda of 44–33 BC' *MAAR* 11 (1933) 7–49; Ronald Syme *The Roman revolution* (Oxford 1939) 149–61; Hallett 1977; Richlin 1983: 81–104.

[97] Veyne 1983. Some scholars have treated Roman invective as rather more significant (in particular Richlin 1983).

[98] Though cf. Hallett and Richlin cited in note 96 and also Earl 1967: 37.

[99] All references to Cicero's letters use Shackleton-Bailey's numbering.

[100] Cf. Baltrusch who suggests that censors often acted from personal or political motives (1989: 13. See too Baltrusch's comments on the punishment of Saturninus, 1989: 18). Even if this is true, it is still significant that such conflicts were articulated in moral terms.

[101] For the notion of symbolic capital, see Bourdieu 1984: 291.

yield apparently contradictory evaluations of some types of behaviour. Leading men of the republic were among those most often characterised as outstanding for their 'immorality'. The attempt to control such individuals by castigating their vices at the same time created an association between immorality and power. This paradox will be explored further in later chapters.

The parading of moral norms and assertions of their transgression were strategies frequently adopted by members of the late republican elite, strategies which continued to be used, to some extent, by the upper classes under the principate. Yet the political structures, in which debates about morality were so closely intertwined, were transformed by the advent of autocracy. Under the principate, the position of aristocrats was subject to new dangers. It would be misleading to suggest that the elite in the last fifty years of the republic always felt secure. But while the proscriptions of the dictator Sulla or the triumvirs were temporary, if traumatic, the emperor's position came to be seen as permanent and institutionalised. Politics shifted from the forum and senate to the Palatine.[102]

Gradually the emperor withdrew from the sort of competitive accusations of immorality which had characterised political disputes under the republic. Until around 23 BCE, Augustus continued to produce attacks on his opponents' morals and defences of his own in the republican vein. Thereafter, further justification of his earlier career perhaps seemed unnecessary, even counter-productive.[103] But Augustus did not ignore those who criticised him. Occasionally (but conspicuously) he had vituperative pamphlets destroyed. Cassius Severus' works were publicly burned, their author exiled. Augustus was the first to prosecute libel under the treason law, according to Tacitus (*Ann.* 1.72). He had more effective means than had republican political leaders of dealing with his accusers.[104]

The luxury and vice of emperors were nonetheless a potent topic in

---

[102] On the changing relationship between emperor and senate, see Millar 1977: 275–8, 341–55; Talbert 1984: 163–84, 488–91.

[103] Zwi Yavetz 'The *Res gestae* and Augustus' public image' in Fergus Millar and Erich Segal eds. *Caesar Augustus: seven aspects* (Oxford 1984) 1–36.

[104] Cf. Yavetz 1984: 4–5. Syme drew attention to the (albeit sporadic) severity of some the controls imposed by the Augustan regime (1939: 459–75). Denis Feeney suggests that while some *licentia* was allowed those who wished to speak out against the *princeps*, its limits were never clear ('*Si licet et fas est*: Ovid's *Fasti* and the problem of free speech under the principate' in Anton Powell ed. *Roman poetry and propaganda in the age of Augustus* (Bristol 1992)).

the literature of the principate, though the focus tended to be on the vices of those who were safely dead. The reigning emperor might be criticised by implication but would perhaps have been unwilling to acknowledge he saw something of himself in lurid descriptions of his predecessors.[105] These stories have often been dismissed as trivia, evidence of the frivolity of authors such as the biographer Suetonius.[106] But the attribution of sexual and sumptuary excesses to emperors had particular political connotations. *Incontinentia* was traditionally associated with tyranny.[107] Yet some emperors may have exploited this association, emphasising their absolute power precisely through publicising stories of their sexual and sumptuary excesses.

Modern historians of the ancient world have generally adopted the view expressed by Tacitus, that the luxury and vice of the Roman upper classes reached a peak under Nero before becoming unfashionable under the Flavians (*Ann.* 3.55).[108] The emperor's example may indeed have influenced court fashions. And later rulers were perhaps unwilling to follow in the extravagant footsteps of Caligula or Nero, whose immense unpopularity among the upper classes led to their deaths. But we should remember that most of the literary sources for the earlier period of the first century CE were written under Trajan and Hadrian. It was as well to make the contrast with the present regime explicit. Tacitus' remarks on the new asceticism of the Roman elite should be read with as much caution as his descriptions of earlier excesses. Yet his discussion of the effects of the example set by Vespasian suggests the ideological capital which might still be derived from using 'traditional' means to make Romans virtuous. Complimenting an emperor for setting a good example to his subjects rather than giving them orders was a commonplace of imperial eulogy.[109] Morality was still one of the most important spheres for the representation and negotiation of power relations.

---

[105] Cf. Frederick Ahl 'The art of safe criticism in Greece and Rome' *AJPh* 105 (1984) 174–208.

[106] For a discussion of the vices of the emperor Nero in the context of Greco-Roman traditions of invective, see Tamsyn Barton 'The *inventio* of Nero: Suetonius' (forthcoming).

[107] For the traditional association of luxury with tyrants, see Aristotle, *Pol.* 1314b30; Polybius 6.7.5–8. On literary representations of tyrants, see J.R. Dunkle 'The rhetorical tyrant in Roman historiography: Sallust, Livy and Tacitus' *CW* 65 (1971) 171–4; N.R.E. Fisher 'Hybris and dishonour' *G&R* 23 (1976) 177–93. For a discussion of allegations concerning the vices of emperors, see Wallace-Hadrill 1983: 157–8, 171–4.

[108] E.g. Friedländer 1964 II:284–5 (= Eng. tr. II 145).

[109] Cf. Vell. Pat. 2.126.4; Pliny, *Paneg.* 45–6.

INTRODUCTION

FAMILY, STATE AND MORAL REGULATION

Foucault provides a definition of morality in the second volume of his *History of sexuality*:

> By 'morality' one means a set of values and rules of action that are recommended to individuals through the intermediary of various prescriptive agencies such as the family (in one of its roles), educational institutions, churches and so forth ... With ... qualifications taken into account, we can call this prescriptive ensemble a 'moral code'. But 'morality' also refers to the real behaviour of individuals in relation to the rules and manners that are recommended to them: the word thus designates the manner in which they comply more or less fully with a standard of conduct, the manner in which they obey or resist an interdiction or prescription; the manner in which they obey or disregard a set of values.[110]

Foucault's distinction between prescription and behaviour is in some ways a useful one, but prescription, too, is a process, an aspect of behaviour. His use of the passive 'are recommended' obscures the origin of the 'set of rules and values' which constitute a moral code. The roles of particular individuals or groups in formulating prescriptions, in recommending rules, are highly significant.

Earlier, I stressed the frequency with which Roman moralists appealed to the examples set by earlier generations of Romans. Even among the living, moral authority was closely associated with age. The eldest male ascendant in the family, the *paterfamilias*, was held to be the source of moral authority within the household. The *paterfamilias* was entitled to impose grave sanctions on family members in his legal power, though he might be expected to take the advice of friends and relatives.[111] Paternal authority was used as a model for the authority of magistrates within the state (the senate could be addressed collectively as *patres*) and, later, for the authority of the emperor. Augustus was granted the title *pater patriae* ('father of the fatherland') in 2 BCE.[112]

---

[110] Foucault 1986: 25.

[111] On the family *consilium* as a model for the informal body which advised the emperor, see J.A. Crook *Consilium principis* (Cambridge 1955) 4–7. For examples of such bodies in action see Liebenam *RE* IV: 915–22, s.v. 'consilium'.

[112] Cf. Augustus, *Res gestae* 35. Cicero is said to have been granted this title unofficially after the suppression of the Catilinarian conspiracy (Dio 44.4.4). An official grant of this title had been made to Caesar, according to Suetonius (*Jul.* 85).

What took place within the family was also held to be a legitimate area for debate and criticism by others outside the family circle. Obscene songs (according to some Roman texts) were chanted outside the houses of those whose behaviour was considered anti-social.[113] A Greek writer, Dionysius of Halicarnassus, contrasted Athens and Sparta where, he claimed, citizens were able to behave as they pleased in their own homes, with Rome where it was felt to be to the advantage of the state that the personal lives of its citizens be subject to relentless scrutiny (20.13.2–3).

The pair of magistrates who held the censorship (the most senior of the *patres*, if not the most powerful) are sometimes represented as the foremost agents of this state scrutiny.[114] Plutarch, a Greek writing in the early second century CE, offers the following description of the censorship in republican Rome:

The office was the crown of all other civic honours and was, in a way, the culmination of a great political career. It carried a wide range of powers, including that of examining the lives and morals of the citizens. The Romans believed that no one should be left to his own ways and desires without being subject to inspection and review, either in choosing a wife, or in begetting children, or in the ordering of his daily life, or in entertaining his friends. Rather, they were of the opinion that these things revealed a man's real character more than did his public and political career, so they set men in office to observe, reprimand and punish, in order that no one should turn aside to self-indulgence and neglect his native and customary way of life [τὸν ἐπιχώριον καὶ συνήθη βίον].

(Plut. *Cat.mai.* 16.1–2)

For Plutarch, the most characteristic feature of the censorship was its concern with the perpetuation of the traditional Roman way of life. This passage too emphasises the extent to which concern for what might be termed private morality was seen by Greeks familiar with Roman culture, as well as by Romans themselves, as a distinctively

---

[113] A ritual referred to as the *convicium*. See Hermann Usener 'Italische Volksiustiz' *RhM* 56 (1901) 1–28. Veyne has drawn attention to the similarities between the ritual of the *convicium* and the charivari in early modern Europe (1983 and 1987: 171–4). The *convicium* or *flagitatio* was developed into a literary genre by Catullus, Horace and others. On the charivari, see Jacques Le Goff and Jean Claude Schmitt eds. *Le Charivari* (Paris 1981).

[114] On the censors' responsibility for the morals of, in particular, the elite, see A.E. Astin 'Regimen morum' *JRS* 78 (1988) 14–34.

Roman characteristic.[115] Yet here again the high point of Roman morality is situated in the past.

Censors were elected magistrates. Although all other magistrates were obliged to submit to the censors' decisions, these could be subsequently reversed by other censors.[116] Censorial activity was severely disrupted in the last century of the republic.[117] In spite of this the censorship continued to have a particular resonance. Dio, writing in the early third century CE, observes: 'By virtue of holding the censorship, [the emperors] investigate our lives and morals as well as taking the census' (53.17.7). Though Claudius was the first emperor to take the title of censor, Augustus had paraded his shouldering of censorial responsibility.[118] The censorship may be seen as a convenient office for emperors, associated with tradition but legitimating moral scrutiny of senators and equestrians which could lead to an individual's loss of status. Such decisions on the part of emperors were not likely to be reversed. In the hands of an autocrat, censorial authority took on a new force. Yet the moral authority even of imperial censors had no transcendent justification. The moral in pagan Rome was not generally presented as closely related to the religious.[119] Morality was more associated with politics than with religion. Certainly 'politics' and 'religion' were themselves overlapping categories; the same individuals were magistrates and priests. But it was elected magistrates who were responsible for the establishment and enforcement of moral rules.

Under the principate, the identity of the elite became gradually more diverse, particularly as local elites from all over the empire were

---

[115] The relationship between the censors and their fellow citizens was sometimes presented as parallel to that between the *paterfamilias* and his family. The elder Cato was said to have recommended that men should behave like censors in scrutinising the conduct of their wives (Gellius 10.23). Cf. Cic. *De rep.* 4.6.16.

[116] Cicero (*De rep.* 4.6) emphasises that the censors controlled their fellow citizens by arousing shame rather than by imposing penalties.

[117] See T.P. Wiseman 'The census in the first century BC' *JRS* 59 (1969) 59–65.

[118] Cf. Suet. *Aug.* 27.5. A.H.M. Jones sets out the constitutional details of Augustus' censorial powers, *Studies in Roman government and law* (Oxford 1960) 19–26. On Claudius' assumption of the censorship, see Barbara Levick *Claudius* (London 1990) 98–101. Domitian assumed the title of *censor perpetuus*, according to Dio (67.4.3).

[119] Even J.H.W.G. Liebeschuetz, who lays more emphasis than most scholars on the link between the moral and the religious in ancient Rome, remarks of the moralising element in Roman literature: 'This mass of moral guidance contains remarkably few references to the gods in the role of supervisors of morality' (*Continuity and change in Roman religion* (Oxford 1979) 39 (for a general discussion of morality and religion, see 39–54)).

absorbed into Rome's governing class.[120] From the second century, in particular, members of the elite, even senators, spent less time in Rome and more time in their original provinces. If senators from Achaea came to think of themselves as 'Roman', it was hardly in opposition to 'Greek'. The virtues of Rome's ancestors were becoming a rather less evocative source of authority.

The republican elite was self-regulating, not so much in that individuals were guided by their private consciences but because they were concerned not to imperil the *dignitas* ('social standing') which they enjoyed in the eyes of their peers. In the first centuries CE, one may perceive in texts composed by members of the Roman elite a shift towards a more internalised morality which in some ways prefigures Christian thinking.[121] Veyne sees this concern for the self as an aristocratic reaction to autocracy.[122] This new cult of introspection could be seen as legitimation of the increasing lack of participation on the part of those who considered themselves members of the elite in the political culture of public service which had, in the past, been invoked to justify their privileged position.[123] We could also see this development as itself serving to reinforce the fragmentation of group interests, a philosophy of depoliticisation. Members of the educated elite were being encouraged to turn inwards and away from political concerns. This was a new form of 'self-regulation', of individuals by themselves, rather than of a cohesive social group – though we should not exaggerate the extent to which even the most educated Romans were concerned with self-control. In the pre-Christian Roman empire no-one, not even the emperor, had a monopoly of moral authority. Moralists and philosophers could advise but they had no means of enforcing the norms they advocated. This is one of the most significant differences between the pagan world and the Christian. Christianity brought with it the institutionalisation of morality.

PAGAN AND CHRISTIAN

Christianity flourished and spread from the time of Tiberius, first in the eastern Mediterranean, then in Rome itself and later still in the west. This study will not cover the development of Christian ethics.

---

[120] For this purpose see Hopkins 1983: 120–200.
[121] On this development, see Foucault 1988.
[122] Veyne 1978: 35–63.   [123] Cf. Hopkins 1983: 166.

All the same, it is important to bear in mind that the ways of thinking examined here played a part in shaping the development of some forms of Christian thought (from the second century in particular). The resemblance between Christian and Stoic moral norms has often been noted by modern scholars, though it would perhaps have been denied by both pagans and earlier Christian sects, who tended to emphasise their differences from one another. A reputation for sexual continence gave identity to some groups of early Christians in much the same way as dietary laws did for Jewish communities.[124] Many of the ancient sources which provide highly coloured descriptions of Roman luxury and vice were written by Christian apologists who had an interest in making pagans appear as 'immoral' as possible (the works of Tertullian and Clement of Alexandria are obvious examples). This early Christian attitude to pagan 'immorality' has been an important, though often unacknowledged, influence on later historians' perceptions of Roman behaviour. Christians were responsible for preserving most of the pagan texts we read now. We cannot tell what may have been lost because Christians either had no interest in preserving it or felt that it conflicted with their chosen image of the pagan world. Even so, it is still possible to trace a plurality of voices in the texts that have survived and some at least of these voices the following chapters set out to explore.

---

[124] See Peter Brown *The body and society* (London 1989). Diet was also important for some early Christian groups. On this see, e.g. Gillian Feeley-Harnik *The Lord's table: eucharist and passover in early Christianity* (Philadelphia 1981).

CHAPTER ONE

A moral revolution?
The law against adultery

In 62 BCE, a young and politically ambitious Roman aristocrat, Publius Clodius, is said to have disguised himself as a women in order to infiltrate the rites of the Bona Dea which it was sacrilege for men to observe. His purpose, according to his detractors, was to seduce the wife of Julius Caesar, the Pontifex Maximus, in whose house the ceremony was taking place. A man dressed as a woman, the profanation of religious rites, adultery with the wife of one of the leading men in Rome and the adulterer already notorious for his pernicious and disruptive political dealings – this incident, related or alluded to by numerous Roman authors, summed up the disorder of the final years of the republic.[1] For Roman writers, adultery among the elite was a telling symptom of disease in the body politic.

Another young and politically ambitious, though rather less aristocratic, man effected what was claimed to be the cure, restoring the *res publica* to health, moral as well as political. Rome's first emperor, Augustus, the new Romulus, promised a revolution – a return to the past. In the early days of Rome, wives were chaste; he initiated legislation making adultery a crime. Augustus boasted, in his *Res gestae: Legibus novis me auctore latis multa exempla maiorum exolescentia iam ex nostro saeculo reduxi*, 'Through new laws passed on my proposal, I brought back many of the exemplary practices of our ancestors which were falling into neglect' (8.5). By asserting that the mythical virtues of Rome's past were to be resurrected, Augustus proclaimed the beneficence of his new regime.

Scholars tend to treat Roman law as a domain independent of what

---

[1] Cic. *Ad fam.* 20.15; *Ad Att.* 12.3; 13.3; 18.2–3 (all references to Cicero's letters use Shackleton-Bailey's numbering); *Pro Planc.* 86; Vell. Pat. 2.45.1; Appian *Roman history* 2.14; Sen. *Ep.* 97.2–8; Suet. *Jul.* 6.2, 74.2; Plut. *Cic.* 28–9; *Jul.* 6, 9–10. For Clodius as the archetypal adulterer, cf. Juv. 2.27.

is labelled literature, a series of practical responses to practical problems. It should rather be seen as a symbolic discourse, bearing as much or as little relationship to patterns of behaviour in ancient Rome as the effusions of Roman moralists, and in dialogue with, indeed, part of, moralistic discourse. After setting out the details of the Augustan legislation, I shall explore the relationship between its prescriptions and discussions of adultery in the late republic, before going on to examine the implications of making adultery a criminal offence. The Augustan legislation was an intervention in a highly charged discourse which changed the terms of the debate – not altogether to the legislator's advantage.

CHERCHEZ LA FEMME

Historians ancient and modern commonly depict the late republic as a period when sexual licence flourished. This licence is particularly associated with women of the senatorial elite, the wives, daughters and sisters of Rome's political leaders. Fausta, daughter of the dictator Sulla, Clodia, sister of Publius Clodius, Sempronia, allegedly an associate of the conspirator Catiline, and Servilia, mistress of Julius Caesar and half-sister of the Stoic Cato, are often referred to as examples of women who enjoyed a high degree of sexual freedom.[2]

Scholars have tended to see Augustus' law against adultery as further evidence for this alleged sexual licence and an understandable response to it. P.E. Corbett, whose book *The Roman law of marriage* was published in 1930 and was until recently the standard book on this subject in English,[3] saw the law on adultery as providing: 'a very necessary check upon the growing independence and recklessness of women.'[4] The view expressed by Beryl Rawson, some fifty years later, is perhaps a liberal descendant of Corbett's: 'In their search for a different kind of relationship [from the one they were likely to

---

[2] Cf. e.g. Hugh Last in *CAH* x (1934) 440; J.P.V.D. Balsdon *Roman women; their history and habits* (London 1962) 45–62; Sarah B. Pomeroy *Goddesses, wives, whores and slaves* (London 1976) 159. Charles Seltman (*Women in antiquity* (London 1956) 170) expresses more scepticism.

[3] Now superseded by Susan Treggiari *Roman marriage: iusti coniuges from the time of Cicero to the time of Ulpian* (Oxford 1991).

[4] P.E. Corbett *The Roman law of marriage* (Oxford 1930) 130. Cf. Last (*CAH* x, esp. 440) on the dangers of allowing women too much freedom; V. Arangio-Ruiz 'La legislazione' in *Augustus: studi in occasione del bimillenario augusteo* (Rome 1938) 101–46 (lauding Augustus' attempt to return to 'pristina purezza').

experience in marriage to social equals] some women resorted not only to adultery but also to unions or marriages with men of inferior social status despite the fact that the law (made by men) frowned on some of these relationships.'[5] The latter view might seem more sympathetic and is shared by many modern scholars. We are asked to see the sexual 'misbehaviour' of upper-class Roman women as an understandable response to the constraints a patriarchal social order imposed on even its most privileged women. But, although Rawson sympathises with the adulteress, rather than condemning her, as Corbett does, she shares with him an assumption that the adulteress was indeed an adulteress.

We should be wary of taking Roman claims about the high level of adultery among the elite as straightforward. Before attempting to arouse sympathy for ancient adulteresses, we need to take a closer look at them. These colourful characters are not real people but resonant metaphors for social and political disorder (though we may and should consider the possible consequences of such metaphors for the women they claimed to represent). These fictions served as vehicles for the articulation of anxieties, personal and political.

The symbolic significance of sexual misbehaviour should be acknowledged in our interpretations of attempts to control it. Maybe members of Rome's upper classes were committing adultery more often in the late republic than they had done before (though we have no way of knowing) but Augustus' legislation on adultery should not be seen as a straightforward, common-sense solution to a troublesome social problem. To take such a view is to ignore the symbolic charge of the Augustan moral legislation, which played a central role in establishing the credentials of his autocratic regime. These laws (which covered the regulation of marriage as well as the control of adultery) were a response to the associations Roman moralists of the late republic regularly made between adultery, unwillingness to marry, childlessness and the political disarray which preceded the civil wars. An ode of Horace, first published in 23 BCE, recommended that the man who wished to be acclaimed *pater urbium*, father of civilisation, should take on the task of restraining licence, *refrenare licentiam* (3.24.27–9). To suppress licence was to guarantee political stability.

---

[5] Rawson introduction to B. Rawson ed. *The family in ancient Rome* (London 1986) 27. Cf. Pomeroy who presents Roman adulteresses as champions of free love (1976: 149, 185). Balsdon is charmed but less concerned to empathise with their plight (1962: 45–62).

THE LAW

Augustus was closely associated with the law that bore his name, the *lex Iulia de adulteriis* (the Julian law on punishing adulteries), passed in 18 BCE.[6] For my argument, it is not particularly important whether it was the emperor himself or his advisers who made the original proposal.[7] 'Augustus' here (as often with Roman emperors) is a shorthand. The emperor's conscious intentions are irrecoverable. I propose to explore the general ideological context in which this piece of legislation may have been perceived by both legislator and citizen.

Before discussing the ideological resonances of the adultery law, I shall set out its main provisions. Both the details of its prescriptions and the sanctions it envisaged (as is often the case with Roman legislation) can only be inferred from allusions in literary texts and from excerpts in later legal sources, principally Justinian's *Digest*, compiled in the early sixth century.[8] As regards the legal sources, it is almost impossible to disentangle the provisions of the original legislation from later attempts to interpret and extend it.[9] The writings of the jurists are often especially concerned with procedural questions, such as the time limits for beginning accusations, which are unlikely to have been among the principal concerns of the original

---

[6] The law is referred to variously in legal texts as the *lex Iulia de adulteriis*, the *lex Iulia de adulteriis coercendis*, the *lex Iulia de adulteriis et de stupro*, the *lex Iulia de adulteriis et de pudicitia*. For arguments in favour of this date as opposed to one slightly later, see Last in *CAH* x: 443.

[7] Dio (54.16.3) suggests that Augustus only introduced the legislation under pressure from the senate. Syme sees the impetus for the measure as coming from local Italian elites (tradition-ally associated with provincial respectability in contrast to the urbane licence of Rome) (1939: 453).

[8] The revelant passages are concentrated in *Dig.* 48.5. There is some additional material in Paul, *Sententiae* 2.26 (an anthology of the writings of a second century jurist, compiled around 300 CE), the *Collatio legum Mosaiorum et Romanorum* (composed around 400 CE) and Justinian's *Codex* (of the sixth century).

[9] S. Riccobono's attempt is probably the most convincing (*Acta divi Augusti* (Rome 1945) 112–28). The legal details are discussed by Theodor Mommsen, who terms the adultery law 'eine der eingreifendsten und dauerndsten strafrechtliche Neuschöpfungen welche die Geschichte kennt' (*Römisches Strafrecht* (Leipzig 1899) 688–99); Corbett 1930: 133–46; Pal Csillag *The Augustan laws on family relations* (Budapest 1976) 175–211; L.F. Raditsa 'Augustus' legislation concerning marriage, procreation, love affairs and adultery' in H. Temporini ed. *ANRW* II. 13 (Berlin 1980) 278–339; Amy Richlin 'Some approaches to the sources on adultery at Rome' in Helene B. Foley ed. *Reflections of women in antiquity* (New York 1981) 379–404; Jane Gardner *Women in Roman law and society* (London 1986); Treggiari 1991: 275–98. Raditsa's account of the Augustan legislation is often perceptive but is unconvincing in its attempt to present those who failed to conform to the law as champions of free love rebelling against a Freudian father-figure. Richlin's discussion is a good introduction to the complexities of the sources on adultery. Treggiari gives a clear discussion of the provisions of the law.

legislation. A further problem with any attempt at synthesis is that one is tempted to assume the coherence of later interpretations of the original law, when these may often have been in conflict.

The *lex Iulia de adulteriis* was specifically aimed at punishing the extra-marital affairs of married women.[10] The law prescribed that a father who discovered his married daughter committing adultery in his own house or that of his son-in-law was permitted to kill both the woman and her lover, provided that he himself was a *paterfamilias*, legal family head.[11] If he killed only one of them, he was liable for murder.[12] This requirement may have been deliberately impractical but the law still paraded the father's right to punish his adulterous daughter and her paramour.

A husband, on finding his wife *in flagrante delicto* in his own house, was not permitted to kill her. Husbands, according to the commentary of the jurist Papinian (written in the late second or early third century), were more likely than fathers to act hastily under such circumstances (*Dig.* 48.5.23.4). According to the jurist Paul, a husband could kill his wife's lover, provided the lover was *infamis* (that is to say, a convicted criminal, an actor, a procurer or a gladiator), a prostitute or a slave (*Sent.* 2.26.4).[13] The writings of other jurists sometimes include the family's freedmen in this list.[14] The jurists were of the opinion that, where the husband had the right to kill his wife's lover, he had the right *a fortiori* to injure him (*Dig.* 48.5.23.3, Papinian). If he killed her lover, the husband was required to divorce his wife within three days and initiate proceedings against her for adultery (*Dig.* 48.5.25.1, Macer; 48.5.30.*pr*, Ulpian). Ulpian states

---

[10] It also covered heterosexual relations with unmarried women and widows and homosexual rape, though some persons were excluded on the grounds of social status (*Dig.* 48.5.6, Papinian; 48.5.35, Modestinus; Paul, *Sent.* 2.26.12). These cases are sometimes referred to as *stuprum* in contrast to adultery. However, the jurist Papinian remarks that the terms *adulterium* and *stuprum* are used interchangeably in the law (*Dig.* 48.5.6.1). Accessories to adultery might also be prosecuted under the *lex Iulia*. On this, see David Daube 'The *lex Iulia* concerning adultery' *The Irish jurist* 7 (1972) 373–80.

[11] *Dig.* 48.5.21–4, Papinian and Ulpian; *Coll.* 4.2.3, Paul; Paul, *Sent.* 2.26.1.

[12] *Dig.* 48.5.24.4, Ulpian; 48.5.33.*pr*, Macer.

[13] On *infamia*, see A.H.J. Greenidge *Infamia: its place in Roman public and private law* (Oxford 1894) and Catharine Edwards 'Unspeakable professions: public performance and prostitution in ancient Rome' (forthcoming).

[14] E.g. *Dig.* 48.5.25.*pr*., Macer; *Coll.leg.Mos.et Rom.* 4.3.1–5, Paul. Jurists were in disagreement over whether the husband could kill his wife's lover if the latter were of higher social status than himself (*Dig.* 48.5.25.3, Macer; 48.5.39.9, Papinian). On this aspect of the adultery law, see Eva Cantarella 'Adulterio, omicidio legittimo e causa d'onore in diritto romano' in *Studi in onore di Gaetano Scherillo* (Milan 1972) I 243–74.

that a husband, if he knew of his wife's adultery but did not divorce and prosecute her, could himself be charged with pandering, *lenocinium* (*Dig.* 48.5.2.2; 48.5.2.6). The legal texts are not always consistent but the law was interpreted by some jurists as prescribing that action could be taken against a husband who knew of his wife's adultery but did not divorce her.[15] Obtaining proof that a husband knew of his wife's infidelity cannot always have been easy, but the significance of this provision should not be underestimated.

Augustus' law made adultery a public offence. Like cases of parricide, *vis* (force), murder and treason, cases of adultery were to be tried in a *quaestio perpetua*, a permanent law court set up for the purpose.[16] Thus trials involving the sexual offences which came under the *lex Iulia* would receive maximum publicity. Not all husbands can have been keen to advertise their wives' infidelity in this way but, as we saw, if a man chose not to initiate legal action against his adulterous wife, he himself might be liable to prosecution. For the first two months following a divorce, the husband and then the father had exclusive rights to bring an accusation (*Dig.* 48.5.2.8; 48.5.4, Ulpian). Thereafter anyone could bring a prosecution against a woman (though there were certain conditions which were the subject of extensive discussion by the jurists). If the alleged adulteress was not divorced, her husband had first to be accused and convicted of *lenocinium*, on the grounds that he had kept his adulterous wife instead of divorcing and prosecuting her (*Dig.* 48.5.27, Ulpian). It seems a woman could not be accused of adultery until she was divorced from the husband she was alleged to have been unfaithful to (*Dig.* 48.5.12.10, Papinian; 48.5.27.*pr*, Ulpian). However, her alleged

---

[15] Cf. e.g. *Dig.* 48.5.30.*pr.*, Ulpian. This matter was a source of some disagreement. Another text argues that the husband was not liable if he was only guilty of 'negligence' (*Dig.* 48.5.2.3, 48.5.30.4). Corbett (1930: 142), Last (in *CAH* x: 446), Gardner (1986: 131) and Treggiari (1991: 288–89) argue that the husband could only be convicted if he could be proved to have caught his wife in the act of adultery and not prosecuted her or if he could be proved to have made a profit from her adultery. The term *neglegentia* seems to me open to a wide range of interpretations and we need not suppose that any one of these was rigorously adhered to by Roman judges. On *lenocinium*, see also V.A. Tracy 'The *leno-maritus*' *CJ* 72 (1976) 62–4.

[16] On the *quaestio perpetua*, see the discussions by Peter Garnsey 'Adultery trials and the survival of the *quaestiones* in the Severan age' *JRS* 57 (1967) 56–60 and Richard Bauman 'Some remarks on the structure and survival of the *quaestio de adulteriis*' *Antichthon* 2 (1968) 68–93. None of the trials for adultery mentioned in literary sources is stated to have taken place in the *quaestio*. Where the circumstances of trials are known, they seem to have taken place before the emperor or in the senate (which became established as the places where high-status individuals were tried).

lover could be accused while she was still married (*Dig.* 48.5.40.1, Papinian). No prosecution could be brought once five years had elapsed since the alleged adultery had taken place (*Dig.* 48.5.30.5, Ulpian; 48.5.32, Paul). If a third party prosecution was successful, the informer would receive a part (probably substantial) of the property confiscated. The rest went to the emperor's treasury.

Obtaining evidence of the crime must sometimes have presented difficulties for informers. However, it was permissable in adultery trials for the slaves of the accused to be tortured so that they might give evidence against their owners. Treason was the only other accusation which permitted the use of evidence gathered in this way.[17] Under the *lex Papia Poppaea* of 9 CE, a convicted adulteress could not inherit. Women found in adultery were prohibited from marriage to freeborn Romans (Ulpian 13).[18] They were thus classified with, among others, actresses, prostitutes and procuresses. If convicted of adultery, a woman lost half her dowry and a third of her property, her lover a third of his property. Each was relegated to a separate island (Paul, *Sent.* 2.26.14).

Women who were known to be adulteresses were required to abandon the *stola* – the dress of the respectable Roman matron. Instead they were to wear a *toga* – the dress of the male Roman citizen and also of the female prostitute.[19] The anomalous status of the adulteress was thereby proclaimed. Tony Tanner, in his discussion of adultery in nineteenth-century novels, remarks: 'An unfaithful wife . . . is an unassimilable conflation of what society insists should be separate categories and functions.'[20] The form of dress which for a man indicated his possession of the honourable status of Roman citizen indicated dishonour for a woman, since women could never possess a citizen's political rights. Being a woman and being politically active were, like wife and mistress, unassimilable categories.

How does this compare with the legal position under the

---

[17] Cf. *Dig.* 48.5.28, Ulpian; *Coll.* 4.11.1, Papinian. It is not clear whether this formed part of the original Augustan provisions. Raditsa argues that initially only those prosecuting in the capacity of husbands or fathers were permitted to have slaves tortured but that this was extended to all prosecutors under the Severi (1980: 311). On the torture of slaves, see P.A. Brunt 'Evidence given under torture' *ZSS* 97 (1980) 256–65; Page duBois *Torture and truth* (London 1991).

[18] Cf. *Dig.* 23.2.43.10–13, Ulpian. On this, see Greenidge 1894: 171–6.

[19] Cf. Mart. 2.39; 10.52. Gardner suggests the toga came to be associated with adulterous women, because many of them became prostitutes (1986: 129).

[20] Tony Tanner *Adultery in the novel* (Baltimore 1979) 12.

republic?[21] In the second century BCE, the elder Cato is said to have observed, in a speech on the subject of dowries, that a man, if he finds his wife in adultery, has the right (*ius*) to kill her. But in what sense was this a legal right?[22] V. Arangio-Ruiz suggested that the husband may only have been allowed to kill his wife if they were married *cum manu*, a form of marriage effectively involving the assimilation of the wife to a daughter, which seems to have become increasingly rare in the late republic.[23] At any rate, no examples are known of offended husbands or fathers exercising a right to kill an adulterous wife or daughter. It is by no means clear that this was a generally accepted right. Moreover, although under the republic adultery by a wife was considered sufficient motive for her husband to repudiate her, it entitled him to retain only a small fraction more of her dowry than he was allowed if he were repudiating her for other less serious forms of 'misbehaviour'.[24] During the republic, adultery, it seems, was not treated as a serious offence under Roman law.[25]

Augustus' legislation on adultery was part of a whole programme of moral reform. In the same year, 18 BCE, another law was passed regulating sexual relationships, the *lex Iulia de maritandis ordinibus* (the Julian law to promote marriage in the senatorial and equestrian orders).[26] This was the first of two laws concerning marriage which penalised the unmarried and rewarded those who had children (the *lex Papia Poppaea* of 9 CE modified the earlier law in some respects).[27] These laws prescribed a graduated series of rewards and penalties to discourage childlessness. They also prescribed who might marry

---

[21] The jurist Paul, writing two centuries after the *lex Iulia* was passed, observes that its first chapter abrogated many previous statutes (*Coll. leg. Mos. et Rom.* 4.2.2). Treggiari discusses some possibilities (1991: 277). Cf. Gardner 1986: 123.

[22] Cato *ap.* Gell. 10.23.5 (= frag. 221 Malcovati). Treggiari's discussion of this passage emphasises the possible non-legal uses of *ius* (1991: 268–75).

[23] Arangio-Ruiz 1938: 111.

[24] Ulpian 6.12. It is not entirely clear what these forms of 'misbehaviour' may have been. Corbett suggests excessive wine-drinking (1930: 193). Roman texts frequently present wine-drinking on the part of women as associated with adultery (cf. e.g. Dion. Hal. 2.25.5–7; Val. Max. 2.1.5; Gell. 10.23). On the extent of a family council's powers over married women, see Treggiari 1991: 264–75.

[25] Though there are a handful of occasions in the mid republic when aediles are alleged to have imposed punishments for adultery (these are discussed by Treggiari 1991: 275–77).

[26] An earlier attempt at such a law may have been made around 28 BCE. Propertius 2.7 is often cited as evidence but E. Badian has cast doubt on this, 'A phantom marriage law' *Philologus* 129 (1985) 82–98.

[27] On these laws, see Corbett 1930: 31–9; Michel Humbert *Le Remariage à Rome* (Milan 1972) 138–78; Csillag 1976: 77–174; Raditsa 1980; A.F. Wallace-Hadrill 'Family and inheritance in the Roman marriage laws' *PCPhS* 27 (1981) 58–80; Treggiari 1991: 60–80.

whom. Senators and their ascendent and descendent relatives to the third generation were forbidden to marry ex-slaves. Ex-slaves and all freeborn Romans were forbidden to marry *infames*. Men between the ages of twenty-five and sixty and women between the ages of twenty and fifty suffered legal disabilities, if they were not married (these disabilities were suspended for short periods following bereavement or divorce). The Augustan legislation set up two separate and mutually exclusive categories: on the one hand, people who ought to marry (and would be penalised if they did not), and on the other, people who were discouraged from marrying anyone but their fellow social outcasts.

Laws like this, taken with other evidence, can of course provide valuable clues for anyone attempting to uncover patterns of social behaviour in Augustan Rome. Recent work on the rate of replacement among the senatorial elite, for instance, suggests that senatorial families were failing to reproduce themselves; the prescriptions of the Augustan legislation, setting a target number of only three children ever-born (an insufficient number to ensure overall reproduction of a social group in a preindustrial society with high mortality), lend further support to this argument.[28] But what conclusions about social behaviour can one deduce from the prescriptions of the adultery law?

ADULTERY AND THE COLLAPSE OF THE REPUBLIC

Augustus' establishment of one-man rule in Rome was presented as a restoration of the *res publica*. Though many of the traditional political institutions were retained, signalling the good intentions of the new regime, this might be seen as less a political 'restoration' than a moral and religious one.[29] The virtues of Rome's rustic past, those virtues which, according to Livy and countless other moralising writers, had made Rome great, were to be reinstated.[30]

Idealised representations of early Rome almost invariably present chastity as one of its distinctive characteristics. As we saw in the introduction, Roman moralists constructed a close association

[28] See Hopkins 1983: 95–6.
[29] In the time of Augustus, when *principatus* was only an emergent term, *res publica* cannot yet have had the constitutional associations which it acquired by the time of Tacitus, who contrasts the two as political systems (cf. Fergus Millar 'Triumvirate and principate' *JRS* 63 (1973) 50–67).
[30] Livy *pr.* 7–12. Cf. e.g. Sall. *Cat.* 7; 9; *Hist.* 1.16; Cic. *De rep.* 5.1; Pliny, *NH* 36.111.

between Rome's military successes in extending the empire and the personal virtues of the Roman people. Adultery was rare, they claimed, and treated with the utmost seriousness. Under Romulus, women were condemned to death for adultery, according to Dionysius of Halicarnassus, who wrote in the time of Augustus (2.25.5).[31] Livy, also writing under Augustus, tells of the story of Lucretia, heroine of the dawn of the republic, to whom suicide seemed the only acceptable course, once her chastity had been defiled (1.58). The satirist Juvenal, writing a century later, presents a less rosy picture of the virtues of even the earliest Roman women (for Juvenal, adultery was the first vice to infect human society and marked the end of the golden age of Saturn, 6.19–20).[32] But, even in Juvenal's picture, at least some protection for virtue was offered by poverty; the advent of wealth acted as a catalyst of vice: *nullum crimen abest facinusque libidinis, ex quo|paupertas Romana perit*, 'Since the day when Roman poverty perished, no criminal deed of lust has been lacking' (6.294–5).

Roman authors treat uncontrolled female sexuality as an emblem of the general breakdown of order. Sallust presents as a prominent member of Catiline's conspiracy the aristocratic matron Sempronia (*Cat.* 25). She was, he claims, beautiful, cultivated and charming but also extravagant to the point of prodigality and without the slightest concern for her chastity, *pudicitia*. Sallust's portrait of Sempronia has been seen by some scholars as out of place in his account of Catiline's conspiracy.[33] Rather she should be read as standing for the corruption of Roman morals, which, for Sallust, is the explanation of the conspiracy's origin. The association between adultery and disorder continued to be a resonant one for Roman moralists. Two hundred years later, when Tacitus wanted to evoke the turmoil of Rome in the late 60s CE, he wrote: *pollutae caerimoniae, magna adulteria*, 'sacred rites were defiled; there were adulteries in high places' (*Hist.* 1.2).

---

[31] Horace (*Sat.* 1.3.104–6) describes the transition from brutish disorder to civilisation as marked by cessation from fighting, the building of towns and the institution of laws against theft and adultery.

[32] Though the constantly shifting perspective from which Juvenal criticises women in his sixth satire might justify a reading of the poem as a parody of the moralistic view. For an exploration of the complexities of representations of the female in satire, see John Henderson 'Satire writes "woman": Gendersong' *PCPhS* 35 (1989) 50–80.

[33] F.R.D. Goodyear observes: 'In a work clumsily planned as a whole, Sempronia is the worst blemish' (E.J. Kenney and W. Clausen eds. *Cambridge history of classical literature* II (Cambridge 1982) 275).

Female unchastity was also a recurrent element in discussions of the 'decline' of Roman religion which was said to have been a feature of the later republic. This chapter began with the story of Clodius' infiltration of the rites of the Bona Dea. Female sexual 'purity' in Roman religion (as in many other religions) was constructed as important to the preservation of divine favour. Female impurity disrupted religious activity; the unchastity of Vestal Virgins, for instance, was often associated with times of crisis.[34] Though the chastity of Vestals is of a rather different order from that of the ordinary Roman matrona, rules governing their behaviour do suggest the threat female unchastity was felt to pose to the religious well-being of the state.[35]

The Bacchanalian scandal of the early second century BCE appears in Livy's history as an important episode in the deterioration of religious order. Female sexual misbehaviour plays a major part in this religious crisis.[36] The consul Postumius Albinus is made to address the senate, advocating stricter controls on the worshippers of Bacchus, describing them as follows:

primum igitur mulierum magna pars est, et is fons mali huiusce fuit; deinde simillimi feminis mares, stuprati et constupratores.

To start with, a great many of them are women and they are the source of this trouble; then there are the men who are just like women, debauched and debauchers.

(Livy 39.15.9)

Women are seen as primarily to blame. They are presented as particularly susceptible to religious frenzy. The behaviour of the men involved is characterised as wrong by assimilating them to women.[37] The disruption of Roman religion is inextricably associated with

[34] For discussions of vestal unchastity, see Tim Cornell 'Some observations on the *crimen incesti*' and John Scheid 'Le délit religieux dans la Rome tardo-républicaine' in *Le Délit religieux dans la cité antique. Collection de l'école française à Rome* 48 (1981) 27–37 and 117–71.
[35] On the status of vestals, see Mary Beard 'The sexual status of Vestal Virgins' *JRS* 70 (1980) 12–27.
[36] This episode is discussed by John North, 'Religious toleration in republican Rome' *PCPhS* 25 (1979) 85–103.
[37] On characterisations of men as effeminate, see chapter two below.

feminine sexual immorality.[38] The preoccupations of Livy's narrative reflected and reinforced the concerns of the regime under which he wrote.

Other Augustan writers, too, saw adultery and the neglect of religion as crucial elements in the collapse of Roman society, culminating in the civil war. An ode of Horace begins by lamenting the neglect of traditional religion which allegedly characterised the late republic, before going on to describe an adulteress presented as equally typical of her time:

> fecunda culpae saecula nuptias
> primum inquinavere et genus et domos;
>   hoc fonte derivata clades
>   in patriam populumque fluxit.
>
> motus doceri gaudet Ionicos
> matura virgo et fingitur artibus
>   iam nunc et incestos amores
>   de tenero meditatur ungui;
>
> mox iuniores quaerit adulteros
> inter mariti vina, neque eligit
>   cui donet impermissa raptim
>   gaudia luminibus remotis,
>
> sed iussa coram non sine conscio
> surgit marito, seu vocat institor
>   seu navis Hispanae magister,
>   dedecorum pretiosus emptor.

Generations pregnant with guilt stained first marriages then families and homes; disaster springing from this source flooded over our fatherland and people.
The adult girl, trained in bad ways, loves to learn eastern dances. Already she thrills to the tips of her fingers at the thought of forbidden love.
Soon she is seeking younger lovers among her husband's guests. She isn't choosy but gives illicit pleasure to anyone, hastily in the darkness.

---

[38] Cf. also Cic. *Ad Att.* 18.3. Cicero begins this letter discussing Clodius' trial: *adflicta est res publica empto constupratoque iudicio, vide quae sint postea secuta*, 'the state suffers as the law courts are corrupted with money and sex. See what follows.' He then observes that Lucullus was unable to celebrate the rites of Iuventus (a cult association since its inception with the Luculli) because his wife had committed adultery.

A MORAL REVOLUTION?

Her husband looks on as she rises from her place at any man's bidding, tradesman or captain of a Spanish ship – whoever will pay cash for her disgrace.

(Hor. *Carm.* 3.6.17–32)

The woman is driven entirely by lust; her husband connives at her adultery, hoping to profit by it. The abandonment of traditional sexual morality is linked with the abandonment of ancestral religion. Both are implicated in political crisis and military defeat.[39]

The connection between what we might view as religion and morality was not so strong in Roman religion as it has been in many forms of Christianity. However, Augustus presented himself as a restorer of traditional Roman practices in religion as well as in morals, laying emphasis in his record of his own achievements on his restoration of previously neglected temples (*Res gestae* 20.4). Augustus' claim that religion was in decline in the late republic is parallel to his claim that morals were in decline. Both these assertions served to highlight the importance of his own role as 'restorer'; neither should be treated as straightforward.[40]

Those individuals who were accused of undermining the republic were regularly associated with adultery. Other adulterous matrons besides Sempronia are associated with Catiline (Sall. *Cat.* 24). Some of the most reprehensible of Cicero's opponents, too, are linked with licentious aristocratic women.[41] Cicero describes Clodius' sister, Clodia as a *meretrix*, 'prostitute' (*Pro Cael.* 49). These assertions should not be taken at face value.[42] Rather they were attempts to associate political rivals with the female licence which was perceived as emblematic of threats to the well-being of the state.

Augustus' legislation should also be situated in the tradition of rhetorical invective, discussed in my introduction. The new regime associated the political leaders of the late republic with failure to

---

[39] Cf. *Carm.* 3.24.

[40] Beard and Crawford emphasise the partiality of Augustus' claim concerning the delapidated state of temples in Rome (1985: 28–9). For the details of Augustus' attempts to 'revive' Roman religion, see Pierre Gros *Aurea templa: recherches sur l'architecture religieuse à Rome à l'époque d'Auguste* (Rome 1976).

[41] Cic. *De har. resp.* 9, 27, 38, 59; *Pro Cael.* 1, 18, 31–8, 47–9; *Pro Clu.* 12–18; 188–99; *De domo sua* 95.

[42] As was argued in the introduction, above, we should resist the temptation to assume that there was no smoke without fire. For further discussion of the rhetoric of invective, see chapter two below.

46

control female licence. Its adultery law prescribed action against the complaisant husband. The emperor may be seen as making a claim, in accordance with the conventions of Roman invective, that the Roman republic failed because its governing class was composed of men who were not men enough to control their own wives. But it is not quite the same thing to accuse your rivals of letting their wives run wild and to pass a law making complaisancy a criminal offence. This tension within Augustus' law will be returned to below.

HONOUR, SHAME AND URBANITY?

Many Roman politicians accused their opponents of seducing the wives of other men.[43] Adultery was among the vices of which Cicero himself was accused (Dio 46.18.3–6). The triumvir Pompey, according to his enemies, had adulterous affairs (Plut. *Pomp.* 2.4–5). Suetonius records that Mark Antony accused the young Augustus of adultery (Suet. *Aug.* 69).[44] Catiline's critics asserted he was notorious for his affairs with other men's wives (Sall. *Cat.* 15). In some sense, these stories were thought to reflect badly on their subjects. But drawing attention to a man's disruptive potential by highlighting his propensity for seducing other men's wives also emphasised his power. The sexual power of Clodius, his suspected ability to win the wife of Caesar, might be read as indicating the potency of his political influence, as well as its corrupt nature. Clodius was able to secure his acquittal when on trial for having infiltrated the rites of the Bona Dea, because, claims Seneca, he had at his disposal the sexual favours of so many elite matrons and youths which he offered as bribes to the jury.[45] Sallust suggested that much of the rebel Catiline's support was gained through the influence he exercised over married women.[46] The power these men exercised is represented as illegitimate by those who describe it. Yet the association of political and sexual power

---

[43] Cf. e.g. Cic. *In Cat.* 2.23; *Pro Flacco* 34; *Pro Sest.* 20; *Pro Planc.* 30; *In Pis.* 70; *Pro Cael.* 20, 29, 35; *Phil.* 2.99. On these accusations, see Richlin 1983: 96–104.

[44] Antony and Octavian accused one another of adultery, bribery and luxurious living, through the issuing of edicts, as they struggled for supremacy. Cf. Kenneth Scott 'The political propaganda of 44–30 BC' *MAAR* 11 (1933) 7–49.

[45] Sen. *Ep.* 97.2–9. Cf. Cic. *Ad Att.* 16.5 and Valerius Maximus 9.1.7.

[46] The most notable parallel from the principate is the alleged affair between the ambitious praetorian prefect, Sejanus, and Livilla, wife of Tiberius' son Drusus (Tac. *Ann.* 4.3).

suggests the two could be seen as mutually reinforcing.⁴⁷ Adulterers were villains, but glamorous ones.

Perhaps the nicest indication of the association between political power and adultery is the biographer Suetonius' comment on Augustus' own behaviour:

> adulteria quidem exercuisse ne amici quidem negant, excusantes sane non libidine, sed ratione commissa, quo facilius consilia adversariorum per cuiusque mulieres exquireret.

> *Not even his friends dispute that he often committed adultery, although they excuse him as motivated not by lust but by calculation, so that he could the more easily acquire information about his rivals' plans from the women of their households.*

(Suet. Aug. 69)

Augustus too was advantaged by appearing more sexually attractive than his opponents, by winning over their wives. He encouraged the rumours, it seems. His friends were slightly embarrassed about his affairs with other men's wives, but that is perhaps not surprising in view of his later attempts to portray himself as a crusader against precisely such manifestations of immorality.⁴⁸ Even so they are not represented as regarding his behaviour as a serious vice. What is perhaps most striking about this passage is the way his friends are reported to have excused his conduct. They felt it reflected better on him to be thought to have committed adultery from calculation, *ratione*, than from lust, *libidine*. Augustus was not impelled by unrestrained instincts to shameful indiscretions. He used sex for political ends – a much more acceptable practice.⁴⁹

Adultery caused disruption and threatened the social order. A good Roman citizen did not commit adultery – but at the same time adultery could be associated with power and with masculinity.⁵⁰

---

⁴⁷ Cf. the stories told about emperors: Sen. *Const.* 19.2; Suet. *Calig.* 36; *Otho* 3; Tac. *Ann.* 13.45. Their flagrant adulteries are emblematic of their abuse of their power.

⁴⁸ Cf. Dio 54. 16.6–7, where Augustus himself is alleged to have been embarrassed at having to enforce the adultery law, as his own behaviour had been by no means exemplary.

⁴⁹ Hallett 1977 explores in more detail the possible benefits to Augustus' reputation stories of his adulterous affairs may have had.

⁵⁰ Cicero, in a letter to Caelius, jokes about the adulterous affair of a mutual acquaintance: *Servius Ocella nemini persuasisset se moechum esse nisi triduo bis deprehensus est*, 'Servius Ocella would never have made anyone believe he was an adulterer, if he hadn't been caught in the act twice in three days' (*Ad fam.* 92.2). Adultery could also be associated with effeminacy, however. This is discussed below in chapter two.

Adulterers were viewed with ambivalence. Augustus passed a law against adultery but derived advantage from committing it himself. It does not matter whether the stories told about him are true, for the stories themselves reveal tensions in Roman attitudes to adultery, tensions which were only exacerbated by the *lex Iulia*.

Adulterers might be viewed with admiration as well as suspicion, but admiration is rather less in evidence in representations of adulteresses.[51] Clodia's sexual licence is a major preoccupation of Cicero's attack on her in the *Pro Caelio*. While, even if her lover was a man of her own social class, the offence of the adulteress was often represented as more serious than that of her lover, affairs between women of high status and men of lower status were viewed with horror by moralists.[52] An aristocratic male might have a fairly public affair with a freedwoman without incurring any serious disgrace.[53] No such licence would have been allowed a woman of respectable family who consorted with a freedman.

The fear that illegitimate children may be brought into a man's family is in many societies offered as the justification for a double standard in attitudes to sexual behaviour (that is to say, tolerating male sexual indiscretions while severely disapproving of parallel behaviour on the part of women).[54] Can we find evidence of such concern in Rome? The jurist Papinian's definition of adultery seems revealing. He writes: 'Properly speaking adultery is committed with a married woman, the name being derived from children conceived from another (*alter*)' (*Dig.* 48.5.6.1). But there are few examples in classical Roman texts of directly expressed concern with illegitimate births as a consequence of adultery. As Ronald Syme has remarked, accusations of bastardy are practically unattested in texts of the late republic and early principate (though they are quite common in the

---

[51] Though cf. the stories about Augustus' daughter Julia in which she is represented as making witty replies to her father's criticism of her immorality (Macrob. *Sat.* 2.5). Representations of Julia are discussed further below. On the double standard in sexual morality in Rome, see Treggiari 1991: 299–309. Another vivid illustration of the double standard is Juv. 6.279–85, though one could read this as a *reductio ad absurdum* of male complaints.

[52] Cf. Treggiari 1991: 308–9.

[53] As Richlin observes, Cicero expresses disapproval of Mark Antony's affair with the freedwoman Cytheris but was quite prepared to attend a dinner party in their company (1981: 384). For further examples of freedwomen as mistresses of members of the senatorial elite, see Susan Treggiari *Roman freedmen during the late republic* (Oxford 1969) 140, 142.

[54] Cf. e.g. on early modern Britain, Keith Thomas 'The double standard' *Journal of the History of Ideas* 20.2 (1959) 195–216 and Lawrence Stone *The family, sex and marriage* (London 1977) 501–7.

A MORAL REVOLUTION?

third and fourth centuries).[55] The poems of Martial and Juvenal occasionally claim that a particular man is not the father of his wife's children (an example of this is discussed below) but there are no instances of similar accusations in the surviving works of Roman historians and orators.[56] Roman aristocrats are virtually never accused of not being the children of their mothers' husbands.[57] This is rather curious when Roman aristocratic wives are so frequently portrayed as adulterous. No one seems to have doubted that the Emperor Claudius was the father of Messalina's children.[58]

Contraception, abortion and exposure might account for the offspring of adultery being few.[59] Husbands may have refused to recognise a child they did not believe to be their own. Until accepted by its father, a Roman baby did not, legally speaking, exist. A poem of Martial is addressed to a woman whose baby, according to Martial, has been rejected by both her husband and her lover (10.95). The child would then be exposed and perhaps brought up as a slave. Suetonius refers to a child cast out by her mother's ex-husband (the

[55] Ronald Syme 'Bastards in Roman aristocracy' *PAPhS* 104 (1960) 323–7 (= *Roman papers* II (Oxford 1979) 510–17). Cf. Ronald Syme 'No son for Caesar?' *Historia* 29 (1980) 422–37 (= *Roman Papers* III (Oxford 1984) 1236–50). This situation is markedly different from that in classical Athens, where orators regularly claimed that their opponents were not the sons of their ostensible fathers (see W. Süss *Ethos* (Leipzig 1910) 248–9). This is striking in view of the otherwise extensive use Roman orators made of the Athenian rhetorical tradition. For a discussion of attitudes to adultery in classical Athens, see David Cohen 'Separation, seclusion and the status of women in classical Athens' *G&R* 36 (1987) 3–15.

[56] Mar. 2.91; 2.92; 8.31; 10.102; Juv. 6.76–81.

[57] Brutus is perhaps an exception to this. He was rumoured to be the son of Julius Caesar but this was a rumour which was thought to reflect well on him rather than otherwise (Syme 1980). Cf. the story that Nymphidius Sabinus, praetorian prefect under Nero, boasted that he was the bastard son of the emperor Caligula (Plut. *Galba* 19). However, some jokes recorded by diverse sources do suggest Romans sometimes made allegations of bastardy against particular individuals (Plut. *Cic.* 25 (concerning the son of Crassus) and 26.6–7 (Metellus Nepos); Val. Max. 9.14. ext. 3 (joke made by provincial about a proconsul)). The resemblance of a child to its mother's husband was sometimes celebrated as proof of her chastity (Cat. 61.214–18; Hor. *Carm.* 4.5.23. Cf. Ovid, *Trist.* 2.351. Denis Feeney has kindly drawn my attention to further instances of this in Martial 6.27 and a fragment of Seneca's *De matrimonio* quoted by Jerome *Adv. Iovin.* 1.49).

[58] For Messalina's adulteries, see e.g. Tac. *Ann.* 11.26–38; Suet. *Claud.* 26; Juv. 6.116–32; 10.329–42. Barbara Levick suggests no-one would dare to accuse the emperor's wife of committing adultery until some time after she had given birth to an heir (*Claudius* (London 1990) 56). It is not clear why this should be so.

[59] On contraception, see Keith Hopkins 'Contraception in the Roman empire' *Comparative Studies in Society and History* 8 (1965) 124–51. On the association of abortion with adultery, see Sen. *De ben.* 3.16; Juv. 6.594–601; Suet. *Dom.* 22. Cf. Suzanne Dixon *The Roman mother* (Sydney 1987) 239 and ch. 3 generally. On exposure, see Suet, *Aug.* 65.4 (Augustus refused to allow the child of his grand-daughter Julia to be reared after her condemnation for adultery). Cf. John Boswell *The kindness of strangers: the abandonment of children in western Europe from antiquity to the Renaissance* (New York 1988).

emperor Claudius), after he had already accepted and begun to rear her:

> Claudiam ex liberto suo Botere conceptam, quamvis ante quintum mensem divortii natam alique coeptam, exponi tamen ad matris ianuam et nudam iussit abici.

> *Claudia was the child of his freedman Boter and, though she was born within five months of the divorce [from Urgulanilla] and he had begun to bring her up, he ordered her to be exposed naked at her mother's door and disowned.*

(Suet. *Claud.* 27.1)

Suetonius presents this as a highly unusual incident. Once a child had been recognised by a woman's husband it was effectively his. Yet there must often have been room for doubt about biological paternity.

Why did this arouse so little apparent concern among the Roman elite, in contrast to other societies? Continuity of blood line does not seem to have been a major preoccupation of Roman families. Some wealthy Romans chose to adopt as heirs the adult offspring of other families – one way of avoiding the expense of bringing up children, many of whom might die before they reached maturity.[60] Legal texts suggest many Romans were content to leave their property to a freedman (who would bear the family name), rather than a blood relative.[61] Moralists present childlessness as a state which many found socially desirable.[62] To return to the question of doubtful paternity, it may be that, if name rather than blood relationship was of primary importance, once a child was recognised as a Claudia or a Claudius, the identity of his or her biological father became unimportant.

Yet there are perhaps indirect manifestations of a concern with biological paternity to be traced in Roman texts of this period. Women are often associated with poisoning by Roman moralists.[63]

---

[60] The number of families involved in this practice seems to have been around 5% (Hopkins 1983: 49). While this may be a lower figure than is usually implied, adoption was still perceived as a fairly common means of perpetuating one's family name.

[61] See David Johnston *The Roman law of trusts* (Oxford 1988) 88–92.

[62] E.g. Hor. *Sat.* 2.5.28–44; Juv. 3.126–36; 4.19; 5.137–45; 6.548; 12.98–120; Pliny, *NH* 14.5; Sen. *Ad Marc.* 19.2; *Const. sap.* 6.1; Tac. *Hist.* 1. 73; *Dial.* 6.

[63] Livy relates that, in 331 BCE, 160 *matronae* were convicted of poisoning (8.18.8). Cf. e.g. Val. Max. 2.5.3; Juv. 5.146–8; 6.614–47; Pliny, *NH* 22.92; Amm. Marc. 28.11; Orosius 3.10. The association between women and poisoning is discussed by Nicholas Purcell 'Livia and the womanhood of Rome' *PCPhS* 32 (1986) 78–105, at 95.

We might see this association as a manifestation of concern with women's capacity to 'pollute' their husbands' lines by conceiving children in adulterous relationships. Quintilian quotes a remark of the elder Cato:

> si causam veneficii dicat adultera, non M. Catonis iudicio damnata videatur, qui nullam adulteram non eandem esse veneficam dixit?

> *If an adulteress is on trial for poisoning, should we not see her as already condemned by the judgement of Marcus Cato, who claimed that every adulteress was as good as a poisoner?*

(Quint. *Inst.* 5.11.39)[64]

On one level, Cato's statement might be read as an assertion that adultery was as bad as poisoning, a woman capable of one would be capable of the other too. We might see it, too, as an allusion to the association often made between adultery and abortion (procured by drugs).[65] But we might also read this as a suggestion that adultery was in a sense the same as poisoning – though we might wonder why Roman anxieties about paternity manifested themselves in this way.

Representations of adulteresses tend to focus on rather different concerns. To return to the double standard: the idea of a woman attracted to a man who was her social inferior was deeply disturbing to Roman moralists.[66] A woman who had sex with her slave called into question the values of the social order in a way that a woman who slept with her husband's social equals did not. Many texts relate stories of the terrible attraction depraved elite women feel towards slaves and other lowly persons.[67] An epigram of Martial is addressed to a man called Cinna, whose wife has given birth to seven children, each of whom, claims Martial, has been fathered by a different one of Cinna's slaves.[68] The poem begins:

> pater ex Marulla, Cinna, factus es septem
> non liberorum: nam neque tuus quisquam
> nec est amici filiusve vicini . . .

> *Cinna, Marulla has made you the father of seven – not children for there is no son of yours, nor of friend or neighbour . . .*

(Mart. 6.39)

---

[64] = Cato 240, Malcovati.   [65] Cf. Dixon 1987 ch. 3.
[66] Pliny, *Ep.* 6.31.4–6 (affair between the wife of a *laticlavus* and a centurion); Plut. *Galba* 12.
[67] E.g. Cic. *Pro Cael.* 31; 36; 38; 49; Juv. 6.76–81; Mart. 8.31; Pet. *Sat.* 69.3; 75.11; 126.5–11.   [68] Similar jibes are made in Mart. 8.31; Juv. 6.76–81.

Martial suggests that it would have been less shameful for Cinna, if his wife had committed adultery with a friend or neighbour. The force of the epigram depends partly on the implication that Cinna is not man enough to control his wife's behaviour. But one point of the jibe seems to be that Cinna's wife prefers slaves to someone of her husband's social class.

As we shall see in the next chapter, masculinity, for Romans, was crucially bound up with social status (to a much greater degree than femininity, which was regularly assimilated to slavery and childhood). Female sexuality was a potent danger for Roman moralists because it might disrupt status distinctions. Sexual relationships between high status women and low status men were an affront not only to the individual husband but to the social order. At the same time, what posed a threat to the good of the state as a whole, posed the greatest threat to those who had the largest interest in the state, whose identities were most closely bound up in its political fabric, men of the senatorial and equestrian elite. Images of women with a taste for degraded lovers were a focus for male anxieties about the social hierarchy and their own places within it.

Augustus' legislation against adultery also displayed a sensitivity to the significance of social hierarchy. Inferior social status aggravated the lover's crime. The injured husband might kill his wife's lover with impunity, if the lover was of low status. Augustus' adultery law was in part a claim to guarantee social hierarchy.[69] Even in the details of its prescriptions the law displayed its concern with the preoccupations of Roman elite men.[70]

But the law implied, too, that men were often to blame for their wives' infidelity. Complaisant husbands appear in satire and history.[71] In the following passage, Juvenal blames the husband's complaisance on his wife's wealth:

[69] Similar concern with the reinforcement of social differentials may be traced in other Augustan measures, in particular those relating to regulation of membership of the senate (on this see Claude Nicolet 'Augustus, government and the propertied classes' in Millar and Segal eds. 1987: 89–128) and the *lex Iulia theatralis*, on the assignment of seating at the theatre (discussed in chapter three below).

[70] Roman law in many cases withheld protection from *infames*, while slaves were subject to entirely different regulations from those governing free citizens (on *infames* see Greenidge 1894 and Edwards (forthcoming b); on slaves see W.W. Buckland *The Roman law of slavery* (Cambridge 1908)).

[71] E.g. Juv. 1.55–57. Cf. Hor. *Carm.* 3.6.17–32 (quoted above), *Sat.* 2.5.81–3; Tac. *Ann.* 6.45; 13.45; 15.48; 15.59; Apul. *Apol.* 40, 75; Dio 63.28. On representations of the complaisant husband, see Tracy 1976a.

'optima sed quare Caesennia teste marito?'
bis quingena dedit. tanti vocat ille pudicam,
nec pharetris Veneris macer est aut lampade fervet:
inde faces ardent, veniunt a dote sagittae.
libertas emitur. coram licet innuat atque
rescribat: vidua est, locuples quae nupsit avaro.

*'How is it that Caesennia's husband swears she's a perfect wife?' Because
she's brought him a fortune. That's his price for calling her chaste. He's no
victim of Venus' arrows and torches. It's his wife's money he's in love with.
Money buys her freedom. Now she can make eyes at men or write billets-
doux while he's sitting there. The rich woman who marries a man in love
with her money enjoys a widow's rights.*

(Juv. 6.136–41)

Notions of sexual and economic freedom are elided. Money buys a
woman the right to indulge her desires as she pleases. What are the
implications of this for the husband? A man who is poorer than his
wife is less of a man (another reminder that Roman notions of
masculinity are bound up with perceptions of power). This is one of
many variations on the theme of adulterous wife and her effeminate
spouse. Those who permit their wives to commit adultery, it is often
implied, do so because they have no interest in playing a sexually
'active' role but would rather be penetrated by other men.[72]

The cuckolded husband is rarely represented sympathetically in
Roman texts. In mime and satire, in particular, he seems to have been
a figure of fun. But to what extent was an aristocratic husband's
prestige dependent on his wife's fidelity?[73] Julius Caesar's response to
the Bona Dea scandal was to divorce his wife (though there was said to
be little evidence that she had been unfaithful to him). In general,
Roman elite husbands are presented as responding to their wives'

[72] Though often the same men are accused of both adultery and seeking to be penetrated by
other men (see chapter two). The power of well-dowered wives who dominate their husbands
was a frequent theme of Roman comedy. Cf. Treggiari 1991: 184.
[73] In many societies, a man's honour is at least in part dependent on the chastity of female
members of his family (cf. J.G. Peristiany ed. *Honour and shame: the values of Mediterranean
society* (Chicago 1966); Julian Pitt-Rivers *The fate of Shechem* (Cambridge 1977) ch. 2
'Honour and social status in Andalusia'). This seems to have been so to a limited extent
among the elites of early modern Europe (cf. Stone 1977). Elite Roman fathers and brothers
do not appear to have lost prestige to a significant degree as a result of the sexual
misbehaviour of their daughter and sisters. Macrobius records an anecdote about Sulla's son
Faustus, who, far from feeling that his honour was besmirched by his sister's adultery,
allegedly made puns on the names of her two lovers, though one might also read this as a
joking illustration of Faustus' own decadence (*Sat.* 2.2.9). Cf. Treggiari 1991: 311–19.

54

adulteries by either tolerating them or else, like Caesar, by initiating a divorce.[74] The men who people the pages of Cicero and Tacitus do not burst into their wives' bedrooms to take violent revenge (even when licence was granted by the law).

A husband's violence against his adulterous wife could be viewed with sympathy. The jurist Papinian reports a rescript of Antoninus Pius, emperor in the mid second century CE.

> ei, qui uxorem suam in adulterio deprehensam occidisse se non negat, ultimum supplicium remitti potest, cum sit difficillimum iustum dolorem temperare, et quia plus fecerit quam quia vindicare se non debuerit, puniendus sit.

> *It is possible to remit the aggravated death penalty to a man who does not deny that he killed his wife whom he had caught in adultery, since it is extremely difficult to temper one's just grief, and he is to be punished because he did more [than he should have done] rather than because he ought not to have avenged himself.*

> (*Dig.* 48.5.39.8)[75]

But this text cannot tell us how often husbands avenged themselves so violently, nor does it reveal the influence of social class (or regional custom) on their responses.

Tacitus describes with apparent approval the reactions of (idealised) German tribesmen to cases of adultery. Among these people, he writes, cases of adultery are very few. It is the husband who punishes the adulteress:

> abscisis crinibus nudatam coram propinquis expellit domo maritus ac per omnem vicum verbere agit; publicatae enim pudicitiae nulla venia: non forma, non aetate, non opibus maritum invenerit.

> *He shaves off his wife's hair, strips her in the presence of kinsmen, throws her out of his house and beats her through the whole village. In fact, they have no mercy on the woman who prostitutes her chastity. Neither beauty, youth, nor wealth can find the woman a husband.*

> (Tac. *Germ.* 19)

[74] On Julius Caesar, see Suet. *Jul.* 74; Plut. *Cic.* 29. Other examples of divorces said to have been initiated as a response to the wife's adultery include Pompey's divorce of Mucia (Suet. *Jul.* 50), Lucullus' divorce of Claudia (Plut. *Luc.* 34; Cic. *Pro Mil.* 73); Cato's divorce of Atilia (Plut. *Cat. min.* 24). For husbands' toleration of a wife's adultery, see e.g. Tac. *Ann.* 2.85; Suet. *Tib.* 35.2.
[75] All translations of passages from the *Digest* are taken from that edited by Alan Watson. Cf. Paul, *Sent.* 2.26.5; *CJ* 9.9.4 (Alexander Severus).

A MORAL REVOLUTION?

Punishment is physical, public and the woman is ostracised from society. But could primitive, if noble, German tribesmen really be models for Roman senators?

The Roman husband's customary right to exact vengeance from his wife's lover was paraded in some texts of the late republic and principate.[76] In the satires of Horace and Juvenal, adulterers, when caught, are castrated, beaten or subjected to homosexual rape by the woman's husband or his slaves.[77] Adulterers might be forced to submit to anal penetration with a mullet.[78] But, as we have seen, however much educated men enjoyed reading about violent punishments, such practices do not find their way into Cicero's letters or Tacitus' histories.[79] The poet Ovid mocks the figure of the jealous husband: *rusticus est nimium quem laedit adultera coniunx*, 'The man's a boor who's too offended by his wife's affairs' (*Am.* 3.4.37). Such a response is presented as sadly unsophisticated, inappropriate in civilised society.[80] Augustus' law, which imposed penalties on husbands who tolerated their wives' adultery, implied husbands did not mind when their wives were unfaithful. Rather, perhaps, the urbane upper classes of the late republic and early principate regarded violent revenge as uncivilised and inappropriate. Rome was a city where men walked about the streets unarmed (in theory at least). Violence was for the battlefield, not the bedroom.

Texts of the first and second centuries CE increasingly focus on the internalisation of morality. Foucault has suggestively explored the shifting preoccupations which can be traced in discussions of sexual morality over this period (though he perhaps exaggerates the extent to which these philosophical texts represent the views of most

[76] This right is also assumed in several of Plautus' comedies, e.g. *Mil.* 1394–1427; *Curc.* 25–38; *Poen.* 862–3.
[77] E.g. Hor. *Sat.* 1.2.45–6; 2.7.46–71; Juv. 10.314–17. Cf. Val. Max. 6.1.13; Sen. *De ira* 1.21.3; Calp. Flacc. *Decl.* 11. On these punishments, see Richlin (1981: 381–94) and Treggiari (1991: 271). Adultery seems often to have been the subject of mimes. On this see Richlin (1983: 215) and R.W. Reynolds 'The adultery mime' *CQ* 40 (1946) 77–84.
[78] Parallel to the *raphanidosis* (anal rape with a horse radish) of Greek old comedy. Anal rape as a punishment is discussed by Richlin 1981: 393–4 and (on *exempla*) 389–91. These actions were represented not only as attempts to degrade the adulterer and cause him physical pain but also to reassert the threatened masculinity of the husband by forcing the adulterer into a sexually subordinate position (for the politics of sexual positions, see chapter two below).
[79] This diversity of representations of adultery in different literary genres is emphasised by Richlin 1981. The only example of a known high-status individual of the late republic allegedly involved in the violent avenging of an adultery is the historian Sallust who was said to have been beaten when he was discovered in bed with Fausta the wife of Milo (Gell. 17.18).
[80] This kind of attitude is treated ironically by Seneca (*De ben.* 1.9.3).

members of the Roman upper classes).[81] The writings of Stoics, such as Seneca, Epictetus and Musonius Rufus, advocate austere norms of sexual morality.[82] But their interest is in the moral harm the adulterer inflicts on himself. Epictetus advised that a man should not commit adultery, firstly because in doing so he will make himself a worse man, and only secondly because he will forfeit the trust of his friends and neighbours (2.2). Virtue was a matter of self-control; good behaviour which was merely a result of necessity did not count as virtue. Seneca quotes the poet Ovid: *quae quia non licuit, non dedit, illa dedit*, 'The woman who did not succumb because she could not, she succumbed' (*De ben.* 4.14.1).[83] In Seneca's *De matrimonio*, marriage and adultery are above all states of mind: *nihil est foedius quam uxorem amare quasi adulteram*, 'Nothing is more shameful than to love your wife as if she were your mistress' (*De matr.* 85). From this point of view, the terms of Augustus' legislation were crude, indeed meaningless. Virtue could never be instilled through legislation.

Roman representations of husbands' responses to their wives' infidelity are difficult to evaluate. Sexual power and other kinds of power are closely associated in the texts examined here. It is impossible to disentangle suggestions that a man's wife was unfaithful from attempts to suggest that he was politically or socially weak. We cannot tell which Roman discussions of sexual misbehaviour are to be interpreted metaphorically. Elite adultery in ancient Rome, I have been arguing, was not readily tolerated by all but a few moralists, as some historians have implied. If it had been, Roman texts would not be so insistently preoccupied with it. Rather, discussions of adultery were a means of articulating a variety of associated concerns – with masculinity, power and, on a more general level, patriarchy itself. The apparent implication of moralising writers – and of the Augustan legislation – is that Roman men were often not men enough to control their wives. It had become socially acceptable, moralists alleged, for elite women to have extramarital affairs. This lamentable shift in morals was to be reversed with a return to the customs of an earlier time. In some respects, suggesting a contrast between old-fashioned severity and new sophistication does cast light on the multifarious

---

[81] Foucault 1988, esp. 39–68.
[82] These texts are discussed by Treggiari 1991: 215–24. On Musonius, see also Cora Lutz 'Musonius Rufus, the Roman Socrates' *YClS* 10 (1947) 3–147, (on adultery) 84–97.
[83] Quoting Ovid, *Am.* 3.4.4.

and divergent texts which discuss adultery. But it is impossible to divide the Roman elite into those who followed one line and those who followed the other. Augustus himself, it seems, combined the two.

SEXUAL POLITICS

An ode of Horace presents the *princeps* as guarantor of prosperity, peace and morality. Under his beneficent rule, oxen graze in safety and:

> nullis polluitur casta domus stupris,
> mos et lex maculosum edomuit nefas,
> laudantur simili prole puerperae,
> culpam poena premit comes.

Households are chaste, polluted by no adulteries. Custom and law vanquish guilty wrong-doing. New mothers are praised, whose infants resemble their fathers. Punishment follows close on crime.

(Hor. *Carm.* 4.5.21–4)

The Augustan law was parading the values which were supposed to have informed the behaviour of Romans in the virtuous past, as we have seen.[84] Aeneas, the hero of Virgil's epic and the alleged ancestor of the Julian family, is pictured in the first book of the *Aeneid* founding the settlement which was to become Rome: *moresque viris et moenia ponet.* 'He established *mores* and walls for his men' (*Aen.* 1.264). The moral legislation was a central pillar of the newly refounded Roman state.

Augustus was inaugurating a new golden age, *aurea saecula* (*Aen.* 6.791–807). In the *ludi saeculares*, the games held (in theory) once a

---

[84] The final poem in Horace's collection of odes includes the following tribute to the age of Augustus, which:

> Ianum Quirini clausit et ordinem
> rectum evaganti frena licentiae
> iniecit emovitque culpas
> et veteres revocavit artes,
>
> per quas Latinum nomen et Italae
> crevere vires . . .

closed the doors of Janus, put a bridle on runaway licence, banished crime and revived the ancient qualities through which the Latin name and the force of Italy grew strong . . .

(Hor. *Carm.* 4.15.9–14)

century, which were celebrated in 17 BCE (the year after the moral legislation), a hymn was sung composed by the poet Horace: *Iam Fides et Pax et Honos Pudorque priscus et neglecta redire Virtus audet.* 'Now Faith and Peace, old-fashioned Honour and Virtue, long neglected, dare to return.' (*Carm. saec.* 57–9). Those who lived on the Aventine hill in Rome made offerings of first-fruits, as though they were primitive farmers[85] – not so much the revival of tradition as its invention. Ronald Syme observes: 'The whole conception of the Roman past on which [Augustus] sought to erect the moral and spiritual basis of the New State was in a large measure imaginary or spurious.'[86] Yet the *princeps* was taking over and adapting the political vocabulary of the republic. His programme of 'restoration' is foreshadowed in a passage from Cicero's *Pro Marcello*, addressed to Julius Caesar:

> constituenda iudicia, revocanda fides, comprimendae libidines, propaganda suboles, omnia, quae dilapsa iam diffluxerunt, severis legibus vincienda sunt.

> *The reestablishment of the courts, the restoration of credit, the suppression of licence, the production of children, all that now suffers from disorder and neglect must be brought under control through vigorous legislation.*

(Cic. *Pro Marc.* 23)

Just as credit crises and the breakdown of the legal system were inextricably associated with sexual excess, so the reestablishment of order must take place in all these spheres at once.

The law ostensibly set out to discourage men who had designs on the wives of others. It permitted fathers and husbands to avenge themselves violently under some circumstances. But making adultery a criminal offence also emphasised its disruptive power. The norms the emperor sought to impose were close to those advocated by the staunchest republican moralists. Like them, he claimed that sexual morality should be subject to much stricter control. But who was to exercise that control? State intervention in cases of sexual and sumptuary misdemeanours was not altogether alien to the traditions of republican Rome (as we saw in the introduction). Since the early republic, the censors had had a degree of authority over what we

[85] Zanker highlights the irony of this ritual (1988: 168). On the *ludi saeculares* in relation to images of the Augustan regime, see Zanker (1988: 167–238) and Syme (1939: 443).
[86] Syme 1939: 452–3.

might term private morality.[87] Cicero, in the *Pro Marcello*, exhorted Julius Caesar to restrain licence but, in his treatise on the ideal state, *De republica*, he argued that the censors should instruct men to control their own wives (4.6). Tacitus, in his treatise on German tribes, praised their severe attitude to adultery, as we have seen. Cases of adultery were not in themselves symptoms of society's moral corruption, for Tacitus; women were always untrustworthy (their males lovers are not mentioned). But a society was revealed as sound or corrupt in its responses to such cases. Among the Germans, the punishment of adultery was entirely in the hands of the woman's family. *Plus ibi boni mores valent quam alibi bonae leges*, 'Good customs are more efficacious there than good laws in other places' (Tac. *Germ.* 19). Tacitus represented the power over sexual morals claimed by the emperor as profoundly sinister. His summary of the history of law in Rome culminates with Caesar Augustus and his moral legislation: *acriora ex eo vincula*, 'From then on the shackles grew tighter' (Tac. *Ann.* 3.28).

Augustus' legislation did not exclude families from exercising a certain degree of authority when it came to punishing the sexual misbehaviour of their female members. Husbands and fathers were permitted to use violence and encouraged to prosecute. Augustus' law paraded the moral obligation of the family to preserve its honour. Husbands were punished for failing to control their wives. But how far was the law concerned with the protection of the individual husband? An attack on the rights of husbands and fathers was an attack on the power of the state; the state claimed the right to intervene, *velut parens omnium*, 'as if it were the universal father' (Tac. *Ann.* 3.28). Augustus was now *pater patriae*, 'father of the fatherland' – the ultimate *paterfamilias*. The whole state had become his household.[88]

Augustus' law was a subtle manipulation of currents in the ideological debates of the republic. The emperor was restoring the republic,

---

[87] Treggiari emphasises the limited nature of these interventions as they are represented in later texts (1991: 292–3).

[88] Augustus was granted the title *pater patriae* in 2 BCE, some months before Julia's alleged adulteries became a public scandal. Andrew Wallace-Hadrill describes Augustus as treating the family as 'a microcosm of the state' ('Propaganda and dissent? Augustan moral legislation and the love poets' *Klio* 67 (1985) 180–4). This is an association to be found in other cultures too, but the particularities of the position of the *paterfamilias* in Roman society lend this analogy a particular force (for other parallels between household and state, see chapter four below).

bringing back the old times when Roman wives, under the careful vigilance of their husbands, were always virtuous. But how could a state be thought virtuous where adultery, to be controlled, had to be made a criminal offence? How could husbands be imagined strong and vigilant, if the threat of punishment was necessary to make them exercise proper control over their own households? Augustus' law made adultery seem more, not less, dangerous. Behaviour that infringed the new legislation acquired a new significance. With reference to his daughter and granddaughter, the emperor called: *culpam inter viros et feminas vulgatam gravi nomine laesarum religionum ac violatae maiestatis*, 'an offence common between men and women by the stern names of impiety and treason' (Tac. *Ann.* 3.24). The law against adultery bore a disconcerting resemblance to that against treason – and adultery itself now took on a much more intimate association with political subversion.

The most notorious offender against Augustus' adultery law, so Roman writers claimed, was his only child, Julia.[89] Her licentious behaviour flagrantly undermined his attempts to reform Roman morals. The father of the Roman state sent his own daughter into exile. Seneca presents her as a mirror image of her father (*De ben.* 6.32).[90] The categories set up by his legislation, she subverted. He divided women into two classes: wives and prostitutes – those whom one might marry and those with whom one might have sex outside marriage. Julia was married but sold her sexual favours to whoever would buy them.[91] By day, the voice of the state spoke in the forum. On the same rostra, those words were nightly disobeyed by the emperor's daughter. In the words of Velleius Paterculus, *quidquid liberet pro licito vindicans*, 'Whatever she desired she claimed as her right' (Vell. Pat. 2.100.3). Her sexual licence, Syme suggests, was a

---

[89] The question of whether this was a pretext for the suppression of a treasonous plot is much discussed. For the argument that there was a plot, see Ronald Syme 'The crisis of 2 BC' *Bayerische Akademie der Wissenschaften* 7 (1974) 3–34 (= Syme *Roman Papers* III (Oxford 1984) 912–36). Syme also argues for the possibility of a treasonous plot in connection with the younger Julia's banishment on the grounds of adultery in 8 CE (Ronald Syme *History in Ovid* (Oxford 1978) 201–11). Others see the elder Julia's alleged adultery as the central issue (e.g. Raditsa 1980; Arther Ferrill 'Augustus and his daughter: a modern myth' in Carl Deroux ed. *Studies in Latin literature and Roman history* II (Brussels 1980) 332–46).

[90] Other texts referring to this episode include: Vell. Pat. 2.100.1–5 (which Seneca seems to echo); Sen. *De clem.* 1.10.3; *De brev. vit.* 4.5; Pliny, *NH* 7.149; 21.9; Tac. *Ann.* 1.53; 3.24; 4.44; Suet. *Aug.* 65.1; *Tib.* 11.4; Dio 55.12–16; Macrob. *Sat.* 2.5.

[91] On representations of aristocratic women (and, in particular, female members of the imperial family) as prostitutes see Edwards (forthcoming b).

perverse variation on traditional aristocratic claims to *libertas*.[92] Yet even the most perverse claim to *libertas* might cast a sinister reflection on the regime which silenced it.

Augustus was making full use of the symbolic associations of controlling sexual misbehaviour. The *lex Iulia de adulteriis* was the last word in rhetorical invective. During the time of the triumvirate, Augustus (then Octavian) had written obscene verses against an aristocrat Pollio, as was customary among the Roman upper classes. But Pollio did not respond in kind: *non est enim facile in eum scribere qui potest proscribere*, 'It is no light matter to write poems against a man who can proscribe you' (Macrob. *Sat.* 2.4.21). There were dangers in bandying insults with an autocrat, for the bounds of licence were shifting, the penalties for transgression hard.

Accusations of adultery led to the removal of several prominent individuals from Rome. Inconvenient aristocratic women could be disposed of with accusations of adultery and treason (Appuleia Varilla, Tac. *Ann.* 2.50; Claudia Pulchra, 4.52) or adultery and poisoning (Aemilia Lepida, 3.22).[93] Men could be accused of committing, or being an accomplice in the commission of, adultery with female members of the imperial family.[94] The criminalisation of adultery contributed to the institutionalisation of the emperor's dynastic ambitions – hardly the most republican of projects. Was adultery with the emperor's daughter perceived as infiltration of the imperial house? Or was it the ultimate challenge to the emperor's attempt to restore morals?

[92] Syme 1939:426. The statue of Marsyas, presented as the scene of Julia's disgrace by Seneca, was traditionally associated with *libertas* (cf. Serv. ad *Aen.* 3.20).
[93] On these adultery trials, see A.J. Marshall 'Women on trial before the Roman senate' *EMC* 34 (1990) 333–66.
[94] A number of aristocrats were punished for their alleged adulteries with the elder Julia (Iullus Antonius, Quinctius Crispinus, Sempronius Gracchus, Appius Claudius Pulcher, Cornelius Scipio) and the younger Julia (D. Iunius Silanus). Many take the view that Ovid was exiled in part for his involvement in the adultery of the younger Julia (J.C. Thibault *The mystery of Ovid's exile* (Berkeley 1964) 38–67). Under Caligula, M. Aemilius Lepidus was accused of adultery with the emperor's sisters Julia and Agrippina, as well as treason. According to Dio (60.8), the philosopher Seneca was exiled for adultery with Caligula's sister Julia (though cf. schol. on Juv. 5.109). This question is discussed by Miriam Griffin *Seneca: a philosopher in politics* (Oxford 1976) 59.

CHAPTER TWO

Mollitia:
Reading the body

The ancient Romans have been so domesticated that many modern western men (fewer women, perhaps) have been able to imagine themselves, their rusty Latin refreshed, easily adapting to life in the time of Cicero or the younger Pliny. But language is not the only barrier which separates us from the Romans. Entire vocabularies of gesture differ from one culture to another. For Romans, a particular physical movement could have a meaning quite at variance with one a modern Briton might attribute to it – even indicating a category of behaviour for which we have no close equivalent.

Cicero is supposed to have said of Julius Caesar:

> . . . *that a tyrannical purpose was evident in most of Caesar's political plans and projects. 'On the other hand,' he said, 'when I look at his exquisitely arranged hair and see him scratching his head with one finger, I find it impossible to believe that this man would ever conceive of so great a crime as the overthrow of the Roman constitution.'*

> (Plut. *Jul.* 4.4)

According to Cicero, Caesar used to scratch his head with one finger – for us a movement of little significance. But Cicero represented this as an indication that Caesar was not a man to be frightened of, that he posed no real threat. What was the connection? Scratching one's head with one finger was a sign of *mollitia*, which may provisionally be translated as 'softness' or 'effeminacy'. This term, in the late republic and early principate, evoked a particular complex of associations, which will be the focus of this chapter.[1] *Mollitia* in a man was

---

[1] For other instances of scratching the head with one finger, see Lucilius 882–4 Marx; Sen. *Ep.* 52.12; Juv. 9.133; Licinius Calvus *FPL* 18 ed., Morel. On the importance of the language of gestures for deciphering character in the Greco-Roman world, see Maud W. Gleason 'The semiotics of gender: physiognomy and self-fashioning' in D.M. Halperin, J.J. Winkler, F.I. Zeitlin eds. *Before sexuality: the construction of erotic experience in the ancient Greek world* (Princeton 1990) 389–415. On the history of gesture, see too Jan Bremmer and Herman Roodenburg eds. *A cultural history of gesture* (Oxford 1991).

63

sometimes taken to imply an inclination to submit oneself sexually to other men, sometimes an inability to act in a forceful 'manly' way. Power and sexual passivity seemed, for Cicero and many other Romans, incompatible – and yet they were often associated with one another, for some of the most powerful men in Rome were accused of *mollitia*.

Many of Cicero's speeches contain accusations of effeminacy, sometimes involving attacks on the sexual behaviour of the victim of the accusation. Those against Clodius and Antony are among the most vivid.[2] The second Philippic gives a highly coloured description of Mark Antony's youth:

> sumpsisti virilem, quam statim muliebrem togam reddidisti. primo vulgare scortum, certa flagitii merces, nec ea parva; sed cito Curio intervenit, qui te a meretricio quaestu abduxit et, tamquam stolam dedisset, in matrimonio stabili et certo collocavit. nemo umquam puer emptus libidinis causa tam fuit in domini potestate quam tu in Curionis.

> *You took on a man's toga and at once turned it into a whore's. At first, you were a common prostitute, the price of your infamy was fixed – and not small either; but soon Curio turned up, drew you away from your meretricious trade and, as if he had given you a matron's robe, established you in lasting and stable matrimony. No boy bought for sexual gratification was ever so much in the power of his master as you were in Curio's.*

(Cic. Phil. 2.44–5)

Like the young lover in numerous Roman comedies, Curio rescues his beloved from the threat of a life of prostitution to make her his wife. Unfortunately, in this case, the blushing bride is not a well-born maiden mistakenly sold into slavery at an early age, but a young man (the son of an impoverished Roman consular).[3] Cicero contrives to make a stable, lasting relationship sound far more reprehensible than prostitution – Antony's emotional attachment to Curio, he implies,

---

[2] Other examples include: Cic. *Phil.* 2.55 (Antony); *In Verr.* 2.5.81 (Verres); *Pro Milone* 55 (Clodius); *In Cat.* 2.4, 8 (Catiline); *De har. resp.* 42 (Clodius); *De domo sua* 49 (Clodius); 60 (Gabinius); 139 (Clodius); *De prov. cons.* 9 (Gabinius); *Ad Att.* 14.5 (Curio); 86.2 (Clodius). Cf. Richlin 1983: 85–6, 96–104; Saara Lilja *Homosexuality in republican and Augustan Rome* (Helsinki 1982) 93–7; Françoise Gonfroy 'Homosexualité et l'idéologie esclavagiste chez Ciceron' *DHA* 4 (1978) 219–65.

[3] For Cicero's evocation of comic plots, see, too, his representation of Clodia as an author and actor of mimes (*Pro Cael.* 64–5). For other ironical invocations of the idea of a homosexual wedding, see Juv. 2.117–42; Suet. *Nero* 28–9; Mart. 12.42; Tac. *Ann.* 15.37.

reduced him to a position of slave-like dependence. Whereas it was generally expected that in a sexual relationship between males, the older 'active' partner would pursue the younger 'passive' one, here Antony is described as running after Curio. He is behaving like a woman, without even the marginally redeeming female virtue of waiting to be sought after.[4]

What are we to make of this and similar accusations? Roman writers associated effeminacy with political, social and moral weakness. In patriarchal societies, it is not uncommon for men to compare to women other men they wish to humiliate. But in what sense were Romans comparing men to women? Often the same men were accused of effeminacy and adultery.[5] We might more readily think of the male adulterer as having an excessive interest in playing a male (sexually 'active') role – rather than being too 'feminine'. Why did Roman writers so frequently associate adultery and effeminacy? This is one of several paradoxes associated with Roman discussions of *mollitia*. I think we can go part way towards unravelling some of them, but first we need to dispense with an assumption which has dominated many modern responses to Roman uses of the term *mollitia*.

Roman discussions of *mollitia* and related notions have generally been taken to mean that many men in ancient Rome (at least among the upper classes) took part in homosexual activity or at least regarded such behaviour as commonplace.[6] But the myth of Rome's unlimited sexual licence has recently been challenged. Paul Veyne observes: 'Sexuality in the ancient world and sexuality in our own day are two structures which have nothing in common and are not even to be compared. They are not to be placed on a scale ranging from the repressive to the permissive, to conform with the liberal fiction of

---

[4] In Latin love elegy, slavery is often invoked as an analogy for the relationship between the poet and his mistress (e.g. Prop. 1.1.27–8; 1.9; Tib. 1.5.5–6; Ov. *Am.* 1.3.5–6. Cf. R.O.A.M. Lyne *The Latin love poets* (Oxford 1980) 78–81; Paul Veyne *Roman erotic elegy; love, poetry and the west* (Chicago 1989) 132–50). The usual elegiac scenario presents the man (conventionally the dominant partner) as slave to the woman – a piquant inversion of relations of domination as traditionally conceived, which also serves to problematise the relationship between power and sexual desire (see D.F. Kennedy *The arts of love* (Cambridge 1993) ch. 4).

[5] Antony was frequently represented as an habitual womaniser (cf. Griffin 1985 ch. 2).

[6] For surveys of the historiography of homosexuality in ancient Rome, see Ramsay MacMullen 'Roman attitudes to Greek love' *Historia* 31 (1982) 484–502, at 35, and Amy Richlin 'Not before homosexuality: the materiality of the *cinaedus* and the Roman law against love between men' (forthcoming).

optimistic rationalists.'[7] To examine attitudes to sexuality in the ancient world with the intention of determining whether 'they' were more liberated than 'us', is to neglect the fact that 'their' preoccupations were quite different from 'ours'.[8] The question posed by John Boswell, for instance, in his book on attitudes to homosexuality in antiquity and the early middle ages (published in 1980) – how tolerant were the Romans of homosexuality? – is, I feel, misleading.[9] His book undertakes to look at homosexuality in Rome in terms of attitudes to those who were perceived as homosexual – a group which Boswell seems to conceive of as unproblematically equivalent to those who see themselves as 'gay' in contemporary western societies. There is little to suggest that Romans ever saw people with exclusively homosexual preferences as a distinct social group.[10] An apparently identical physical act can take on radically different meanings in different cultures.[11] We should not embark on an examination of Roman attitudes to different sexual practices from the assumption that they constructed sexuality in the same ways as we might do.[12]

[7] Veyne 1978 at 52, my translation. (But of course Veyne at the same time suggests their comparability by designating them both 'sexualities', as Duncan Kennedy points out to me.) Veyne's contribution to the study of sexuality in the ancient world has been rather overlooked by some recent scholars, whose concentration on ancient Greece and interest in contemporary gay activism has perhaps led them to focus rather on Foucault's work (David Halperin, for instance, referring to the appearance of K.J. Dover's *Greek homosexuality* in 1978, identifies this year as the start of a new era in the study of ancient sexuality, without noting that 1978 also saw the appearance of Veyne's article in *Annales* (*One hundred years of homosexuality* (New York 1990) 4). Foucault himself freely acknowledged his debt to Veyne, in the introduction to *The history of sexuality* II: *The use of pleasure* (London 1986) esp. 8. For arguments against seeing the history of sexuality in terms of a shifting balance between licence and repression, see Foucault 1978.

[8] The alien nature of patterns of sexual behaviour in the ancient Greek world has been well emphasised in recent years: J.J. Winkler *The constraints of desire* (New York 1990); D.M. Halperin *One hundred years of homosexuality* (New York 1990); Halperin, Winkler and Zeitlin 1990.

[9] John Boswell *Christianity, social tolerance and homosexuality* (Chicago 1980). Boswell has since modified his position somewhat ('Concepts, experience and sexuality' *Differences: a Journal of Feminist Cultural Studies* 2.1 (1990) 67–87). For more sophisticated statements of an 'essentialist' position see Richlin forthcoming (on Rome).

[10] This point is stressed by Veyne 1978, MacMullen 1982 and Foucault 1986 and 1988. Though cf. the case made by Richlin forthcoming.

[11] See e.g. Kenneth Plummer ed. *The making of the modern homosexual* (London 1981) Plummer intro; Jeffrey Weeks *Sex, politics and society* (London 1981).

[12] 'Sexuality' is a problematic term. A recent book on the construction of erotic experience in the ancient Greek world is entitled *Before sexuality* – though the editors' introduction is somewhat equivocal on the significance of the title (Halperin, Winkler and Zeitlin 1990: 5–20). Some are unwilling to use the term 'sexuality' with reference to periods earlier than the nineteenth century, which certainly saw a major shift in constructions of the erotic (Foucault 1979; Peter Gay *The bourgeois experience: Victoria to Freud* (Oxford 1984–6); Stephen Heath

Recognising this affects our perceptions not only of how Romans thought about and talked about sex but also of their sexual behaviour and desires. The Freudian or Kinseyian view, that sex drive exists at a constant level in any population group, rising and falling in accordance with the life-cycle of the individual, has been radically called into question in recent decades. There are good grounds for supposing that human sexuality is not a straightforward biological given but varies significantly in form and intensity between cultures.[13] We cannot assume a constant framework of human sexual practices or even of desires to which we might relate Roman attitudes to sex. John Gagnon and William Simon, in a study of modern theories of sexuality, suggest that Freudian preoccupations can have a distorting effect. They argue: 'It is just as plausible to examine sexual behaviour for its capacity to express and serve non-sexual motives as the reverse.'[14]

This chapter sets out to examine not sexual behaviour in ancient Rome (which is irrecoverable) but Roman discourses about sexual behaviour and how those discourses were deployed in the pursuit of non-sexual (as well as sexual) ends. What will, I hope, emerge is the impossibility of separating off discourses about sex from other discourses, in particular those relating to gender but also those relating to oppositions between sophistication and vigour, between Greek and Roman. No Roman author ever calls himself effeminate in surviving Latin literature.[15] Yet many male Romans seem to have adopted ways of dressing, of speaking, even of walking, which laid them open to charges of effeminacy. How is it that some Romans cultivated forms of behaviour which others saw as effeminate? The apparent ambiguity of some forms of behaviour suggests the difficulty members of Rome's educated upper classes seem to have felt in

The sexual fix (London 1982); A.I. Davidson 'Sex and the emergence of sexuality' Critical Enquiry 14 (1987–8) 16–48). However, there is no convenient substitute for the term sexuality in the sense of the cultural interpretation of erotic experience, which is how I use it here. Of course, the use of any single term to refer to categories of experience in the ancient as well as the modern worlds has essentialising implications, but these are to some extent at least unavoidable.

[13] See e.g. John Gagnon and William Simon Sexual conduct: the social sources of human development (London 1973). Cf. Foucault who argues that apparently restrictive prescriptions relating to sexual behaviour may create rather than repress forms of sexuality (1979). For an example of a society characterised by what might seem from a western point of view to be a very low level of sexual activity, see Karl G. Heider 'Dani sexuality: a low energy system' Man 2 (1976) 188–201.   [14] Gagnon and Simon 1973: 17.

[15] See Richlin forthcoming on the silence of the cinaedus.

distinguishing between sophistication, elegance and urbanity on the one hand, and effeminacy on the other. It also suggests the implication of ideas of *mollitia* in a whole range of other discourses we might not immediately associate with sexual behaviour.

Scholars have used discussions of *mollitia* in attempts to establish Roman attitudes to homosexual behaviour. But when Roman men accused one another of being *mollis*, how far were they reacting to, or making allegations about, their specifically sexual behaviour? This chapter argues that accusations of *mollitia* were not so much responses to 'effeminate' sexual behaviour as attempts to humiliate. The terms referring to *mollitia* and related notions have a much broader frame of reference than the specifically sexual. This is not to say that there was no relationship between accusations of *mollitia* and certain sexual practices. But I would argue that in many cases to accuse a man of being susceptible to sexual penetration by other men was more a vivid metonymy for a generalised and pejorative claim that he was effeminate rather than an accusation that could be directly related to the sexual preferences of the victim of the insult.

THE SIGNS OF MOLLITIA

Accusations of *mollitia* are characterised by certain recurring features.[16] The victim of the accusation is alleged to be over-careful in his dress, often affecting 'feminine' and/or exotic clothes. Martial mocks the scarlet and violet robes of his male acquaintances – 'real' men, he implies, wore white togas and sober-coloured cloaks (1.96). Juvenal castigates an orator for wearing clothes of the diaphanous silk associated with courtesans (2.65–81).[17] The 'effeminate' man is perfumed, bathes more often than is necessary and depilates his legs.[18] We should note the frequent occurrence of Greek terms for

---

[16] For a vivid evocation of 'effeminate' appearance in general, see Seneca, *NQ* 7.31.1–3. On effeminate characteristics, see Richlin forthcoming, Gleason 1990.

[17] On effeminate dress, see too: Cic. *In Verr.* 2.5.31, *In Cat.* 2.22–3; *Phil.* 2.76; Quint. *Inst.* 5.9.14; Sen. *Ep.* 90.20, *De ben.* 7.9 (expressing disapproval of transparent dress worn by women, too), *Const. sap.* 18.3; *Ad Helv.* 16; Gell. 6.12.4–5. These texts are discussed by V.A. Tracy 'Roman dandies and transvestites' *EMC* 20 (1976) 60–3.

[18] The elder Pliny is critical of the use of luxurious perfumes (*NH* 13.18–25). On the use of perfume, see J. Colin 'Luxe oriental et parfums masculins dans la Rome Alexandrine' *RBPh* 33 (1955) 5–19, and R.J. Forbes *Studies in ancient technology* III (Leiden 1965) 1–50 'Cosmetics and perfumes in antiquity'. On the moral dangers of bathing, see Sen. *Ep.* 86.6–13. On depilation, see Mart. 3.74; 10.65; Gell. 6.12; Sen. *NQ* 1.16–17; Athenaeus 13.564f–5f. Cf. Richlin 1983: 41,168, 188–9.

cosmetics and perfumes, which signified not only the foreign provenance of some of these substances but also the ambivalence with
which some Romans regarded them. The 'effeminate' man walks in a
mincing way, like a dancer or a woman.[19] Women, too, might be
disapproved of for wearing perfume, cosmetics and transparent
dresses, and for dancing.[20] Such behaviour was sometimes presented
by moralists as characteristic of bad women rather than women in
general. This dimension of the contrast between masculine and
feminine modes of self-presentation and behaviour through which
discussions of effeminacy are articulated is highly significant and will
be discussed below.

Often, too, the effeminate man is represented as plucking out his
beard in order, so moralists claimed, to appear more youthful.[21] The
younger Seneca expostulates:

> non videntur tibi contra naturam vivere qui commutant cum feminis
> vestem? non vivunt contra naturam qui spectant, ut pueritia splendeat
> tempore alieno? quid fieri crudelius vel miserius potest? numquam vir
> erit, ut diu virum pati possit? et cum illum contumeliae sexus eripuisse
> debuerat, non ne aetas quidem eripiet?

> *Don't you think that men live contrary to nature who adopt a feminine
> style of dress? Don't men live contrary to nature who try to look fresh and
> boyish when they're far too old? What could be more cruel or pathetic? Will
> he put maturity off for ever so that he may give other men pleasure? Can't
> he, even as a grown man, abstain from practices his sex should never have
> licensed him to engage in in the first place?*

(Sen. *Ep.* 122.7–8)

Youth was associated with sexual passivity (though such behaviour
Seneca presents as reprehensible even in young men). Those who
strove to look young were suggesting by their behaviour a positive
valuation of youthful looks over a mature appearance, which we
might interpret as posing a threat to the ethic of reverence for age and
respect for *mores maiorum*. Suetonius records that the emperor Otho
would apply moist bread to his face every day in order to keep his skin

---

[19] Cf. Phaedrus appendix 8; Macrob. *Sat.* 2.3.16. For Roman disapproval of dancing, see
Macrob. *Sat.* 3.14.6–7.
[20] See Maria Wyke 'Woman in the mirror: the rhetoric of adornment in the Roman world' in
Léonie Archer, Susan Fischler, Maria Wyke eds. *Illusions of the night: women in ancient
societies* (forthcoming).
[21] On the semiotics of hair, see Gleason 1990: 401–2.

smooth and soft like that of a boy (*Otho* 12.1).[22] The desire to look younger than one's age was seen as particularly inappropriate in one who, as emperor, should inspire respect and obedience. Such behaviour undermined the traditional associations between authority, seniority, masculinity and *Romanitas*.

SEXUAL PRACTICES

Accusations of effeminacy are, I suggested, usually interpreted by modern scholars as implying something about the specifically sexual tastes of the 'effeminate'. Although the association Romans made between effeminacy and particular sexual practices is not as straightforward as it might at first seem, before examining its problematic aspects in more detail I want to look at what it meant to accuse a man of wishing to play a 'female' sexual role. Sexual relationships were constructed as relationships of domination and subordination, of superiority and inferiority, in Roman moral and social discourse.[23] Veyne stresses that Romans never saw the love of women and the love of boys as opposites, as mutually exclusive options. What mattered was whether one took an 'active' or a 'passive' role. To be 'active' was to be 'male'.[24] No Roman portrays himself as willingly playing a 'passive' role.[25]

Several terms of abuse could suggest sexual passivity, for instance, *pathicus, concubinus, cinaedus*.[26] Invective asserting the sexual passivity of one's male enemies took a variety of forms, some of which were evidently perceived to be more serious than others.[27] Cicero regularly accused his male opponents of submitting themselves in their youth

---

[22] On Otho, see too Juv. 2.99–109. On bread poultices, see also Juv. 6.461–73.

[23] A.E. Housman drew attention to the differentiation of 'active' and 'passive' male sexual roles in Latin literature ('*Praefanda*' *Hermes* 66 (1931) 402–12). The 'domination and subordination' model seems more pervasive in Roman culture than Greek. See Eva Cantarella *Secondo natura: la bisessualità nel mondo antico* (Rome 1988) esp. 130–3.

[24] Paul Veyne 'Homosexuality in ancient Rome' in Philippe Ariès and André Béjin eds. *Western sexuality: practice and precept in past and present times* (Oxford 1985) 26–35, quotation from 29. On perceptions of sexual roles in classical Athens, see K.J. Dover *Greek homosexuality* (London 1978); Foucault 1986; Halperin, Winkler and Zeitlin 1990; Halperin 1990; Winkler 1990; David Cohen *Law, sexuality and society: the enforcement of morals in classical Athens* (Cambridge 1991). On Greece and Rome, see Cantarella 1988.

[25] As Richlin points out (1983: 38, 65, 226 and forthcoming).

[26] See Richlin forthcoming for a more extensive list.

[27] See Richlin (1983: 220–2) for a detailed discussion of the hierarchy of insults, with many examples. Cf. Veyne 1985: 30–1.

to be penetrated by other men (as in the speech against Antony, quoted above). To imply that a man continued to play a 'passive' sexual role into adulthood was a much graver charge.[28] Worst of all was to imply that he used his mouth to give sexual pleasure to others, particularly women.[29]

It seems to be the case that citizen men who enjoyed being penetrated ran the risk of exposing themselves to legal and civic disabilities. This may well have been the offence covered by the republican *lex Scantinia*.[30] The praetor's edict included in the category of those not permitted to represent others in the praetor's court (classed with those who have hired out their services to fight with wild beasts and those condemned on a capital charge) *qui corpore suo muliebria passus est*, 'the man who has suffered his body to be used like that of a woman' (*Dig.* 3.1.1.6, Ulpian).[31] A passage in the writings of the Jurist Paul refers to the fine a man might incur if he allowed another to commit *stuprum* against himself, that is, he allowed himself to be penetrated (Paul, *Sent.* 2.26.12–13). These legal restrictions are suggestive but they do not necessarily mean men who enjoyed being penetrated were any more of a social group than, for instance, adulteresses.

A paradoxical feature of accusations imputing 'effeminate' sexual behaviour to males is that a 'passive' sexual role was not thought to be a source of sexual pleasure for men. Ovid suggests that mature women are to be preferred to boys as sexual partners for the following reason:

[28] It also seems to have been more acceptable to desire to penetrate boys or young men (who had not yet grown beards) rather than older men. Cf. Sen. *Ep.* 122; Suet. *Galba* 22; Athenaeus 13.605d; Lucian, *The ignorant book collector* 25. It is sometimes suggested that boys were castrated in order to make them more attractive (e.g. Mart. 9.8; Stat. *Silv.* 2.6.38–41). Seneca accuses the really perverse of castrating themselves (*NQ* 7.31.3).

[29] Cf. Richlin 1983: 55. Foucault's analysis of Artemidorus, *The interpretation of dreams*, is consistent with this (1988: 4–36), though Artemidorus' assertion that some dreams are to be interpreted as having an 'inverted' value suggests that we cannot necessarily expect to extract a clear picture of sexual morality from his treatise. For further discussion of Artemidorus' treatment of sexual dreams, see the discussions by S.R.F. Price ('The future of dreams: from Freud to Artemidorus' *P&P* 113 (1986) 3–37) and Winkler 1990: 17–44. On oral sex, cf. Dover (1978: 101) who refers to Galen's statement: 'We are more revolted by cunnilinctus than by fellatio' (12.249 Kühn, tr. Dover).

[30] For this interpretation of the various allusive references to this legislation (in particular that in Juv. 2.36–44), see Richlin forthcoming, who discusses the legal position of the sexually 'passive' male citizen in detail. Contrast Boswell (1980: 65–8) and Lilja (1982: 112–21) who argue that the *lex Scantinia* did not make illegal homosexual relations between adult males.

[31] The *lex Iulia municipalis*, a law of Julius Caesar relating to local government, disqualified from standing for office, among others: *queive corpore quaestum fecit, fecerit*, 'one who has prostituted or shall have prostituted himself' (*CIL* 1 593, l.123).

illis sentitur non inritata voluptas:
quod iuvet, ex aequo femina virque ferant.
odi concubitus, qui non utrumque resolvunt;
hoc est, cur pueri tangar amore minus.

They need no encouragement to take their pleasure: let both man and woman feel what delights them equally. I hate embraces which fail to satisfy both partners. That is why for me loving boys holds little attraction.

(Ov. *Ars.* 2.681–4)

Boys, unlike mature women, were not thought to make sexual demands.[32] There seems to be no discussion in Latin texts of what boys were supposed to find attractive in a male lover.[33]

Male sexual 'passivity' was associated with young slaves, who had no choice but to submit to the wishes of their masters. The assumption that male slaves might be called upon to provide sexual gratification for their masters, and might actually have been bought for that purpose, is a common one.[34] The distinction between 'active' and 'passive' roles in sex between males was profoundly implicated in the distinction between free and slave. Françoise Gonfroy sets out the rhetorical techniques by which Cicero assimilates the servile, the feminine and the sexually passive in attacks on his opponents.[35] Feelings of contempt for sexual passivity, for slaves and for women were made mutually reinforcing by this elision.

'Activity' and 'passivity' in a sexual context are hardly unproblematic terms.[36] It all depends, Veyne remarks, on whether one takes

[32] For similar comparisons, see Prop. 2.4.17–22, Juv. 6.36–7. Cf. the contrast between Encolpius' sexual encounters with Giton and those he has with women in Petronius, *Satyricon* (discussed by T. Wade Richardson 'Homosexuality in the *Satyricon*' *C&M* 25 (1984) 105–27). The lack of erotic feeling on the part of the male passive partner is also a commonplace in Greek literature. See Dover 1978: 52–4.

[33] Richlin 1983: 38 and forthcoming. Contrast the insistent and disapproving speculation on the part of Roman moralists as to what women find desirable, discussed in chapter two above. Medical writers and others sometimes offer explanations as to why men should deliberately seek to be penetrated by other men. Caelius Aurelianus (a fifth-century writer who incorporates substantial amounts of material from the second-century medical writer Soranus) attributes this tendency to a diseased mind (*De morbis chronicis* 4.9). Cf. Aristotle, *Nic. eth.* 1148b27. The former text is discussed in detail by P.H. Schrijvers *Eine medizinische Erklärung der männlichen Homosexualität* (Amsterdam 1985).

[34] Cf. e.g. Sen. *Contr.* 4.pr.10; Pet. *Sat.* 63.3; 75.11; Sen. *Ep.* 47.7; Plut. *Roman questions* 101. Cf. B.C. Verstraete 'Slavery and the dynamics of male homosexual relationships in ancient Rome' *Journal of Homosexuality* 5.3 (1980) 227–36; Veyne 1985: 30–1; Cantarella 1988: 134–8. [35] Gonfroy 1978.

[36] Several recent discussions of sex in ancient Athens have used the terms 'penetrative' and 'receptive', in an attempt to avoid the negative associations of passivity. I have chosen to use 'active' and 'passive', precisely because passivity plainly did have negative associations for the authors of virtually all the texts examined here.

'stabbing' (*sabrer*) or 'eating' (*manger*) as one's analogy.[37] 'Eating' occasionally appears as a metaphor for sexual intercourse.[38] Some texts focus on the threat posed by the sexually voracious female – a suggestion that the penetrator need not always have a monopoly of power.[39] This is a striking feature of invective against old women (a frequent theme, especially of satire). The sexually greedy old woman is represented as wholly repulsive.[40] Male power over women had to be striven for. Texts produced (and largely bought and read) by Roman men presented as the most sexually significant question, who penetrated whom. This preoccupation with penetration, characteristic of certain genres in particular of Latin literature, might be seen as an attempt to shore up the penetrator's insecure claim to domination. This may help explain, too, the intense disgust and disapproval with which oral sex was viewed, since it problematised the assignment of 'active' and 'passive' roles. The status of 'stabbing' as the natural metaphor for sex was open to contestation.

PENETRATION AS METAPHOR

Some texts do seem to describe individuals as effeminate only in their sexual tastes. It would be a mistake to take this small number of texts as evidence that sexual behaviour was the central concern of all accusations of effeminacy, for accusations couched in apparently similar terms can serve very different purposes, but these texts are interesting on their own account. The figure of the hypocritical philosopher or moralist who looks stern, rugged and masculine but enjoys playing a 'passive' sexual role appears in the work of Martial, Juvenal and other authors.[41] Part of the point in these texts is that

---

[37] Veyne 1978: 53.
[38] See J.N. Adams *The Latin sexual vocabulary* (1982) 138–41.
[39] Cf. representations of love as slavery in elegy, referred to in note 4 above.
[40] Richlin 1983: 109–16. She observes: 'It seems at least possible that invective against *vetulae* constitutes a sort of apotropaic satire that attempts to belittle and control the power of old women, pitting the phallus against the threat of sterility, death and chthonic forces' (1983: 113).
[41] E.g. Quint. *Inst.* I.pr.15; Juv. 2.9–19; Mart. 1.24; 1.96; 6.56; 9.464; Lucian, *The ignorant book-collector* 23. These texts are discussed by Richlin (1983: 138–9, 201–2) and Gleason (1990: 405–8). This seems to be a variation on the idea of the moralist as debaucher (as opposed to debauchee in these texts). The hypocritical moralist was represented as corrupting the young by making them become his passive sexual partners (perhaps to be related in turn to the idea of the philosopher who corrupts the minds of his pupils). For examples of moralists as sexual corruptors, see the figure of Eumolpus in Petronius, *Satyricon*. Cf. Athenaeus 13.565e.

73

those who appear stern but take decadent pleasure in perversely submitting themselves to others are hypocrites. They pretend to be manly but underneath they are effeminate. These people, Martial and Juvenal both assert, are, because of their hypocrisy, worse than those who are effeminate in their appearance as well as in their sexual tastes.[42]

Yet in these texts, sexual preference is taken to be the final test of whether or not these men are effeminate. Here we can perhaps gain some clues to Roman attitudes to men who played a 'passive' sexual role (though we learn nothing about the extent of such behaviour). Richlin describes Juvenal's second and ninth satires as containing: 'an elemental expression of hostility on the part of the norm against the abnormal.'[43] Certainly Boswell's assertion that 'Romans were extraordinarily dispassionate about sexuality' seems implausible.[44] Roman texts present the question of who penetrated whom not as insignificant but as a highly emotive issue.

Stanley Brandes' anthropological study of male sexual ideology in an Andalusian town sets out patterns of invective in this provincial Spanish community of the mid twentieth century, which seem very similar to those we can trace in ancient Roman texts. Among the Andalusians interviewed by Brandes, to liken a man to a woman in a specifically sexual way is to offer him a grave insult. Parallel to the Roman male concern with being sexually dominant (manifested, for instance, as we have seen, in accusations of passive homosexual behaviour made against political opponents) is the preoccupation of the men in the Andalusian community studied by Brandes with the fear of anal penetration. He remarks: 'Men show themselves to be constantly aware that the anus can be used in homosexual encounters in which the passive partner is perceived as playing the feminine role and indeed as being converted symbolically into a woman. It is this sexual transformation that men fear. As a defence, male speech forms reveal a constant attempt to force masculine rivals into the feminine role in a never-ending quest to avoid adopting this role themselves.'[45]

Similar insults are widely attested in ancient Rome, evident not

---

[42] Richlin forthcoming.   [43] Richlin 1983: 201.

[44] Boswell 1980: 62. This, he argues, gives particular value to Latin literature as a source for the study of 'gay people and gayness in a cultural setting'.

[45] Stanley Brandes 'Like wounded stags: male sexual ideology in an Andalusian town' in Sherry B. Ortner and Harriet Whitehead eds. *Sexual meanings: the cultural construction of gender and sexuality* (Cambridge 1981) 216–39 at 232.

only in Cicero's speeches but also in Catullus' poems and graffiti on the walls of Pompeii, as well as a wide range of other contexts.[46] Accusations of effeminacy may be seen as diluted threats of rape. In the context of these insults, sex is a vivid metaphor for power. The phallus is a source of interpersonal dominance, suggests Richlin, who goes on to observe: 'The sexual threat is thus a metaphor for the assertion of a questioned dominance.'[47] Looking at parallels with the community studied by Brandes can reinforce our sense of the metaphorical status of these accusations. Brandes observes: 'Men generally think of strategic weakness in daily affairs, be they economic or political, in terms of potential anal penetration.'[48] But no-one in this Spanish community (so far as the anthropologist is aware) ever admits to having been anally penetrated himself.

Accusations of certain forms of sexual misbehaviour made by Romans can be read as claims to dominance by the accuser over the accused. To be penetrable was to be weak.[49] To be penetrated was to be aligned with the female, the 'other'. It was not the only respect in which a man could be like a woman but in many cases it was made to stand for other aspects of effeminacy. Penetrability could be invoked at such a level of abstraction that men were often accused of being effeminate while having an excessive interest in penetrating women.

GENDER AND SEXUALITY

Conceptions of sexuality in ancient Rome are inseparable from conceptions of gender. The work of Veyne and Foucault has generated valuable ways of reading Roman sexuality. Both take pains not to treat sexuality as an isolable phenomenon but as an aspect of culture which must be related to other strands in a society's discursive practices. Yet both tend to treat the idea of gender as itself unproblematic. It is clear (even from their own work) that Roman conceptions of sexuality and gender are intimately linked. If we are to treat

---

[46] Richlin 1983: 81–104; Lilja 1982: 88–138.
[47] Richlin 1983: 140–1.   [48] Brandes 1981: 233.
[49] Halperin, discussing the Greek world, argues for seeing 'the apparent refusal of Greek males to discriminate categorically among sexual objects on the basis of anatomical sex . . . [not] as a sexuality at all but . . . rather as a more generalised ethos of penetration and domination, a socio-political discourse, structured by the presence or absence of its central term, the phallus' (1990: 34–5).

sexuality as culturally constructed, then surely gender, too, should be examined as a cultural product.[50]

Recent work in anthropology and sociology has stressed the cultural construction of both sexuality and gender. Sherry Ortner and Harriet Whitehead, in their introduction to a collection of anthropological studies entitled *Sexual meanings*, state as the premise of the book that: 'natural features of gender and natural processes of sex and reproduction furnish only a suggestive and ambiguous backdrop to the cultural organisation of gender and sexuality.'[51] Gender, sexuality and reproduction should be treated as symbols, invested with meaning by the society which uses them. The issues raised by Ortner and Whitehead are fundamental to a better understanding of Roman discussions of *mollitia* and effeminacy. Traditionally, as I suggested above, scholars have used references to men behaving in an effeminate manner to determine, firstly, how widespread homosexual practices were in ancient Rome,[52] and, secondly, how acceptable they were *qua* sexual activity.[53] We cannot hope to find an answer to the first question. The second question may look more promising but it too implies the possibility of treating sexual behaviour as an isolable sphere of activity.

A.E. Housman, Veyne and others have stressed the fundamentally different attitudes expressed in Roman texts to those taking 'active' and those taking 'passive' roles in homosexual acts. Their assertion of the crucial importance of the differentiation of 'active' and 'passive' sexual roles is largely based on ancient texts which discuss effeminacy. Men who took a 'passive' part in homosexual activity are, I have been arguing, often portrayed as assimilating themselves to women –

---

[50] Recent studies of ancient Athenian discourses have laid greater emphasis on the interrelationship of conceptions of gender and sexuality there (Winkler 1990; Halperin 1990: esp. ch. 5). Winkler in particular makes effective use of anthropological parallels in exploring these areas.   [51] Ortner and Whitehead 1981: 1.

[52] Gordon Williams suggests that, despite the frequent occurrence of references to homosexual acts in Latin literature, Roman poets were exclusively heterosexual in their own lives, only including such material in their work because it was an integral part of the Greek literary tradition they used as a model (*Tradition and originality in Roman poetry* (Oxford 1968) 549–57). For a critique of this approach, see Kennedy 1992 ch. 2. At the other extreme from Williams, Boswell argues that homosexual behaviour was common and unproblematic in ancient Rome (1980).

[53] MacMullen is surely right to argue that we should speak of Roman attitudes, rather than the Roman attitude, to homosexual behaviour (1982). However, he too wants to see those engaging in homosexual behaviour as a recognisable social group defined in terms of its sexual preferences. Richlin forthcoming also argues for seeing sexually 'passive' males as an identifiable social group.

hence the frequency of such terms as *effeminatus* in discussions of behaviour of this kind. The relative value Romans placed on the attributes they symbolically associated with men and with women has crucial implications for the significance of Roman references to sexually 'passive' behaviour and effeminacy in general in men. We can only hope to understand the charge of descriptions of men behaving 'like women' if we examine them in the context of the complexes of attributes associated with 'male' and 'female' behaviour.

In many cases it is very difficult to pin down an exact meaning for 'sexual' terms of abuse. Boswell, in the course of his study of attitudes to homosexuality, argues against privileging the specifically sexual associations of certain terms, suggesting that the Greek term μαλακός (similar in meaning to *mollis*), for instance, need not be read as meaning 'passive homosexual' but rather connotes a whole complex of associated ideas.[54] The implications of this (which are not explored by Boswell) are highly significant. While a word such as μαλακός or *mollis* in some contexts suggests a man who wears perfume, shaves his legs and wears clothes made of silk, rather than someone who likes to be penetrated by other men, this mode of self-presentation was inevitably associated with certain sexual practices. However, we cannot assume that such behaviour was seen as immoral only because it was associated with certain sexual practices.[55] It is impossible to disentangle attitudes to ways of behaving which are so frequently associated with one another in ancient texts. Cowardice in battle, for instance, may well have seemed more shameful to some Romans than allowing oneself to be penetrated by another man.[56] All these forms of behaviour are presented as 'effeminate'.[57] Those who are thought prone to one are often accused of others too. Attitudes to sexual passivity in men at once colour and are coloured by attitudes to other kinds of behaviour seen as 'unmanly'.

Ortner and Whitehead point out that a feature of the organisation

[54] Boswell 1980: 339.
[55] Cf. Veyne who observes: 'The passive individual's effeminacy was not the result of his perversion, far from it; it was simply one of the results of his lack of virility, and this was still a vice, even where no homosexuality was present' (1985: 30).
[56] For the association between effeminacy and cowardice, see Cic. *Pro Mur.* 31; Suet. *Otho* 12; Plut. *Otho* 9; Tac. *Ann.* 13.30. This idea is played on in Hor. *Epist.* 2.1.156–7. Cf. Halperin on the Greek world. He suggests: 'War not love reveals the inner man' (1990: 37).
[57] Cf. Boswell (1980: 76).

of gender ideas to be found in many cultures is that: 'very commonly the same axes that divide and distinguish male from female (and indeed rank male over female) also cross-cut the gender categories, producing internal distinctions and gradations within them.' This suggests, they claim, that: 'many axes of gender distinction are not in fact unique to the domain of gender but are shared with (both derived from and imported to) other important domains of social life.'[58] An example of this might be the quality of self-control, *continentia*, as it is represented in Roman texts. While a 'good' woman would be one who exemplified this virtue to a degree greater than did inferior women, it was a virtue exhibited to the greatest degree by men. Cicero, defining *continentia*, writes that it consists in avoiding behaviour which is unmanly – *parum virile* (*De fin.* 2.47).[59]

For a Roman to suggest that a man was behaving like a woman was to imply that he was inferior to other men. Conversely, to suggest that a man was inferior to other men in that he was promiscuous, luxurious, lazy or cowardly, was to imply that he was in some ways like a woman. The way accusations of effeminacy are articulated and the part they play in Roman moral discourses may, in the end, tell us far more about how Romans conceived of the differences between men and women than about how common homosexuality was in ancient Rome or even how acceptable specific sexual practices were. Accusations of effeminacy drew attention to the difference between men and women, investing it with a powerful moral resonance and thereby serving to reinforce and legitimate male power over women.

MALE AND FEMALE

Romans accused of effeminacy are portrayed in a range of ways. Some elements in this kind of description are articulated in terms of the physical difference between men and women (the axis of youth as opposed to age cuts across this contrast – for a man, to look younger is to look more feminine). Other elements relate to the cultivation of an appearance particularly associated with women, for instance wearing soft clothes, perfume and cosmetics. Still other effeminate characteristics relate to qualities of personality to which women were con-

---

[58] Ortner and Whitehead 1981: 9.
[59] The highest praise Seneca can offer his mother is that she lacks all feminine flaws (*Ad Helv.* 16).

sidered to be more prone than men: timidity, laziness and self-indulgence, for instance.[60] Seneca's discussion of the qualities mothers and fathers encourage in their children discloses a desire to align women with leisure as opposed to business, retirement as opposed to public life and indulgence as opposed to toil (the opposition of youth and maturity also plays a part here – Seneca accuses mothers of trying to prevent their children from growing up):

> non vides quanto aliter patres, aliter matres indulgeant? illi excitari iubent liberos ad studia obeunda mature, feriatis quoque diebus non patiuntur esse otiosos et sudorem illis et interdum lacrimas excutiunt; at matres fovere in sinu, continere in umbra volunt, numquam contristari, numquam flere, numquam laborare. patrium deus habet adversus bonos viros animum et illos fortiter amat.

> *Do you not see how fathers show their love in one way and mothers in another? The father orders his children to be woken up so that they can get busy early. Even on holidays he won't let them be idle and he urges them on, drawing from them sweat and sometimes tears. But the mother wants to cuddle them in her lap, keep them out of the sun and have them always be happy, never to cry, never to struggle. God is like a father to good men and has a manly love for them.*

(Sen. *De prov.* 2.5–6)

Indolence is represented as characteristic of women – Seneca's mothers encourage their children to be like themselves, soft and idle. The inactivity of women could sometimes be positively viewed, as an advertisement for the wealth of their families, but women, without suitable occupation, were also liable to be perceived as dangerous, because especially susceptible to the temptation of misdeeds, ranging from adultery to ruinous expenditure on adornment.[61] Good women sat at home and spun (the emperor Augustus, according to Suetonius (*Aug.* 73), proclaiming his wish to return to the customs of earlier days, paraded the fact that he wore clothes spun by his female

---

[60] On the association of cowardice with women, see e.g. Val. Max. 2.7.9. Women exemplify bravery only exceptionally. Valerius Maximus elsewhere observes of Lucretia, the mythical figure who committed suicide in shame after being raped by Tarquin, that she was possessed of an *animus virilis* (a virile spirit) which had entered her female body in error (6.1.1; cf. Cic. *De off.* 1.61).

[61] On female idleness, see, too, Columella, *De re rust.*12 *pr.* Cf. Jean Maurin '*Labor matronalis:* aspects du travail feminin à Rome' in Edmond Lévy ed. *La Femme dans les sociétés antiques* (Strasbourg 1983) 135–55.

relatives). Specifically feminine characteristics could never be an unambiguously good thing for Roman moralists.[62]

Accusations of effeminacy are often associated with imputations of luxuriousness.[63] Some moralists maintained that homosexual practices, like other elements in the life of luxury, such as rare wines, gems and perfumes, had come to Rome owing to the corrupting influence of Greece and Asia.[64] But luxury itself was especially associated with women who were thought highly susceptible to its attractions.[65] The diversion of wealth to private ends, instead of its use for the public good, is a recurring concern of Roman moralising, as we shall see in chapters three and four. Again, it was seen as a particularly feminine characteristic to value private concerns over the good of the state.[66] Here, too, accusations of effeminacy were intertwined with allegations of other vices which formed a complex of behaviour implicitly associated with women.

The tensions and ambiguities in Roman delineations of 'feminine' characteristics help to explain some of the contradictory features of accusations of effeminacy. Women are always 'inferior' to men if they are judged according to their position along axes of the kind set out by Ortner and Whitehead. Accusations of effeminacy sometimes imply that 'effeminate' men are being criticised for behaving as one would expect the worst women (rather than all women) to behave. This is consistent with an 'axes' model, but this model, as Ortner and Whitehead themselves imply, cannot be made to cohere with all attributions of personal qualities. For some characteristics, though negatively valued in men, are represented as positive qualities in women. Seneca may seem to criticise the way mothers, as opposed to fathers, treat their children, but this should not be taken to imply that, in his view, maternal nurturing is entirely reprehensible. Similarly, some Roman moralists express unease when women aspire to quali-

---

[62] Pierre Bourdieu notes the ambiguity of even the virtues of the dominated. Among the Kabyle, the table manners deemed appropriate to women are at the same time despised (*The logic of practice* (Oxford 1990) 77).

[63] E.g. Polybius 31.25.2–5; Cic. *In Verr.* 5.81; *In Cat.* 2.23; Sen. *Ep.* 114; 122; Dio 62.6.4–5.

[64] E.g. Polybius 31.25.2–5; Cic. *Tusc.* 4.70.

[65] See e.g. Val. Max. 9.1.3; Pliny, *NH* 12.84; Sen. *De ben.* 7.9. Cf. the speech attributed to the censor Cato in a debate on whether the *lex Oppia* (a sumptuary law aimed at women) should be repealed (Livy 34.1–8). On the *lex Oppia* see Wyke forthcoming and Phyllis Culham 'The *lex Oppia' Latomus* 41 (1982) 786–93.

[66] Ortner and Whitehead remark that the opposition of self-interest and the public good is one of the principal binary oppositions through which gender distinctions are articulated in many cultures (1981: 7).

ties which, in men, might be approved of.[67] Seneca and other Roman writers, in discussions of the difference between men and women, elide the difference between 'good' and 'bad' female qualities, for not to do so might raise awkward questions about their claims that it is always wrong for men to behave like women. This tactic of elision is especially manifest in accusations of effeminacy. Thus the apparent incoherence of accusations of effeminacy – the same people are accused of being both sexually passive and sexually insatiable – makes more sense if we look at effeminacy – 'being like a woman' – as a wholly negative term when applied to men. Whatever qualities were undesirable in a male member of the Roman elite were termed 'feminine'.[68]

INCONTINENTIA

In the eyes of Roman moralists, the effeminate were like women in playing a 'passive' sexual role but at the same time they were like women in having an excessive interest in sex. The appetites of the effeminate were uncontrollable. They were adulterers as well as catamites. The multiple associations of effeminacy engendered tensions within some passages of invective, as for instance here, where the elder Seneca attacks the exquisite oratorical style fashionable among his contemporaries:

> torpent ecce ingenia desidiosae iuventutis nec in unius honestae rei labore vigilatur; somnus languorque ac somno et languore turpior malarum rerum industria invasit animos: cantandi saltandique obscena studia effeminatos tenent, [et] capillum frangere et ad muliebres blanditias extenuare vocem, mollitia corporis certare cum feminis et immundissimis se excolere munditiis nostrorum adulescentium specimen est. quis aequalium vestrorum quid dicam satis ingeniosus, satis studiosus, immo quis satis vir est? emolliti enervesque quod nati sunt in vita manent, expugnatores alienae pudicitiae, neglegentes suae. in hos ne dii tantum mali ut cadat eloquentia: quam non mirarer nisi animos in quos se conferret eligeret. erratis, optimi iuvenes, nisi illam vocem non M. Catonis sed oraculi creditis . . . 'Orator est, Marce fili, vir bonus dicendi peritus.' ite nunc et in istis vulsis atque expolitis et nusquam nisi in libidine viris quaerite oratores.

[67] Such as athletic prowess or a high level of literary learning. Cf. Juv. 6.398–456; Mart. 7.67; 7.70.
[68] Hence, too, the frequent assimilation of the non-man, the eunuch, to the female (e.g. Quint. *Inst.* 5.12.17–20; Clem. Alex. *Paedagogus* 3.19.2).

Observe the indolent young men of today: their brains sleep. Not one of them can stay awake in the pursuit of a worthwhile project. Their minds are possessed by sleep, laziness and an industry in the pursuit of wicked ends more reprehensible than sleep and laziness. Lubricious pleasure in singing and dancing rules these effeminates. Their preferred way of living leads them to arrange their hair exquisitely, to mould their voices until they are as sweet as those of women, to compete with women in the softness of their bodies, decking themselves out with filthy fineries. Can you think of any one of your contemporaries who is enough of a man, leaving aside the question of his talent or industry? All their lives they remain as weak and soft as the day they were born, assaulting one another's chastity, neglectful of their own. Let the gods not permit so great an evil as that eloquence should fall to them – a quality for which I would have little respect if it was not judicious in selecting its exponents. Cato's well-known saying should be accorded oracular status . . . 'An orator, son Marcus, is a good man skilled in speaking.' Go then and see if you can find an orator among the smooth and hairless of today, men only in their lusts.

(Sen. *Contr.* 1. pr.8–9)

This passage invokes many of the features of representations of effeminacy examined so far. The objects of Seneca's indignation are indolent and torpid. They lavish attention on their personal appearance, arranging their coiffures with infinite care and removing unwanted body hair. They disdain the kinds of activities (such as military training) which would make their bodies hard and masculine. They wear cosmetics (their skin has a feminine softness) and ornaments. Their voices affect a feminine sweetness. Their sexual appetites are given free rein – they debauch each other. Their manner of speaking Seneca characterises as feminine (and therefore corrupt). But the final sentence of this passage is disconcerting. It is in their lusts, and in their lusts alone, that these effeminates can claim to be true men, *viri* – irony, perhaps, but, even so, a profoundly problematic assertion for those who wish to maintain that discussions of effeminacy were essentially concerned with sexual roles.[69]

Epictetus, according to Arrian, chastised a young man, alleging that he cultivated an effeminate appearance in order to appeal to

---

[69] Cf. the story related by Gellius of the comments made by a philosopher on a rich man whose manner and appearance were effeminate, though he lived an upright life (*incorruptus . . . et a stupro integer*). The philosopher remarked: *nihil interest quibus membris cinaedi sitis posterioribus an prioribus*, 'It makes no difference with what parts of your body you debauch yourself, front or rear' (Gell. 3.5).

women (*Discourses* 3.1.27–33). The possibility of becoming a *cinaedus* is raised (though it is quickly dismissed) but Epictetus is presented as assuming that an effeminate appearance will be found attractive by lascivious women.[70] Juvenal is highly suspicious of friendships between women and men who look like *cinaedi*:

> horum consiliis nubunt subitaeque recedunt,
> his languentem animum [servant] et seria vitae,
> his clunem atque latus discunt vibrare magistris,
> quicquid praeterea scit qui docet. haud tamen illi
> semper habenda fides: oculos fuligine pascit
> discinctus croceis et reticulatus adulter.
> suspectus tibi sit, quanto vox mollior et quo
> saepius in teneris haerebit dextera lumbis.
> hic erit in lecto fortissimus.

On the advice of cinaedi, *women marry then quickly divorce; in their society they dispel boredom or enliven business; from them, they learn to wiggle their hips – and whatever else the teacher knows. But beware! That teacher is not always what he seems: that man who wears make-up and dresses like a woman is an adulterer. Suspect him the more for his soft voice and effeminate gestures – he is a valiant man-at-arms in bed.*

(Juv. 6.O17–24)

The unwary husband might not suspect a man who looks like a catamite of having designs on his wife. Juvenal is aware of and plays with this apparent paradox. There was plainly some tension between the ideas, associated here, of effeminacy (again manifested in voice, gestures, make-up and dress) and adultery. But this is not an isolated instance of the association. This oxymoronic combination is to be found in the work of Lucilius, Ovid and Clement of Alexandria, among others.[71] Sexual excess of all kinds was associated in accusations of effeminacy.

---

[70] Cf. Pet. *Sat.* 126.

[71] Lucilius 1058 Marx (*moechocinaedi*); Ovid, *Ars* 3.433; Clem. Alex. *Paedagogus* 3.15.2 (though Clement was a Christian writing in the second century, he expresses many concerns typical of pagan elite texts). Other examples include: Pet. *Sat.* 75; Mart. 5.61; 12.91; Macrob. *Sat.* 2.4.12 (Augustus is said to have called Maecenas effeminate in a verse which mimicked the florid style supposedly characteristic of Maecenas' own compositions. The verse ended 'in short you seducer of unfaithful wives'). For literary *mollitia*, see below. The association between effeminacy and excessive interest in penetrating women is discussed by Richlin (1983: 3, 4, 222). Cf. Dover who observes that, in classical Athens, the same men were thought to be attractive both to older men and to women (1978: 72).

Such accusations served in part to parade the perversity of the women attracted to such men. Indeed, women were sometimes alleged to be attracted to eunuchs, because of their smooth cheeks and effeminate appearance – and also because sex with eunuchs did not carry the risk of pregnancy.[72] The association of lasciviousness with women helps to explain the bi-sexual promiscuity of which the effeminate are so often accused.[73] Accusations of effeminacy, I have been arguing, need not be seen as essentially concerned with sexual 'passivity'. The picture painted by Veyne of all sexual actors in the ancient world being exclusively active or passive, or even as being perceived as such, is an oversimplification. The question of how far the roles actually adopted in homosexual relationships were exclusively 'active' or 'passive' is impossible to answer (though certainly when an anecdote is intended to elicit disapproval of both partners they are accused of *mutuum stuprum*, 'mutual debauchery', suggesting, presumably, that each penetrated the other).[74] Veyne claims: 'to be active was to be male, whatever the sex of the passive partner.'[75] It seems though, that 'to be male' was a rather more complex business even in specifically sexual contexts.

PUBLIC INTEREST, PRIVATE PLEASURE

Those accused of submitting themselves to other men were often held to have done so in order to derive some advantage from a man of power and influence.[76] As Cicero's allegations about Antony's behaviour suggest, advantage was perhaps felt to be a more reasonable justification for such behaviour than pleasure or affection (*Phil.* 2.44,

[72] E.g. Mart. 6.67; Juv. 6.366–7. Cf. Claudian, *In Eutropium* 2.84–90. On alleged relations between women and eunuchs in the later Roman empire, see Hopkins 1978: 194. Women's lack of interest in reproduction is one of the favourite objects of moralists' concern (e.g. Pliny, *NH* 24.18; Juv. 6.592–601; Sen. *Ad Helv.* 16; Gell. 12.1.9).
[73] Adultery is regularly associated with other kinds of crime in allegations made about women by Roman writers. See chapter two above.
[74] Suet. *Calig.* 36. There are numerous allusions to groups of young males which might be read either as references to mutual exchanges of homosexual roles or else to combinations of active role-playing with female partners and passive with male (the *moechocinaedus* again?), e.g. Cic. *In Cat.* 2.23 (*Hi pueri tam lepidi et delicati non solum amare et amari . . . didicerunt*, 'these elegant and precious boys learnt not only to love and be loved . . .'); Sen. *Contr.* 1.pr.8–9 (quoted above); Sen. *Ep.* 99.13 (*qui suam alienamque libidinem exercent mutuo stupri*, 'those who satisfy their own lust and that of others in mutual *stuprum*').
[75] Veyne 1987: 204.
[76] E.g. Cic. *De har. resp.* 42 (Clodius); Suet. *Caes.* 49; 52; *Aug.* 68; 71; *Otho* 2.2; *Vit.* 3.2; *Dom.* 1; Dio 57.19.5 (Sejanus).

quoted above). If a man desired financial or political advantage, then at least he was still showing an interest – if in a rather misguided way – in the proper concerns of the upper-class Roman male, rather than pursuing aims which called the value of political activity itself into question by suggesting other pursuits might be more attractive.

Indeed, even those alleged to be overfond of their own wives might be accused of effeminacy. Plutarch describes Pompey's behaviour after his marriage to a woman considerably his junior:

> *Soon, however, Pompey himself weakly succumbed to his passion for his young wife, devoting himself almost exclusively to her, spending his time with her in villas and gardens and neglecting affairs of the forum. One result of this was that even Clodius, who was at that time a tribune of the* plebs, *despised him and undertook the most daring measures ... So when Pompey made an appearance at a public trial, Clodius, accompanied by a mob of rude and insolent villains, took up a conspicuous place and put them questions of the following kind: 'Who is the general with no self-control?', 'Who is the man who runs after other men?', 'Who scratches his head with one finger?' They, like a chorus trained in their answers, as he shook his toga, would reply to each question, shouting out 'Pompey!'*

(Plut. *Pomp.* 48.5–7)

Pompey's intense interest in his new wife led him to neglect public affairs and laid him open to charges of effeminacy.[77] He was accused of lacking self-control, of desiring other men and of making the characteristic gesture of the effeminate – scratching his head with one finger. Erotic distraction, dependence on a woman (even one's wife) were felt to divert a man from his public responsibilities.[78] In neglecting the public good for the pursuit of his private desires he became like a woman, in Roman eyes.[79]

The physical consequences which were believed to result from excessive sexual activity should perhaps be related to this anxiety about the neglect of the public good. Peter Brown suggests the belief that excessive sexual activity diminished one's capacity to be a man in other ways is to be explained by the connection medical writers made between the loss of heat which they believed to result from sexual

---

[77] Cf. Plut. *Pomp.* 53; Val. Max. 4.6.4. Though devotion to one's wife could be more positively viewed, cf. Lucan on Pompey (*Bellum civile* 8).

[78] An idea persistently played on in Latin love elegy (see below).

[79] Cf. the idea that avarice (obsessive concern with building up private wealth – implicitly at the expense of one's commitment to the community) makes men effeminate – Sall. *Cat.* 11.3; Gell. 3.1.

85

activity and a reduction in energy.[80] Rather than see this as an explanation, it is more plausible to view the claims made by medical writers as a parallel manifestation of the commonly held view that excessive indulgence in sex diminished a man's potency in other respects.[81] Male actors and gladiators were sometimes infibulated to prevent them from having sexual intercourse, when they were supposed to be conserving their energies for public performance.[82] Quintilian's description of the regime an orator should follow in order to perform well may be seen as reflecting a similar concern:

augentur autem sicut omnium, ita vocis quoque bona cura, neglegentia minuuntur. sed cura non eadem oratoribus quae phonascis convenit; tamen multa sunt utroque communia, firmitas corporis ne ad spado-num et mulierum et aegrorum exilitatem vox nostra tenuetur; quod ambulatio, unctio, veneris abstinentia, facilis ciborum digestio, id est frugalitas, praestat.

The good qualities of the voice, like all other things, are improved by attention and harmed by neglect. However, the orator and the singer do not require the same training, although the two skills have much in common. In both cases, physical robustness is essential to prevent the voice from dwindling to the feeble shrillness that characterises the voices of eunuchs, women and the sick. This strength may be attained through walking, rubbing down with oil, abstinence from sexual intercourse, an easy digestion – that is to say the simple life.

(Quint. *Inst.* 11.3.19)

Sexual indulgence of all kinds sapped a man's strength and made him like a woman, unable to take part in public life.[83] Veyne dismisses statements like that of Quintilian as a minority view, only to be found among political thinkers who 'arrived at puritanical conclusions because they felt that all forms of love and lust, homosexual or not, were uncontrollable and enervated the citizen-soldier.'[84] But there is

[80] Peter Brown 'Late antiquity' in Veyne 1987: 243 (relevant medical texts include Soranos 1.30–1). There is a close parallel to this in the belief held by some Hindus that any discharge of semen weakens the male body. A man's strength, on this view, is entirely dependent on his reserves of semen (G. Morris Carstairs *The twice born* (London 1957) ch. 5).
[81] Cf. the belief in the debilitating consequences of sexual intercourse for the man held by members of the Andalusian community studied by Brandes (1981).
[82] On infibulation (the insertion of a pin through the foreskin), see Celsus 7.25.2; Mart. 7.82; 9.27.12; 14.21.5; Juv. 6.73–5, 379. For more details, see *RE* s.v. 'infibulatio'.
[83] Cf. Mart. 7.82. Aline Rousselle discusses Roman views on factors affecting the strength of the voice, 'Parole et inspiration: le travail de la voix dans le monde romain' *History and Philosophy of the Life Sciences* 5 (1983) 129–57.   [84] Veyne 1985: 27.

enough of an overlap between the concerns expressed here and the taunts shouted at Pompey by the crowd to make us wonder if the 'majority' thought very differently.

Roman discourses about effeminacy, as we have seen, were often more concerned with likening men to women generally, than with castigating certain types of specifically sexual behaviour. However, the anxiety with which the texts examined here often seem to be charged could perhaps be attributed to the threat posed by behaviour, including sexual behaviour, which called into question the natural attribution of distinct roles to men and women. A lengthy but illuminating passage from the younger Seneca on the subversion of 'natural' patterns of gender-specific behaviour certainly betrays anxiety, but the 'naturalness' of the gender roles it invokes is made particularly susceptible to deconstruction by the bravura of Seneca's rhetoric:

> maximus ille medicorum et huius scientiae conditor feminis nec capillos defluere dixit nec pedes laborare; atqui et capillis destituuntur et pedibus aegrae sunt. non mutata feminarum natura, sed victa est; nam cum virorum licentiam aequaverint, corporum quoque virilium incommoda aequarunt. non minus pervigilant, non minus potant, et oleo et mero viros provocant; aeque invitis ingesta visceribus per os reddunt et vinum omne vomitu remetiuntur; aeque nivem rodunt, solacium stomachi aestuantis. libidine vero ne maribus quidem cedunt, pati natae, di illas deaeque male perdant! adeo perversum commentae genus inpudicitiae viros ineunt. quid ergo mirandum est maximum medicorum ac naturae peritissimum in mendacio prendi, cum tot feminae podagricae calvae sint? beneficium sexus sui vitiis perdiderunt et, quia feminam exuerant, damnatae sunt morbis virilibus.

> *The great founder of the science and profession of medicine observed that women never lost their hair or suffered from pain in the feet. But in our own day their hair falls out and they are afflicted with gout. This does not mean that women's anatomy has changed, but that it has been subverted; by competing with men in their indulgences, they have also sought to outdo men in their illnesses. They stay up just as late and drink just as much alcohol; they challenge men in wrestling and revelling; they are no less given to vomiting from swollen stomachs and thus throwing up all their*

wine again; nor are they behind men in gnawing at ice to relieve their disturbed digestions. And they even (may the gods and goddesses confound them!) match men in their sexual desires, although they were created to feel love passively. They think up the most impossible varieties of immoral sexual practices, and when they are with men they play the man's part. It is no great surprise then that our observations confound the statement of the greatest and most expert doctor, when so many women are gout-ridden and bald! By their vices, women have forfeited the privileges of their sex; they have spurned their womanly natures and are therefore condemned to suffer the diseases of men.

(Sen. *Ep.* 95.20–1)

The affectation of an inappropriate gender role is represented as a threat to the natural order.[85] But how natural is this order? Almost all the qualities which Seneca portrays here as 'naturally' male (but usurped by women) are hardly the natural attributes of either sex. The only exception might be hair loss (in Roman women perhaps a consequence of lead poisoning).[86] Appeals to nature were a powerful rhetorical weapon, particularly for those imbued with Stoic teaching, but the behaviour of the women Seneca describes challenged cultural rather than natural categories.[87] Seneca was not reacting to naturally anomalous behaviour. He was taking part in the reproduction of a cultural system.

Pierre Bourdieu, discussing the symbolic significance of sexual difference, observes:

Psychoanalysis . . . forgets and causes it to be forgotten that one's own body and other people's bodies are only ever perceived through

[85] Adams (1982: 122) compares the use of *ineo* here with the use of *futuo* with a female subject in Martial (7.70). On Roman representations of sexual relationships between women see Judith P. Hallett, 'Female homoeroticism and the denial of Roman reality in Latin literature' *Yale Journal of Criticism* 3.1 (1989) 209–27 (214–15 on this passage from Seneca).

[86] A.T. Hodge provides convincing evidence against the idea that lead water pipes were responsible but leaves open the possibility of poisoning from other sources, such as the lead carbonate used for cosmetic purposes ('Vitruvius, lead pipes and lead poisoning' *AJA* 85 (1981) 486–91).

[87] 'Nature' is generally used by Roman moralists to justify what they approve of (see chapter four on luxurious building). 'Natural' need not necessarily be a term of approval and indeed in many cultures is not so. It may carry overtones of crudity, rusticity and brutality. Cf. Sherry B. Ortner 'Is female to male as nature is to culture?' *Feminist Studies* 1 (1972) 5–31 = M.Z. Rosaldo and L. Lamphere eds. *Women, culture and society* (Stanford 1974) 67–88. The use of 'natural' as a highly charged term of approval in modern western discourses may be traced back to J.J. Rousseau (see Maurice Bloch and Jean H. Bloch 'Women and the dialectics of nature in eighteenth-century France' in C. MacCormack and M. Strathern eds. *Nature, culture and gender* (Cambridge 1980) 25–41).

categories of analysis which it would be naive to treat as sexual, even if
. . . these categories always relate back, sometimes very concretely, to
the opposition between the biologically defined properties of the two
sexes. This would be as naive as it would be to reduce to their strictly
sexual dimension the countless acts of diffuse inculcation through
which the body and the world tend to set in order, by means of a
symbolic manipulation of the relation to the body and to the world
aiming to impose . . . a 'body geography' . . . or better cosmology.[88]

In almost every culture, the biological difference between the sexes is
a crucial bearer of meaning which can be made to organise whole
systems of values, but those values cannot themselves be inferred
from the biological differences between men and women. The
'mnemonic' role of the body in the reproduction of value systems is
emphasised by Bourdieu. By setting store by the 'seemingly most
insignificant details of dress, bearing, physical and verbal manners',
societies treat the body as a memory. 'They entrust to it in an
abbreviated and practical, i.e. "mnemonic", form the fundamental
principles of the arbitrary content of the culture.' The principles thus
embodied are 'beyond the grasp of consciousness.'[89] Usually, they are
not made explicit and so cannot be challenged.

Roman moral discourse often focuses on such 'seemingly insignificant details'. Seneca emphasises the capacity of the slightest movement to betray the individual's moral disposition:

> omnia rerum omnium, si observentur, indicia sunt et argumentum
> morum ex minimis quoque licet capere; impudicum et incessus
> ostendit et manus mota et unum interdum responsum et relatus ad
> caput digitus et flexus oculorum.

> *If you observe them carefully, the slightest movements can give away*
> *volumes and you can judge character by the most trivial signs. The lecher*
> *reveals himself by the way he walks – or the movements of his hand, or some*
> *remark he makes in passing, or the way he touches his head with one finger*
> *or else the shifty look of his eyes.*

(Sen. *Ep.* 52.12)

Treatises on physiognomics reveal similar preoccupations.[90] The

---

[88] Pierre Bourdieu *Outline of a theory of practice* (Cambridge 1977) 92 (= 1990: 77–8).
[89] Bourdieu 1977: 94. On Bourdieu's notion of the cultural arbitrary, see John B. Thompson
Studies in the theory of ideology (Oxford 1984) 57.
[90] On these treatises, see Gleason 1990: 389–415; Tamsyn Barton *Power and knowledge:*
astrology, physiognomics and medicine under the Roman empire (forthcoming).

body was a place where nature and culture met. It was a text to be deciphered, to be read.

When Cicero prescribed the proper way to dress and comport oneself, he, too, was taking part in the reproduction of a set of values relating to far more than the aesthetics of clothing and posture (*De off.* 1.130).[91] To wear one's toga fastened in a certain way was also to suggest something about one's political intentions and about one's sexual proclivities. These claims must have functioned on an unconscious level most of the time but cultural codes have to become explicit when they are subject to challenge. Julius Caesar, whose dictatorship marked the end of the Roman republic, would not even dress as a conforming member of the senatorial class was expected to. He wore his tunic ungirt and was criticised for this habit by his contemporaries. Dio writes:

> *He prompted gossip because, at that time, although of mature years, he still lavished care on his appearance. He chose to parade about in public in rather loose clothes – and later on he took to wearing shoes which were sometimes high and reddish in colour in the manner of the kings who had once ruled Alba (for he claimed that he was related to them through Iulus) ... Sulla used to look askance at his loose belt – to such a degree indeed that he wished to kill him and when others tried to dissuade him, he declared: 'Well, you can keep him, but do not relax your guard against this ill-girt fellow.'*

(Dio 43.43.1–4)

A detail of Caesar's dress was the most apt sign his enemy could invoke to sum up the nature of the threat he posed to political, social and cultural order.[92] And yet, if we think back to the comments Plutarch alleges Cicero made, again about Julius Caesar, these allegations can also be seen as illustrating the tensions within the discourses about *mollitia*. To be ill-girt (*discinctus*; κακῶς ζωννύμενος) was as much a sign of *mollitia* as scratching one's head with one finger (both traits are linked with over-careful arrangement of the hair in the two passages) but what Sulla saw as a disturbing sign of danger seemed to Cicero a reassuring indication of weakness.

---

[91] Elsewhere Cicero counsels the avoidance of effeminate movements and posture on the grounds that they are unnatural (*De fin.* 5.35). Cf. Quint. *Inst.* 11.3.69–129 on the self-presentation proper to an orator. On the implications of different forms of male self-presentation in terms of civic and social status, see Wyke forthcoming and Florence Dupont *La Vie quotidienne du citoyen romain* (Paris 1989) 267–70, 290–5.

[92] Briefer versions of this story are told by Suetonius (*Jul.* 45) and Macrobius (*Sat.* 2.3.9).

CONTAINING CAESAR

Julius Caesar was the subject of a jibe by Curio. Caesar was: *Omnium mulierum virum et omnium virorum mulier*, 'A man to every woman and a woman to every man' (Suet. *Jul.* 52.3). The *moechocinaedus* appears again, this time not just a fellow one would not want to see hanging around one's wife but one of Rome's most successful generals, a man whose power was so great as to prove unbearable to his fellow senators. Similar stories were told about the sexual behaviour of Sulla, Catiline, and indeed Curio himself, powerful – and dangerous – men. Those whose personal ambitions fundamentally weakened the stability of the republic were also its most glamorous, exciting figures, covertly envied by those who would never dare to emulate them.[93] The accusations of sexual excess made against them may be seen as a way of containing the power of the most powerful men in Rome – an attempt to reassert the (always already) contested dominance of senatorial consensus. But at the same time their political uncontrollability was further emphasised by the stories told about their uncontrollable sexual appetites.

Uncontrolled sexuality, as manifested in both adultery and homosexual activity, was felt to pose a threat to the moral order of the state. Those whose lack of self-control led them to these forms of sensual indulgence were the protagonists in Roman narratives of the tragedy of the republic – and vice versa. Velleius Paterculus, writing under the emperor Tiberius, comments:

> bello autem civili et tot, quae deinde per continuos viginti annos consecuta sunt, malis non alius maiorem flagrantioremque quam C. Curio tribunus plebis subiecit facem, vir nobilis, eloquens, audax, suae alienaeque et fortunae et pudicitiae prodigus, homo ingeniosissime nequam et facundus malo publico cuius animo neque opes ullae neque cupiditates sufficere possent. hic primo pro Pompei partibus, id est, ut tunc habebatur, pro re publica, mox simulatione contra Pompeium et Caesarem, sed animo pro Caesare stetit. id gratis an accepit centies sestertio fecerit, ut accepimus, in medio relinquemus.

> *It was the tribune Gaius Curio, though, who more than anyone else was responsible for sparking off the civil war and all the terrible events which followed in succession for the next twenty years. Curio was a man of noble birth, eloquent, reckless, prodigal both of his own fortune and chastity and those of other people, a man most ingenious in perversity, who used*

[93] Cf. Veyne 1987: 205.

eloquence for the subversion of the state. No wealth and no pleasures were enough to satisfy him. First he was on Pompey's side, that is to say, on the side of the republic, as it was then regarded. Then he made out that he was opposed to both Pompey and Caesar but in his heart he supported Caesar. Whether his conversion was spontaneous or due to a bribe of 10,000 sesterces as is reported, we leave open.

(Vell. Pat. 2.48.3–4)

Men whose unbridled lust for power led them to be forces of political disruption were also accused of sexual behaviour which was socially disruptive (causing women to deceive their husbands and men to be distracted from their public duties). Their actions were also culturally disruptive. Roman moralists perceived a connection between cultural changes (with which they associated homosexual relationships among the upper classes) and prosperity, on the one hand, and political breakdown on the other. Real Romans only had sex with their wives and even then not too often.

EFFEMINACY AND HELLENISATION

As we have already seen from earlier chapters, Roman moralists attributed a key role in the process of moral decline to increasing contacts with Greece and the near east which came about as a consequence of Rome's military expansion. Sallust, in his monograph on Catiline's conspiracy, outlines the process by which eastern softness infected previously manly Romans:

L. Sulla exercitum quem in Asia ductaverat, quo sibi fidum faceret, contra morem maiorum luxuriose nimisque liberaliter habuerat. Loca amoena, voluptaria, facile in otio ferocis animos molliverant.

Lucius Sulla, in order to make loyal to him the army he had brought into Asia, had allowed his soldiers luxury and licence foreign to the ways of our ancestors and, in their leisure hours, the warlike spirits of those men were easily softened by the charms and pleasures of those places.

(Sall. *Cat.* 11.5)

The east, with its pleasures, made soft – *mollis* – Sulla's soldiers, undermining their capacity to fight.[94] Luxury and licence were alien

---

[94] Cf. the enervating delights of Capua and their pernicious consequences for Hannibal's army (Livy 23.18.12). Dio makes the British leader Boudicca criticise the softness of the Romans in contrast to the rugged Britons (62.6.4–5). For a fuller discussion of Roman views on the effects of pleasure, see chapter five below.

to *mores maiorum*, 'the ways of Rome's ancestors'.

The associations of pleasure in Roman moralistic texts will be examined more closely in a later chapter but it is worth briefly noting here the complex of elements which were seen as making up a distinctively Greek life of pleasure – imported wine and perfume, leisure, feasting, love and literature.[95] This was a 'soft' life, *mollis* – as Roman elegists self-consciously asserted – a life which was defined, at least partly, in opposition to the more authentically 'Roman' life of frugality and military virtue. Some genres of literature were 'softer' than others.[96] Particular literary styles might also be described as feminine (though no-one ever suggests this is how women write).[97] This characterisation of literary styles as 'masculine' and 'feminine' is to be found in earlier Greek texts; in Roman texts, too, it is often implicated in disagreements over the relative merits of 'Attic' and 'Asiatic' oratorial styles – a debate which cannot be simply mapped onto an opposition between Greek and Roman – but the parallels often drawn between the Greek and the feminine are nevertheless revealing.

The qualities attributed to Greeks themselves in Roman texts are often at least implicitly 'feminine'. Lacking physical and moral strength, they are presented as resorting to deceit and flattery to secure their ends. Giving advice to his brother (about to begin his period of office as proconsul of Asia), Cicero warns against the slippery ways of Greeks and Asiatics, which are to be connected, he says, with their lack of political power (*Ad Q. fr.* 1.16). By implication, those who have been conquered behave like other dominated groups, women and slaves. The satirist Juvenal attributes to Greeks in particular the sexual insatiability which, as we have seen, so often appears in Roman texts as a trait of the effeminate (3.109–12). An effeminate appearance and excessive preoccupation with one's toilet could be presented as typical of a Greek. Martial attacks a man whose

---

[95] Griffin 1985 ch. 1.

[96] For the gendering of elegy as feminine (in opposition to masculine epic) see in particular M. Wyke 'Reading female flesh: *Amores* 3.1' in Averil Cameron ed. *History as text: the writing of ancient history* (London 1989) 111–43, and Kennedy 1993 ch. 2.

[97] Cf. Sen. *Contr.* (quoted above); Cic. *Brut.* 167; Sen. *Ep.* 114.8; Quint. *Inst.* 2.5.10–11; 5.12.17–22 (where Quintilian likens the 'unnatural' allure of a florid style to that of a castrated youth); Mart. 2.86; Persius 1.13–23; Gell. 6.14.11; Plut. *Ant.* 2.3–5; ps.-Lucian, *Amores* (discussed by Foucault 1988: 243). On employment of cosmetics as metaphor, see T.P. Wiseman *Clio's cosmetics: three studies in Greco-Roman Literature* (Leicester 1979) 3–8. Wyke discusses Ovid's appropriation of bodily *cultus* as an analogy for the *cultus* which characterises his own text, inverting the rhetorical strategies of moralists (forthcoming). On descriptions of literary style as effeminate, see Gleason 1990.

effeminate self-presentation – his hair is curled, his legs shaved, his voice lisping – is a predictable consequence of his place of birth, Corinth.[98] The poet, by contrast, a native of Spain, is bristlingly masculine (10.65). Descriptions of Greeks and Grecising Romans as effeminate or *mollis* have sometimes been linked by modern scholars with Roman claims that homosexuality was a Greek practice which was adopted in the later republic by some Romans.[99] Certainly Roman texts often refer to homosexual acts using Greek terminology and, in particular, there is a wide range of Greek words which seem to have been used to mean sexually 'passive'.[100] But the use of Greek terms signals Roman ambivalence rather than the literal foreignness of the behaviour in question.

There was never a time when Rome was not subject to Greek influence but there are significant differences between the way homosexual acts are discussed in Greek and in Latin texts. The god Priapus, though a Greek import, developed a peculiarly Roman form.[101] Herms and phalluses, to which an apotropaic function is regularly ascribed, were a common feature of Roman towns and countryside. Catullus' threats to rape his detractors are not paralleled in the works of earlier Greek poets but are echoed rather by insults scratched on Pompeian walls. I suspect that the 'anti-Greek' rhetoric that has come to be associated with accusations of effeminacy was grafted onto an established Roman practice (described above) of attempting to humiliate one's rivals by likening them to women, sometimes in specifically sexual ways.

Of course any import, whether an artefact or a practice, takes on a new meaning in a new context.[102] But we do not have to believe Roman men took the idea of penetrating one another from Greece (though possibly some fashionable Romans may have been more inclined to enter into a homosexual relationship with a social equal because such affairs were associated with Greek sophistication). Many of the supposedly 'Greek' practices moralising Romans disapproved of as effeminate were also castigated by Greek moralists in

[98] Corinth was particularly associated with softness. Cf. e.g. Cic. *De rep.* 2.4.7–8.
[99] Cicero *Tusc.* 4.33 (on homosexual relations as a peculiarly Greek practice, see Cic. *De rep.* 4.4.4; *Tusc.* 4.70; 5.58; Nepos *pr.*4; *Alcibiades* 7.2.2–3). Cf. Lilja 1982: 123–4.
[100] Listed by MacMullen 1982.
[101] Cf. Richlin 1983 ch. 1, 'Roman concepts of obscenity'.
[102] Cf. Marshall Sahlins *Culture and practical reason* (Chicago 1976); Arjun Appadurai 'Commodities and the politics of value' in Appadurai ed. *The social life of things* (Cambridge 1986) 3–57.

similar terms.[103] For them, the soft life was not distinctively Greek.[104] So why did Romans so often associate Greekness and *mollitia*?

A cultural inferiority complex in relation to the Greeks may be sensed in many Roman texts, as we have seen. Cicero, in his philosophical works, sometimes makes claims for the ability of Romans to challenge Greek cultural preeminence (for instance, *De fin.* 1.10; *De nat. deor.* 1.8) but more often he settles for championing Roman moral superiority. Greeks have carried the palm for literature and philosophy, but Romans outdo them in morals and on the battlefield (*Tusc.* 1.1.2). Here, again, we see an elision of the meanings of *virtus* – courage, virtue, and, importantly for the current discussion, manliness. Romans, unlike Greeks, were real men.

For many educated Romans, familiarity with Greek literature, Greek art and Greek customs (as well as the purchase and consumption of Greek goods) was a crucial source of prestige, of cultural capital (as we saw in the introduction). For that reason 'Greece' posed a threat to the stability of Roman elite society. Gendering Greek culture as 'feminine' and philhellenes as 'effeminate' can be seen both in general terms as a strategy to defuse the threat to Rome's cultural identity and, in terms of conflicts between individuals, as a strategy to limit the value of Greek sophistication to those Romans who possessed it to an unusual degree.

Priapus threatened to defend his territory with his erect phallus. It makes sense to link the idea that a Roman must never submit to being penetrated by another man with the Roman military ethic of conquest.[105] Sexual passivity and military defeat were closely associated.[106] The analogy between sex and war is a central preoccupation of Latin love elegy but elegy also turned around the metaphor, playing on the idea of the male lover as dominated by his mistress.[107] Propertius writes: *nullus liber erit si quis amare volet*, 'The man who wants to be in love will never be free' (2.23.24). And Greece, too,

---

[103] Dover 1978: 74.
[104] Though contrast Polybius 31.25.2–5 who does present homosexual relations as a Greek custom new to Rome.   [105] Veyne 1978, 1985; Cantarella 1988: 130–3.
[106] E.g. Juv. 2.159–70 – the barbarian's romanisation is symbolised by his submitting to satisfy the lusts of a tribune (though Juvenal contrasts this with what he ironically presents as the more usual situation – the sexually passive but militarily active Romans conquer the more moral barbarians). Cf. the associations of effeminacy with cowardice discussed above. This should all be connected with the association of passive sexual experience and slavery.
[107] For the analogy between love and war, see e.g. Ov. *Am.* 1.9 (which begins: *militat omnis amans*, 'Every lover is a soldier').

made her conqueror her slave: *Graecia capta ferum victorem cepit et artis\intulit agresti Latio*, 'Captive Greece possessed her rugged captor and invaded rustic Latium, armed with arts' (Horace, *Epist.* 2.1.156–7).[108]

A taste for homosexual relations might be associated with the 'Greek' literary life.[109] Conversely, effeminacy suggested urbanity, as opposed to rusticity – and urbane did not have to be a pejorative term.[110] Elite Romans of the late republic and early principate had to perform a balancing act. To be as coarse and simple as the Romans of earlier days were believed to have been was to invite ridicule. A similar fate lay in store for those who were over-cultivated. Seneca compares those orators who imitate the style of texts written in the days of the Gracchi (the late second century BCE) with those whose speech is over-elaborate and contains an excessive number of neologisms and obscure usages. He remarks: *tam hunc dicam peccare quam illum; alter se plus iusto colit, alter plus iusto neglegit; ille et crura, hic ne alas quidem velit*, 'One approach is as mistaken as the other; one is inappropriately elaborate, the other inappropriately unpolished – the former shaves his legs, the latter not even his armpits' (*Ep.* 114.14). So much for nature as an arbiter of propriety.

In choosing to negotiate the delicate balance between Greek and Roman, sophistication and vigour, in terms of the supposedly straightforward distinction between 'male' and 'female', Romans exposed the problematic nature of their conceptions of gender. It might seem easy to identify Romans as characteristically masculine. Yet to identify Greeks and Greek culture as feminine was to compromise too much of Roman culture and society. Gellius tells a story about Hortensius, a contemporary of Cicero and one of the leading orators of his day:

---

[108] The term *capere* – 'to take' – has both martial and marital associations. It seems that in a Roman wedding, the forcible abduction of the bride might be enacted (described by Festus 364–5 Lindsay). Cf. the rite by which a new Vestal Virgin, in a symbolic wedding, was transferred into the college (Beard 1980: 14).

[109] The gymnasia Cicero associated with homosexual affairs were centres of intellectual as well as athletic activity in Greece (*Tusc.* 4.70).

[110] Cf. the positive, if self-mocking, use of *mollis* in elegy (e.g. Prop. 1.7.19; Ov. *Am.* 1.1.19). *Mollis* could even, in certain contexts, have positive associations in the work of the elder Pliny (e.g. *NH* 2.190). The Christian polemicist, Minucius Felix, plays on the association of urbanity and effeminacy – for pagan Romans, he says, *impudicitia* is *urbanitas* (*Octavius* 28.10–11).

. . . quod multa munditia et circumspecte compositeque indutus et amictus esset manusque eius inter agendum forent argutae admodum et gestuosae, maledictis compellationibusque probris iactatus est multaque in eum, quasi in histrionem, in ipsis causis atque iudiciis dicta sunt. sed cum L. Torquatus, subagresti homo ingenio et infestivo, gravius acerbiusque apud consilium iudicum, cum de causa Sullae quaereretur, non iam histrionem eum esse diceret sed gesticularium Dionysiamque eum notissimae saltatriculae nomine appellaret, tum voce molli atque demissa Hortensius, 'Dionysia,' inquit, 'Dionysia, malo equidem esse quam quod tu, Torquate, ἄμουσος ἀναφρόδιτος ἀπροσδιόνυσος.'

Because he dressed very foppishly, arranged his toga carefully and exactly and when he was speaking used his hands to excess in lively gestures [he] was the object of jibes and embarrassing taunts; and even when he appeared in court, many jokes were made at his expense, alleging that he resembled an actor. However, when, during Sulla's trial, Lucius Torquatus, a rather boorish and uncouth person, not only called Hortensius an actor, with a great deal of noise and bluster, in the presence of the jurors, but also said he was a pantomime and a Dionysia (the name of a notorious dancing girl), then Hortensius replied, in a soft and gentle tone: 'I would rather be a Dionysia, Torquatus, indeed I would, than be like you, a stranger to the Muses, to Aphrodite and to Dionysus.'

(Gell. 1.5.2–3)[111]

A soft voice, a rare one, that spoke for sophistication, philhellenism and even the feminine. This may be as close as a Roman text ever comes to suggesting virility need not be the ultimate virtue.

[111] Cf. Val. Max. 8.10.12.

97

CHAPTER THREE

Playing Romans:
Representations of actors and the theatre

Disapproval of acting and the theatre was a distinguishing Roman characteristic, in the eyes of many ancient authors. The significance Romans attached to the different ways actors were viewed in Greece and in Rome is indicated by Cornelius Nepos, in the preface to his Lives, where he sets out some of the principal contrasts between Greek and Roman culture:

> magnis in laudibus tota fere fuit Graecia victorem Olympiae citari; in scaenam vero prodire ac populo esse spectaculo nemini in eisdem gentibus fuit turpitudini. quae omnia apud nos partim infamia, partim humilia atque ab honestate remota ponuntur.

> *Almost everywhere in Greece, it was thought a high honour to be proclaimed victor at Olympia. Even to appear on the stage and exhibit oneself to the people was never regarded by those nations as something to be ashamed of. Among us, however, all those acts are regarded either as disgraceful or as base and inconsistent with respectability.*

> (Nepos pr. 5)

While Greeks admired actors, according to Nepos, to display oneself on stage, to make a spectacle of oneself, was considered by Romans to be shameful. Other writers, too, saw differing attitudes to the theatre as a significant indicator of the contrast between Greek and Roman culture.[1]

---

[1] There are incidental references in a range of authors: e.g. Livy 24.24.3; Cic. *De rep.* 4.13; Augustine *De civ. dei* 2.11; 2.13 (Cicero and Augustine specifically contrast Rome with Athens). After the time of Menander the Greek theatrical profession, which had previously been largely Athenian, became Panhellenic, as the theatre increased in popularity throughout the Greek-speaking world. On attitudes to the theatre in the Greek-speaking world of Nepos' day, see G.M. Sifakis *Studies in the history of Hellenistic drama* (London 1967) and Arthur Pickard-Cambridge *The dramatic festivals of Athens* (2nd edn., Oxford 1968) esp. ch. 7.

The theatre occupied a problematic space in Roman life. In Nepos' preface, it is implicated in marking cultural distinctions between 'Greece' and 'Rome' (a role it has sometimes played in modern texts too).[2] It was also involved in the negotiation of other distinctions within Roman society. Acting was incompatible with *honestas*, 'honour', and *dignitas*, 'social standing', the qualities which were supposed to mark out those of senatorial and equestrian status above all. Moralists characterised the theatre as a storehouse of obscenity, a place where lust, laughter and political subversion were incited in almost equal measures. Actors were viewed as base persons, of ambiguous and venal sexuality, whose words could not be trusted. Here, too, Roman law reflected and reinforced the attitudes of moralists, for actors were subject to numerous legal disabilities.

Theatre has been regarded in many societies as a dangerous phenomenon. Plays attract large and volatile gatherings of people. Drama may often provide the medium for public expressions of sentiments contrary to the governing regime. Players are frequently travellers, not especially susceptible to local authorities. And the successful actor's capacity to suspend the disbelief of his or her audience is often regarded with ambivalence.[3] But there are particular features which distinguish Roman anxieties about the theatre.

The theatre was profoundly unRoman, many Romans asserted. Yet, dramatic performances in Rome were a central part of major religious festivals. They were paid for in part by the state treasury and in part by individual magistrates and, later, the emperor. Leading Romans watched the performances, seated in the front rows of the auditorium. The theatre was a central Roman institution and yet it was regarded by many of Rome's governing class with deep suspicion. Why this ambivalence?

Many Roman writers suggested that the theatre was not indigenous to Rome but an import, not to be trusted. The poet Horace and other critics attacked the 'bad taste' of Roman theatrical shows (contrasting

---

[2] See e.g. Margarete Bieber *The history of the Greek and Roman theater* (Princeton 1961).

[3] Compare, for instance, the views of Puritans in early modern England and those of Calvinists in sixteenth-century Geneva. On attitudes to the theatre in these and other cultures see: Peter Burke *Popular culture in early modern Europe* (London 1978) 94–198; Michael D. Bristol *Carnival and theatre: plebeian culture and the structure of authority in Renaissance England* (New York 1985); Peter Stallybras and Allon White *The politics and poetics of transgression* (London 1986) 61–79 (on the association between the theatre and disorder). See too E.K. Chambers (*The Elizabethan stage* (Oxford 1923) 248–64), who discusses Puritan disapproval of acting, noting Puritans' citations of Roman precedent in support of their views.

them with the Greek theatre). I shall argue that these are not explanations of Roman hostility to the theatre but rather further manifestations of that hostility. Roman elite anxieties about the theatre should be related to the specific socio-political role of the theatre in Rome. The theatre was often the means for mediating tensions between rulers and ruled in Roman society but it was also a place where these tensions were at their most obvious. For the Roman elite, the theatre was both alluring and threatening. It was a place where the wealthy and influential could display their riches and power. But it was also a place where authority could be challenged. The highly charged nature of social interaction in the theatre had implications for the way people perceived the position of actors, who were regarded at once as among the lowliest members of Roman society and as celebrities. By focusing on the contradictions in Roman attitudes to actors, we can go some way towards explaining why some members of the elite, and even the emperor himself, chose to appear on stage.

DRAMATIC INVASION?

Some accounts, both ancient and modern, of the history of theatre in Rome imply that Roman ambivalence to the theatre is to be connected with its foreign origins. Livy's history explains the beginnings of the theatre as follows:

> . . . ludi quoque scaenici, res nova bellicoso populo – nam circi modo spectaculum fuerat – inter alia caelestis irae placamina instituti dicuntur; ceterum parva quoque, ut ferme principia omnia, et ea ipsa peregrina res fuit. sine carmine ullo, sine imitandorum carminum actu, ludiones ex Etruria acciti ad tibicinis modos saltantes haud indecoros motus more Tusco dabant.

> . . . Among other efforts to placate the angry gods, they are said to have instituted dramatic entertainments. This was a new departure for a warlike people, whose only spectacles had been those of the circus; but indeed, it began in a small way, as most things do, and besides was imported from abroad. Without singing, without imitating the actions of singers, players who had been brought in from Etruria danced to the music of the flautist and performed graceful movements in the Tuscan manner.

> (Livy 7.2.3–4)

Livy goes on to remark that the Latin word for actor, *histrio*, is derived from an Etruscan word, *ister*. His emphasis on the Etruscan origins of the theatre – *peregrina res fuit* – has parallels in the accounts of Valerius Maximus, Tacitus, Tertullian and Augustine.[4]

It seems likely that Italian theatre developed first in the south of the peninsula, later spreading to Rome itself.[5] Little is known of drama among the Etruscans, though it would not be surprising if Etruscan practices had some influence on the development of Roman theatre.[6] The true origins of Roman theatre must remain obscure for us – as for Roman writers of the late republic and early principate. Their speculations tell us more about their own ambivalence to the theatre. Livy seems to have used the antiquarian Varro as his principal source on this subject. However, he distorted Varro's account so as to place much greater emphasis on the Etruscan rather than Roman origins of the theatre.[7] The Etruscans are often represented in Roman texts as foreign and dangerous and yet, at the same time, Italian, the source from which tyranny and decadence came to Rome, but also the origin of venerable religious institutions.[8] Besides the theatre, gladiatorial games were sometimes represented as originating in Etruria.[9] The attribution of Etruscan origins had a particularly ambivalent resonance.

Livy claims that the theatre was alien to those who were by nature warriors – *res nova bellicoso populo*. Other sources suggest Livy was

---

[4] Val. Max. 2.4.2; Tac. *Ann.* 14.20; Tertullian *De spect.* 5.2; Augustine *De civ. dei* 3.17. Cf. also Plut. *Mor.* 289d (*Roman questions* 107), quoting the historian Cluvius Rufus. Other texts stress the development of a primitive form of theatre from rustic festivals: Virg. *Georg.* 2.380–96; Tibullus 2.1.51–8; Donatus *Com. Gr. Frag.* ed. Kaibel 67–71; Diomedes ed. Keil I 488–92. E. Rawson argues that these latter texts unjustifiably privilege Rome itself in their accounts of the development of the Italian theatre, picking up on a Greek tradition (as exemplified in Aristotle, *Poetics* 1449a–b6) which, with rather more justification, gave prominence to Athens ('Theatrical life in republican Rome and Italy' *PBSR* 53 (1985) 97–113 = Rawson 1991: 468–87).   [5] Rawson 1985b: 112–13.

[6] Though such influence is probably exaggerated by e.g. William Beare *The Roman stage* (3rd edn., London 1964) 16–23.

[7] See J.H. Waszink 'Varro, Livy and Tertullian on the history of Roman dramatic art' *VChr* 2 (1948) 224–42.

[8] For ancient characterisations of the Etruscans, see, e.g. Strabo 5.2.2; Livy 5.1.6 (on the Etruscan preoccupation with religion); Diod. Sic. 5.40 (quoting Posidonius on their propensity for luxury, feasting and sensual indulgence). Some of the kings of Rome were alleged to have come from Etruria. The Roman republic was established when the last of their number, Tarquin, was assassinated by Brutus.

[9] Georges Ville also discusses the texts which argue for Etruscan origin. He suggests Campania is more likely (*La Gladiature en occident des origines à la mort de Domitien* (Rome 1981) ch. I). See, too, Thomas Wiedemann *Emperors and gladiators* (forthcoming).

not alone in constructing fighting and acting as mutually exclusive activities. Ovid, in the *Fasti*, observes that scenic games are not honours appropriate to Mars, the god of war (5.595–8). Actors, Livy emphasises, were not permitted to be soldiers (7.2.8). Acting was seen as the inversion of fighting, its antithesis. Actors accomplished nothing. The theatre was an empty show of action without real consequences. Actors were dissemblers, people who pretended to be what they were not. They were praised precisely for their ability to deceive. These were not qualities desirable in a Roman soldier. In the third century CE, soldiers were singled out as liable for capital punishment if they appeared on stage (*Dig.* 48.19.14). Romans represented themselves as essentially a military people.[10] Actors were neither soldiers nor full citizens. Acting was essentially 'unRoman', essentially 'other'.[11]

Roman writers frequently constructed a connection between the importation of 'foreign' goods and practices and the decline of Roman morals. This association is prominent in the accounts of the development of the theatre in Rome given by both Livy and Tacitus. Livy ends his discussion of the origins of drama in Rome by lamenting the crippling extravagance of the theatrical shows in later times (7.2.13). Tacitus' account, which also begins by alluding to the original 'importation' of the theatre from Etruria, constructs an even stronger connection between the 'foreignness' of the theatre and its deleterious effect on morals. Shows are a conduit through which the worst foreign influences flow into Rome. Nero instituted a theatrical competition on the Greek model. Tacitus describes reactions:

> spectaculorum quidem antiquitas servaretur, quotiens praetores ederent, nulla cuiquam civium necessitate certandi. ceterum abolitos paulatim patrios mores funditus everti per accitam lasciviam, ut quod usquam corrumpi et corrumpere queat, in urbe visatur, degeneretque studiis externis iuventus, gymnasia et otia et turpis amores exercendo . . .

> *'As for the shows', the objectors said, 'they should carry on in the old Roman way, whenever the praetors celebrate them, and citizens should*

---

[10] The soldier-citizen ideal was to be found in Athens and other Greek cities. In Rome, however, it was still more significant. Cf. M.I. Finley *Politics in the ancient world* (Cambridge 1983) 129; Nicolet 1980: 89.

[11] Florence Dupont (*L'Acteur-roi* (Paris 1985): 44, 96) emphasises the 'otherness' of acting for Romans.

be under no obligation to compete. Our ancestral morals, already in a state
of gradual deterioration, have been quite overturned by this imported
laxity! It causes everything potentially corrupting or corruptible to be on
show in the capital – foreign influence demoralises our young men, making
them pursuers of idleness, gymnastics and shameful love affairs . . .'

(Tac. *Ann.* 14.20)

Tacitus' account implicates the Greek theatrical tradition as a corrupting influence.[12] The association of the theatre with foreign
influence, pernicious idleness and perverse sexuality is a frequent
one. For Roman moralists, the theatre was not authentically Roman.
We should be cautious before accepting at face value a Roman
author's assertion that something is foreign. Late republican moralists implied that Roman men only became sexually interested in
other men in subservience to Greek fashion.[13] To describe something
as 'foreign' and 'extravagant' was as much an expression of distrust as
an explanation of why distrust was felt.

DRAMATIC DECADENCE?

Some scholars have argued that the low status of actors and the
ambivalent, or even hostile, attitudes to the theatre expressed by
many of the literary elite are to be explained by the low quality of
Roman theatre. Margarete Bieber, for instance, sees the Roman
theatre as a debased imitation of the Greek.[14] Theatre in Rome
(implicitly like the city itself) was overblown, grotesque, derivative.
Inferior even in the days of Plautus and Terence, according to this
view, it declined, characterised by still greater tawdriness under the

---

[12] The first literary drama to be staged in Rome was said to have been a Greek play translated
into Latin by Livius Andronicus and put on in the *ludi Romani* of 240 BCE. Cf. Hor. *Epist.*
2.1.156–67. Suetonius emphasises that the early dramatists were 'part-Greek': *antiquissimi*
doctorum . . . idem et poetae et semigraeci erant – Livium et Ennium dico (*Gramm.* 1). Much
Roman comedy and tragedy was based, if somewhat loosely, on Greek models.

[13] On this, see chapter two above. A view similar to that expressed by some Roman moralists
perhaps lies behind Beare's remark: 'In truth, the development of the theatre and the
weakening of the marriage tie were two aspects of the impact of Hellenism on Roman life'
(1964: 34).

[14] Bieber 1961: 156–7; 166. Cf. the comments often made comparing plays of Plautus with lost
Greek forerunners, to the discredit of the former. For a more positive view of the use made by
Plautus of his Greek models, see Segal 1987 and Niall Slater *Plautus in performance*
(Princeton 1985).

principate.[15] Roman audiences cared little for character or plot; what they wanted was licentious spectacle, argues Bieber. In what has been a standard textbook on the Roman theatre, W. Beare wrote:

> Short, amusing, topical, utterly unrestrained by any considerations of technique or decency, yet capable of adopting on occasions the most sententious style, the mime came nearer than any other form of drama to the real tastes of the Roman populace.[16]

The 'immorality' of the Roman theatre is explained in terms of the degraded tastes of the Romans.

One major problem with attempting to trace the history of the theatre in Rome is that few texts of Roman plays survive. We have no complete comedies composed after the time of Terence (who wrote in the early second century BCE).[17] The *Octavia* and the plays attributed to Seneca are the only tragedies whose texts have been preserved.[18] Many have doubted whether the latter, in particular, were ever performed. Other dramatic texts survive only in fragments. Over the period for which we have reliable evidence (from the mid third century BCE to the end of the second century CE), it seems there were major changes in the types of drama performed in public and in private. In the earlier period, tragedy and comedy, modelled, though not always closely, on classical Greek tragedy and Greek new comedy appear to have been popular.[19] Some tragedies were composed on mythological subjects, others, known as *praetextae*, on subjects from Roman history.[20] These types of comedy and tragedy seem to have been succeeded under the principate (at least in the context of public theatre) by mime (a form of comic drama which could be written or improvised).[21] Pantomime (which often had tragic themes and was

---

[15] E.g. Beare 1964: 233, 238; Bieber 1961: 227. Some Romans, unsurprisingly, were of the opinion that the theatre had declined (e.g. Cic. *De leg.* 2.30).

[16] Beare 1964: 154. Cf. e.g. Friedländer 1964 II: 230 (Eng. tr. II: 92); Bieber 1961 *passim*.

[17] On the history of Greek and Roman New Comedy, see R.L. Hunter *The New Comedy of Greece and Rome* (Cambridge 1985).

[18] On earlier Roman tragedies, see R.J. Tarrant 'Senecan drama and its antecedents' *HSCPh* 82 (1978) 213–61.

[19] For a picture of Roman drama in the mid republic, see A.S. Gratwick in E.J. Kenney and W.V. Clausen eds. *Cambridge history of classical literature* II (Cambridge 1982) 77–137.

[20] On *praetextae*, see H. Zehnacker 'Tragédie prétexte et spectacle romain' in *Théâtre et spectacles dans l'antiquité. Actes du colloque de Strasbourg* (Leiden 1981) 31–48.

[21] Under the principate, tragedies seem often to have been composed for recitation rather than performance (see Tarrant 1978). On mimes, see H. Reich *Der Mimus* (Berlin 1903). Some of the longer fragments of mimes are examined by Beare (1964 appendix L). See too Reynolds 1946. J.C. McKeown emphasises the wide range of types of production which went under the name of mime ('Augustan elegy and mime' *PCPhS* 25 (1979) 71–84).

generally sung by one or more performers while others mimed the actions) was also popular in the public theatres but was more particularly associated with private performances in the houses of the wealthy. Other forms of comic performance, such as the Atellan and Oscan dramas, went through various stages of popularity.[22]

Because so little has survived of most forms of drama, we are reliant on ancient descriptions. Horace criticises the low tastes of contemporary audiences. The temptation to draw a contrast between Rome and Greece, which often assails modern scholars, is reinforced by Horace's appeal to Aristotelian canons of taste. Aristotle argued in the *Poetics* that proper theatre should achieve its effects through words, while spectacle should be subordinate (1453b1–2). Horace regrets that Roman theatre does not comply with these prescriptions:

> nam quae pervincere voces
> evaluere sonum, referunt quem nostra theatra?
> Garganum mugire putes nemus aut mare Tuscum;
> tanto cum strepitu ludi spectantur et artes
> divitiaeque peregrinae, quibus oblitus actor
> cum stetit in scaena, concurrit dextera laevae.
> 'dixit adhuc aliquid?' 'nil sane'. 'quid placet ergo?'
> 'lana Tarentino violas imitata veneno.'

> *For what voices have ever managed to rise above the din with which our theatres resound? You might imagine it was the roaring of the Garganian forests or of the Tuscan sea; such clamour accompanies the entertainment, the works of art and the foreign finery, and, when, swallowed up in this, the actor sets foot on the stage, loud applause at once. 'Has he said something already?' 'Not a word.' 'Then why this response?' 'It's his woollen robe, made the colour of violets by Tarentine dye.'*

> (*Epist.* 2.1.200–7)

Horace goes on to contrast this 'theatre of spectacle' where the audience cares nothing for the words and is only interested in the cost of the props, with the much finer theatre of the Greek poets.

Much of Roman theatre was improvised. Where texts do survive, they may not have been the most important element in theatrical productions. The Roman idea of theatre was unlike the classical Greek theatre which was much more text-based.[23] Roman concep-

---

[22] The different varieties are set out in detail by Bieber 1961 chs. 10, 11 and 15.

[23] Even the plays of Plautus and Terence seem to have had a much greater musical element than did Greek New Comedy. On music in the Roman theatre, see A. Baudot *Musiciens romains de l'antiquité* (Montreal 1973) 57–63.

tions of the theatre were also very different from modern ones.[24] But modern aesthetic judgements, which rate Greek theatre as superior to Roman, have little explanatory value in discussions of the development of Roman attitudes to the theatre. Roman expressions of disapproval focus especially on mime (which, like more elevated forms of drama, seems to have had its origins in the Greek-speaking world).[25] Moralists complain that these plays are vehicles for coarse jokes, preoccupied with love-affairs and adultery (the association of the theatre with sexual licence and laughter will be discussed further below).[26] Other texts present mimes as a source of moralising platitudes.[27] We should not assume when elite Romans express disapproval of a particular form of entertainment that they are impelled by the same motives we would attribute to ourselves.[28] When an educated Roman, such as Horace, referred back to Aristotelian canons of propriety to validate his own disapproval of the theatre enjoyed by the Roman public, he was also displaying his own familiarity with Greek culture, making clear the refinement which distinguished him both from the common people of the city and also from some of its less educated wealthy citizens.

The most savage attacks on the immorality of the pagan theatre are to be found in Christian authors. Augustine is amazed that pagan Romans allow common actors to play the part of Jupiter, and represent him performing shameful deeds (*De civ. dei* 4.26). He and other patristic writers, including Orosius and Salvian, lament the scandalous exhibitions to be seen on the Roman stage and regularly

[24] Cf. Dupont 1985: 3: 'La conception romaine du théâtre était très éloignée de la nôtre attachant plus d'importance à la musique et à la mise en scène, qu' au texte lui-même.' For a full discussion of the way 'bad taste' has traditionally been attributed to the Roman public, see esp. 111–19.
[25] Cf. e.g. Xenophon *Symp.* 9. It seems, however, quite possible that this bore little resemblance to some of the plays which were termed mimes in Rome. See Dupont 1985: 300–2.
[26] E.g. Sen. *Contr.* 2.4; Juv. 6.41–4; Tert. *De spect.* 17; Minucius Felix, *Oct.* 37.12. Valerius Maximus records that the inhabitants of Massilia banned mimes *quorum argumenta maiore ex parte stuprorum continent actus*, 'most of whose plots included sexual misdemeanours' (2.6.7). Ovid, ostensibly defending himself from the charge of having corrupted morals by writing the *Ars amatoria*, suggests his poetry is much less corrupting than mimes 'which take as their theme loves against the law, in which the smart adulterer is always turning up and the clever wife fools her stupid husband' (*Tristia* 2.498–500). Ovid in the same poem emphasises the power of Augustus' temples to corrupt the morals of Roman women.
[27] On this, see E. Rawson '*Speciosa locis morataque recte*' in M. Whitby *et al.* eds. *Homo viator: classical studies for John Bramble* (Bristol 1987) 80–8 = Rawson 1991: 570–81.
[28] This is most obvious in the case of gladiatorial games. On this question see Wiedemann (forthcoming).

point to them as a striking symptom of pagan degeneracy.[29] Tertullian describes all acting as adultery, since the Christian god forbids pretence of any kind (*De spect.* 23). The loud voice of the Christians among those condemning the Roman theatre should perhaps have aroused more scholarly suspicion than it has, for the Roman theatre was closely implicated in the rites of Roman state religion.

SACRED AND PROFANE

'The way to the theatre is from the temples and altars, from that wretched mess of incense and blood, to the music of flutes and trumpets', wrote Tertullian (*De spect.* 10). Drama in Rome had strong connections with the worship of the gods.[30] The antiquarian Varro included his study of the *ludi scaenici*, 'theatrical games', among his *Res divinae* (Augustine *De civ. dei* 4.31). The theatrical games were presented as part of several important religious festivals in the Roman calendar – the *ludi Megalenses* (in honour of the *Magna Mater*, Cybele), the *ludi Ceriales* (in honour of Ceres), the *ludi Florales* (in honour of Flora), the *ludi Apollinares* (in honour of Apollo), the *ludi Plebei* (the games of the people) and the *ludi Romani* (in honour of Jupiter). These were all well established annual events by the end of the republic. The theatrical games began with a sacrifice in the temple of the relevant deity.[31] A *pompa* or procession led from the temple to the theatre.[32] Statues of the gods on special chairs were carried as part of this procession to witness the games held in their honour from prominent positions in the auditorium.[33] As in the case

[29] E.g. Augustine *De civ. dei* 4.26; Orosius *Adv. paganos* 4.21; Salvian *De gubernatione dei* 6; Tert. *De spect.* esp. 17, 23.
[30] Some modern scholars have rather underplayed the connection (as J.A. Hanson emphasises, *Roman theater-temples* (Princeton 1959) 3–5). Others have explored it in some detail. See, for instance, André Piganiol *Recherches sur les jeux romains* (Strasbourg 1923) esp. ch. 6. Jean-Pierre Morel is perhaps overly preoccupied with tracing the origins of Roman drama in ancient rituals ('La *iuventus* et les origines du théâtre romain' *REL* 49 (1969) 208–52). Besides their role in the *ludi*, actors also seem to have been involved in the funeral ceremonies of important men (cf. e.g. Diodorus Siculus *exc.* 31.25.2 on the funeral of Lucius Aemilius in the second century BCE and Suet. *Vesp.* 19.2 on the funeral of the emperor Vespasian).
[31] On sacrifices, see Hanson 1959: 86–7.
[32] H. Versnel discusses similarities and differences between *pompae* for games, funerals and triumphs (*Triumphus* (Leiden 1970) ch. 3).
[33] See Hanson 1959: 15 and ch. 5. Arnobius gives a vivid description of the procession of statues (*Adversus nationes* 7.33).

of a religious ritual, the *ludi scaenici* had to be repeated from the beginning if they were interrupted.[34]

Augustine and other patristic writers were perplexed by pagan Romans' paradoxical attitude to those who played a central role in their religious ceremonies. Contrasting the Roman view with the more consistent position of the Athenians (outlined at 2.11), Augustine asks:

> qua consentanea ratione homines scaenici ab omni honore repelluntur, et ludi scaenici deorum honoribus admiscentur?

> *By what consistent principle can dramatic performers be excluded from all right to honour, if drama is included among the honours paid to the gods?*

> (*De civ. dei* 2.13)

Patristic writers, such as Tertullian, Lactantius, Arnobius and Augustine, had their own reasons for emphasising the link between Roman drama and the worship of pagan gods. Building on the association of the theatre with immorality and licence, they stressed its religious links in an attempt to discredit pagan cults.[35] Their hostility to the theatre may have been partly provoked by parodies of Christian rites which were sometimes staged there.[36] But, while we should beware of accepting all the assertions of early Christian polemicists, there are reasons for thinking pagan Romans themselves saw the theatre as religiously important.

According to Livy's account, drama first came to Rome in 364 BCE. Rome was afflicted with a terrible plague and theatrical games were the last resort of citizens desperate to placate the gods (Livy 7.2.3). Valerius Maximus, writing in the time of Tiberius, tells a similar story (2.4.4) as does Augustine in his discussion of the origins of the theatre in Rome. The theatre was brought to Rome to please the gods. The emphasis some later Romans chose to lay on the alleged religious origins of the theatre suggests its religious associations continued. Cicero (when it suited him) could lay great emphasis on the religious

---

[34] Cic. *De har. resp.* 21–3; Servius *ad Aen.* 8.110.

[35] Though Tertullian's attack on the pagan games, denounced for their indecency and cruelty, might be seen as somewhat compromised by its culmination – a savage picture of the sufferings of the pagans in hell (*De spect.* 30).

[36] E.K. Chambers (*The medieval stage* (Oxford 1903) ch. 1) gives references to such stories in lives of the saints. See too some of the material discussed by Kathleen Coleman ('Fatal charades: Roman executions staged as mythological enactments' *JRS* 80 (1990) 44–73).

importance of the games (*In Verr.* 2.5.36). It has been argued that, under the principate in particular, the theatre was increasingly dissociated from its religious connections.[37] Certainly, Tacitus' account of the origins of the theatre makes no mention of the relationship between the theatre and worship of the gods, in contrast to Livy's version, written a century earlier (Tac. *Ann.* 14.20–1). But there are other indications that the connection was a persistent one. Hanson concludes his book, *Roman theater-temples*, by drawing attention to some late antique references to the place of the theatre.[38] He cites a rescript of 346 CE from the Christian emperor Constantius, which runs as follows:

> quamquam omnis superstitio penitus eruenda sit, tamen volumus, ut aedes templorum, quae extra muros positae, intactae incorruptaeque consistant. nam cum ex nonnullis vel ludorum vel circensium vel agonum origo fuerit exorta, non convenit ea convelli, ex quibus populo Romano praebeatur priscarum sollemnitas voluptatum.

> *Although all superstition must be utterly eradicated, still we do not wish the temples which are outside the walls to be destroyed or despoiled. For since certain plays, or circus spectacles or contests, derive their origin from some of these temples, such structures shall not be torn down, since the regular performance of long-established amusements of the Roman people stems from them.*

> (*C. Th.* 16.10.3)

The connection between the theatre (and other games) and the temples with which they were associated was so close that the temples were necessary, if the games were to survive. An inscription, again dating from after the Christianisation of the Roman empire, illustrates the same point (*CIL* XI 5265). The citizens of Hispellum could not be given the right to hold *ludi* unless they had their own temple. The link between theatres and temples was conceptual as well as architectural.[39]

---

[37] J.-M. André 'Les *ludi scaenici* et la politique des spectacles au début de l'ère antonine' *Association Guillaume Budé. Actes du IXe congrès* (Paris 1975) 468–79.

[38] Hanson 1959: 91–2.

[39] Pompey's incorporation of a temple of Venus into his theatre building in the Campus Martius was perhaps not so cynical as is sometimes suggested (though cf. Gell. 10.1.7 and Tert. *De spect.* 10). On the architectural link in general, see Hanson 1959, esp. chs. 2 and 3; Filippo Coarelli *Guida archeologica di Roma* (Rome 1974); Pierre Gros 'La fonction symbolique des édifices théâtraux dans le paysage de la Rome augustéene' *L'urbs: espace urbain et histoire. Collection de l'école française de Rome* 98 (1987) 319–46.

POLITICAL THEATRE

The theatre played a central part in the religious rituals of the city; it was also an important arena for the display of power and wealth. During the republic, Roman magistrates were expected to provide dramatic performances and the temporary theatres in which they took place (as well as circus games). The curule aediles provided for the *ludi Romani* and the *ludi Megalenses,* the plebeian aediles for the *ludi Plebei,* the *Ceralia* and the *Floralia* and the urban praetor for the *ludi Apollinares.* A subsidy was provided by the state but a large part of the costs seem to have been met from the pocket of the presiding magistrates.[40] Dramatic performances were also given as part of the funeral games commemorating the death of a notable, to celebrate a triumph and at the dedication of temples. Even in the days of Plautus and Ennius, that is in the late third and early second centuries BCE, theatrical performances were being given on almost as many days per year as in classical Athens. Under the principate, an emperor's birthday might be celebrated with the performance of plays, as might his safe return from abroad. The number of days on which theatrical performances were given increased substantially. By 354 CE, Romans could go to the theatre a hundred days per year.[41]

We might wonder if the theatre can really have been important in Rome when only a small proportion of the population of the city (about five per cent) could be accommodated in the three permanent theatres which existed by the end of Augustus' reign.[42] It is worth noting that the population of Attica could not fit into the theatre of Dionysus – hardly a strong argument for the insignificance of Greek tragedy.[43] Roman dramatic festivals lasted several days. Many people

---

[40] The financing arrangements for *ludi* are discussed by Ville (he is primarily concerned with *venationes* but his remarks have relevance for games in general) (1981: 94–9). Cf. too Paul Veyne *Bread and circuses* (London 1990) 208–10.

[41] Bieber gives a full list (1961: 227).

[42] The theatre of Pompey seated about 17,000, that of Marcellus 20,000, that of Balbus 11,500 (in total 48,500). The free population in Rome in the time of Augustus is reckoned to have been around 600,000–700,000, excluding children (assuming a third of the population was slaves). At least by the principate, slaves seem to have had some access to the theatre so they should be included in calculations of the potential audience. On the capacity of the theatres, see Coarelli 1974. On the size of the population of the city of Rome see Hopkins 1978: 96–8.

[43] The Lycurgan theatre of Dionysus in Athens seems to have had room for between 14,000 and 17,000 (Pickard-Cambridge 1968 ch. 6). Slaves were not permitted to watch the plays but the free population of Attica, even in the fourth century, was probably somewhere between 100,000 and 175,000 (Signe Isager and Mogens Herman Hansen *Aspects of Athenian society in the fourth century* BC (Odense 1975) 11–19).

will have seen at least some part of a cycle of *ludi scaenici*. Roman discussions of the theatre cited throughout this chapter attest to its symbolic importance. Leading members of the elite were missed if they did not put in an appearance.[44] Magistrates and, later, emperors were expected to be present.[45]

Seating arrangements at the games were a reflection and reaffirmation of the social hierarchy.[46] Livy relates that in 194 BCE senators first sat separately from the rest of the audience, despite the complaints of the *plebs* (34.44.5; 34.54).[47] In 67 BCE, a tribune of the *plebs*, L. Roscius Otho, proposed the *lex Roscia theatralis* (Roscian law on the theatre) under which the first fourteen rows of seats in the theatre were reserved for senators and equestrians.[48] The theatre was a place to parade distinctions. After his military successes in the east (66–63 BCE), Pompey was granted, as a special mark of honour, the right to wear the purple-bordered toga and golden crown of the triumphant general in the theatre (Vell. Pat. 2.40.4). Priests and priestesses sat in special places at the games, as, under the principate, did the emperor and his family.[49]

The emperor Augustus' *lex Iulia theatralis* (Julian law on the theatre) reiterated the rules about separate seating for senators and *equites*.[50] According to Suetonius, it contained the following provisions:

> facto igitur decreto patrum ut, quotiens quid spectaculi usquam publice ederetur, primus subselliorum ordo vacaret senatoribus, Romae legatos liberarum sociarumque gentium vetuit in orchestra sedere, cum quosdam etiam libertini generis mitti deprendisset. militem secrevit a populo. maritis e plebe proprios ordines assignavit, praetextatis cuneum suum, et proximum paedagogis, sanxitque ne quis pullatorum media cavea sederet. feminis ne gladiatores quidem,

---

[44] See e.g. Cic. *Pro Sest.* 116.

[45] See Zwi Yavetz *Plebs and Princeps* (Oxford 1969) 22–4; Alan Cameron *Circus factions: blues and greens at Rome and Byzantium* (Oxford 1976) 162–9 and 174.

[46] As Hopkins points out in his discussion of the gladiatorial games (1983: 17–18). Regulations governing seating in the theatre seem to have been the most detailed. According to Tacitus, the principle of reserving the first fourteen rows for senators and equestrians applied only to the theatre until the time of Nero, when it was extended to the circus (*Ann.* 15.31). Valerius Maximus speaks of the theatre as an *urbana castra*, 'an army in the city', referring to the regimentation with which the audience was organised (2.4.1).

[47] Cf. Valerius Maximus 2.4.3.

[48] Cf. Plut. *Cic.* 13. See G. Rotondi *Leges publicae populi Romani* (Milan 1912) 374.

[49] Hopkins 1983: 18.

[50] Suet. *Aug.* 44. Rotondi suggests this may only have been a decree of the senate (1912: 462).

quos promiscue spectari sollemne olim erat, nisi ex superiore loco spectare concessit.

The resulting senatorial decree provided that at every public performance, wherever held, the front row of seating must be reserved for senators. At Rome, Augustus would not allow the ambassadors of independent or allied states to sit in the orchestra, when he discovered that some were only freedmen. Besides this, his rules included the separation of soldiers from civilians, the assignment of special seats to married common people, to boys not yet of age and, close by, their tutors; and he refused to allow those dressed in dark cloaks to sit anywhere but the back rows. Also, although, until then, men and women had always sat together, Augustus made women sit behind, even at gladiatorial shows.

(Suet. *Aug.* 44.1–2)

We need not assume all these rules were scrupulously complied with.[51] The preoccupation with the categorisation of Roman citizens is also evident in other pieces of Augustan legislation. Measures to stamp out licence in the theatre were guaranteed an audience – a very public means of displaying authority and control. Later, Domitian, too, in his capacity as censor, is said to have strictly enforced the rules about seating arrangements (Suet. *Dom.* 8.3).[52] Emperors took advantage of the way a Roman audience went to the theatre not only to enjoy the spectacle provided on stage, but also to see the Roman socio-political hierarchy made visible, a still more awesome spectacle.[53]

In ancient times, according to Valerius Maximus, rules governing seating arrangements were not necessary, for all knew their place (4.5.1). In Juvenal's third satire, those of low origin (the sons of auctioneers and gladiators) sitting in seats intended for their betters are presented as a glaring symptom of the disruption of the social order (3.152–9). This passage has been invoked in support of the suggestion that the rules on seating arrangements were generally

---

[51] On the details of this law, see E. Rawson 'Discrimina ordinum: the lex Iulia theatralis' PBSR 55 (1987) 83–114 (= E. Rawson 1991: 508–45). On seating arrangements in general, see also Jerzy Kolendo 'La répartition des places aux spectacles et la stratification sociale dans l'empire romain: à propos des inscriptions sur les gradins des amphithéâtres et théâtres' Ktèma 6 (1981) 301–15; Saara Lilja 'Seating problems in the Roman theatre and circus' Arctos 19 (1985) 67–74.   [52] Cf. Mart. 5.23.

[53] For a suggestive discussion of the theatre as symbolic space see Monique Clavel-Levêque L'Empire en jeux (Paris 1984) esp. 45–6. Seating arrangements at the theatre could function as a vivid metaphor for the Roman social hierarchy (see e.g. Pet. Sat. 126).

ignored but, if these rules were regarded as unimportant, Juvenal's picture would lose its point. An anecdote recounted by Tacitus, concerning the reaction of some barbarian envoys on a visit to Rome, also relies for its significance on the symbolic importance of seating arrangements at the theatre (*Ann.* 13.54). We should note, in passing, Tacitus' observation that the Frisii were unable to appreciate the show itself, since they were quite uneducated. Enjoyment of the theatre could function as something which distinguished Romans from barbarians.[54]

Republican magistrates were expected to be generous in the provision of games of all kinds. Cicero speaks with qualified approval of the munificence of some of his contemporaries (*De off.* 2.57).[55] Public generosity was regularly contrasted with the evils of private luxury (as we shall see in chapter four). But such generosity was not entirely disinterested. Success in subsequent elections was felt to be strongly influenced by lavishness in the financing of *ludi*.[56] Roman historians describe how the competition became fiercer and the display more extravagant towards the end of the republic. Magistrates vied with one another, each striving to appear richer and more generous than his rivals.[57] Cicero emphasises how great a financial burden this could be (*De off.* 2.55–7, 63).[58] The elder Pliny describes, no doubt with some exaggeration, the extraordinarily extravagant theatre built by the aedile Scaurus in 58 BCE.[59] Others are recorded by Valerius Maximus (2.4.6). The younger Cato allegedly made a stand against this movement away from the frugality ascribed to earlier Romans (Plut. *Cat. min.* 46.2–3), but Plutarch stresses how unusual Cato's behaviour was felt to be. In 28 BCE, there were no candidates for the aedileship (according to Dio 53.2.2), as none of those who

---

[54] Cf. Philostratus, *Apollonius of Tyana* 5.9.

[55] Cf. Livy's account of the impressive triumphal games of Paulus in 167 BCE (45.32.8). Paulus is made to claim that a general should be skilled in giving games as well as in warfare.

[56] Shatzman 1975: 85–7.

[57] Cf. e.g. Cic. *De dom.* 111 (Appius Claudius Pulcher *cogitaret omnes superiores muneris splendore superare*, 'aimed by the munificence of his games to outdo all his predecessors'). Veyne discusses the provision of theatrical shows as a manifestation of euergetism (1990: 212–14). This rivalry in the provision of shows was echoed by local magistrates in the provinces. On this, see Clavel-Lévêque 1984: 35.

[58] Elsewhere, he writes to a friend describing with disapproval the lavishness of a particular cycle of *ludi scaenici* (*Ad fam.* 7.1). Cf. Livy's complaints about the luxury of the theatre (7.2.13).

[59] *NH* 34.36; 36.50, 113–15, 189. The debts incurred by Scaurus during his time as aedile were notorious (cf. Asconius *In Scaurianum*). For other examples of extravagant games, see Shatzman 1975: 84–7.

might otherwise have been interested had the resources to stage the lavish entertainments which were by then required.

In the late republic, temporary theatres must have been among the most obvious manifestations of the escalating extravagance which sucked in all but the Catos of Rome's elite. The theatre could be the setting for a magistrate's spectacular financial ruin. Not all aediles went on to secure election as praetor or consul (thus attaining the opportunity to recoup their losses as provincial governors). Yet impressively lavish games could be essential to electoral success. No wonder the elite felt ambivalent towards acting and the theatre.

The temporary theatres built by republican aediles were a symbol of the temporary nature of their own authority. Their theatres were taken down even before they themselves were succeeded by the next year's magistrates, rather than remaining as monuments to the generosity of those who had built them. Pompey's building of a permanent theatre in 55 BCE could be said to prefigure the end of the republic. Soon after this, Julius Caesar began work on a similar theatre (which was eventually finished by Augustus, who named it after his son-in-law Marcellus). These buildings were permanent reminders of the power and wealth of those who built them.[60]

Under the principate, aediles ceased to have charge of the games. Augustus transferred responsibility for all regular cycles of *ludi* to the urban praetor (Dio 53.2). Praetors were forbidden to contribute from their own funds more than twice what was provided by the state towards the cost of the games (Dio 54.2.4).[61] Private individuals no longer gave games. Under Tiberius, the popular assemblies in practice lost control over the election of higher magistrates. Thus the provision of games aimed at the people would have little effect on one's chances of becoming consul, so magistrates had less incentive for generosity. While spending on the regular cycles of *ludi* was restricted, emperors monopolised the provision of extraordinary games, which naturally outshone all others.[62]

By the time of Augustus, it was common practice for the people to make requests of the emperor at the theatre, arena and circus. The

[60] Gros notes of these permanent structures that they were: 'les instruments de définition d'un pouvoir, en rupture croissante avec la tradition républicaine' (1987: 320). He vividly emphasises how impressive Pompey's theatre complex must have been when it was first erected, a vast structure dominating the Campus Martius (1987: 323–4).

[61] Though this prescription seems to have been ignored (Dio 60.3.1–4).

[62] See Veyne 1990: 388–92.

emperor's decision to refuse or accede to these requests was consequently very public and would at once arouse popular favour or disapproval.[63] Why did emperors expose themselves to these potentially threatening situations? In appearing at the circus, arena or theatre, an emperor was parading the fact that he shared the tastes of his people, demonstrating his *civilitas*.[64] In listening personally to requests, an emperor showed he took an interest in his people's concerns. Popular measures would gain maximum publicity performed in front of a large audience assembled for a show. If the crowd went out of control, it was at least easier to impose discipline in a closed than in an open space. Yet emperors, like republican magistrates before them, can hardly have felt at ease when they attended the games. Where an aedile's or an emperor's generosity was on show, it was also on trial.

Under the republic, popular opinion could be forcefully expressed at the games. The crowd might applaud or hiss not only in response to the show but also to mark the arrival of particular individuals in the audience.[65] Cicero's discussion in the *Pro Sestio* of responses to his own exile is the most vivid evocation of the potential of the games as an arena for the expression of public opinion.[66] Certainly Cicero had an interest in exaggerating what he presented as feelings of outrage at his own exile manifested in the theatre. His assertion that it was at the games rather than in the *contiones* (deliberative assemblies) or *comitia* (electoral assemblies) that public opinion was expressed is perhaps doubtful (though it is interesting to speculate what variations there might have been in the composition of the 'public' on these occasions).[67] There are, of course, obvious differences. Demonstrations at the games might be noisy but they did not necessarily change anything. Cicero observes of the audience's response on one occasion that it was 'a unanimous cry, but with hatred rather than

[63] See Cameron (1976: 162–4) who cites, in particular, Josephus *AJ* 19.24. See too Millar 1977: 368–75.
[64] Tacitus suggests Augustus attended the games because it was *civile . . . misceri voluptatibus vulgi*, 'democratic to join in the amusements of the common people' (*Ann.* 1.54. Cf. Tac. *Hist.* 2.91.2; Dio 44.8.2). See the discussion by Yavetz (1969 esp. 99–102; 114; 123–4).
[65] E.g. *Ad Att.* 38.1; 39.2–3 (Caesar entered to no applause and was angered when Curio was received with an ovation); 356.1; 357.2; *Ad fam.* 78.1 (Hortensius was hissed when he entered the theatre); 205.2; *Pro Sest.* 117–18. See F.F. Abbott 'The theatre as a factor in Roman politics under the republic' *TAPhA* 38 (1907) 49–56.
[66] See the perceptive discussion by Nicolet (1980: 363–73).
[67] Cicero observes that at the time of Verres' trial, Rome was full of citizens from all over Italy because of the coincidence of the *comitia*, the games and the census (*In Verr.* 1.54).

power behind it' (*Ad Att.* 39.3).[68] Yet the audience's sentiments could sometimes be hard to ignore.

The arguments so far adduced apply, to a certain extent, to other kinds of games as well as to the theatre. But the theatre had a particular potency as a place for challenging authority. Roman audiences, when they went to see a play, may have valued staging and music more than the words but the words were important, too. The text of a drama could be given a contemporary political meaning, through the interaction of players and audience. Cicero tells of an incident during the *ludi Apollinares* in 59 BCE (at a time when Pompey, together with Caesar and Crassus, was a dominant influence in Rome):

> ludis Apollinaribus Diphilus tragoedus in nostrum Pompeium petu-lanter invectus est: 'nostra miseria tu es magnus' miliens coactus est dicere. 'eandem virtutem istam veniet tempus cum graviter gemes' totius theatri clamore dixit itemque cetera. nam et eius modi sunt ii versus ut in tempus ab inimico Pompei scripti esse videantur.

> *At the games of Apollo, the actor Diphilus set on poor old Pompey quite brutally: 'By our sufferings art thou Great.' There were thousands of encores. 'But that same manliness heartily|In time to come shalt thou lament.' The whole audience shouted out applause as he said those words, and the rest, too. Indeed, the lines almost seemed to have been written specially for the occasion by an enemy of Pompey.*

> (Cic. *Ad Att.* 39.3)

Pompey himself was absent on this occasion but often the individuals focused on were in the audience.[69] Such occurrences must have been profoundly disconcerting, both for the subjects of attacks and for others whose turn might be next.

---

[68] When sentiments were not unanimous, the hierarchisation of seating made it easy to see the source of particular outbursts (e.g. Cic. *Pro Sest.* 115 and *Ad Att.* 39.3, where the equestrians are identified as responsible for giving Curio his ovation). Horace uses the hierarchisation of seating at the theatre to dramatise the difference in tastes between the senatorial and equestrian orders and the rest (*Sat.* 1.10.76–7).

[69] Similar incidents are described by Cicero elsewhere (*Pro Sest.* 118, 120–3; *Ad Att.* 357.2). These stories are discussed by Cameron 1976: 157–61; Traugott Bollinger *Theatralis licentia* (Winterthur 1969) 25–73; Nicolet 1980: 361–73. E. Frézouls suggests that the theatre only became important as a political arena after the abolition of the *collegia* ('La construction du *theatrum lapideum* et son contexte politique' in *Théâtre et spectacles dans l'antiquité. Actes du colloque de Strasbourg* (Leiden 1981) 193–214). As Rawson points out, some of the incidents Cicero refers to took place before the abolition of the *collegia* (1985b: 98, n. 7).

Some Roman tragedies, mythological ones as well as *praetextae*, were composed with contemporary political relevance (for instance, those of Accius in the late second century BCE.[70] Varius' *Thyestes* (a play about fratricide) was staged in the games given by Octavian in 29 BCE to mark his triumph over Antony and Cleopatra at the battle of Actium, the end of the civil war.[71] But older plays might also be appropriated for their potential to resonate with a particular set of circumstances. Cicero's letters reveal that the question of what play was to be performed at the *ludi Apollinares* after the assassination of Caesar in 44 BCE was a vexed one. Accius' *Brutus*, which had as its subject the story of Brutus the regicide, inaugurator of the republic, was not seen as a neutral choice (Caesar's assassin Brutus claimed to be descended from his namesake). Even the eventual selection of Accius' *Tereus* was thought to be a triumph for the killers of Caesar.[72] Comedies, too, might contain contemporary allusions.[73] It is hard to judge how far plays which are now fragmentary, had potential to be interpreted in terms of contemporary politics. It seems that political allusions in both comedy and tragedy had to be implicit. By convention, living persons were not named.[74] *Praetextae*, if concerned with events in the recent past, were generally performed at the funerals of their protagonists.[75] Yet almost any play could be appropriated as a vehicle for the articulation of contemporary concerns. Roman audiences seem to have been highly sensitive to a line's potential for multiple meanings.[76]

Theatres were traditionally the meeting places, in Greek city states,

---

[70] Nicolet 1980: 366–7.   [71] According to a scholiast (Didasc. in cod. Paris. 7530 s. viii).

[72] Cic. *Phil.* 1.36; Appian *Civil wars* 3.24. Cf. Gratwick in *CHCL* II (1982): 127; Cameron 1976: 171; Nicolet 1980: 371–2.

[73] John Henderson explores the resonances of Terence *Adelphoe*, composed for the funeral of L. Aemilius Paullus ('Entertaining arguments: Terence *Adelphoe*' in Andrew Benjamin ed. *Post-structuralist classics* (London 1988) 192–226).

[74] Cf. Cic. *De rep.* 4.12; Augustine *De civ. dei* 2.12. According to Gellius (3.3.15), the playwright Naevius was imprisoned for his libellous references to some leading Romans in his plays. R.E. Smith concludes that later Roman dramatists were consequently unwilling to make explicit reference to their contemporaries ('The law of libel at Rome' *CQ* I (1951) 169–79). This seems highly implausible (the story of Naevius' imprisonment is itself disputed, see H.B. Mattingley 'Naevius and the Metelli' *Historia* 9 (1960) 414–39). Gratwick more plausibly attributes this convention to the theatre managers' concern not to lose future custom by making enemies among those who might later become magistrates (1982: 82).

[75] Balbus was disapproved of for putting on a play in Spain in 43 BCE, celebrating his own achievements (Pollio *ap.* Cic. *Ad fam.* 415).

[76] Nicolet observes 'Roman theatre audiences in the last century of the republic were politicised to a remarkable extent' (1980: 373).

of democratic assemblies (in which, in theory at least, any citizen might speak).[77] This was perhaps one reason why some members of the Roman elite were hostile to the idea of a permanent theatre building. Cicero expresses disapproval of the *libertate immoderata ac licentia*, 'the excessive liberty and licence' associated with democratic meetings in theatres in the Greek world (*Pro Flacco* 15–16.) The relationship between the theatre and other spaces where public speaking took place was a highly problematic one in Rome. Few citizens, even under the republic, are likely to have spoken in public at *contiones* or in the courts. Only the words of magistrates and orators, men of wealth and established position, carried public authority.[78] The speech of actors was, of course, very different from the speech of magistrates. Actors were known to be dissemblers, speaking words which carried no legitimate weight.[79] They were banned from standing for election to magistracies. Yet actors still had an opportunity to command the attention of the Roman people with the words they spoke, an opportunity otherwise denied to all but the governing class. It was perhaps in recognition of the peculiar power of actors that they were branded as *infames* in Roman law – that is to say, 'without reputation' (*fama*).[80] But the etymology of the term also suggests 'without a voice'. The actor's words were drained of legal weight.

The parallels between the speech of an actor and the speech of a magistrate were potentially compromising for the latter. The *levitas* of the player often bore an uncomfortable resemblance to the *gravitas* of the senator. Seneca suggested there was little difference between those who held power in real life and those who played the part of rulers on stage (*Ep.* 76.31). Actors could become persons of any status. They could transcend all the conventions of dress by which members of Roman society were categorised. Their manifest dissimulation suggested others, too, might not be what they seemed. Roman orators considered with some nervousness the similarities between their own profession and that of the actor. Quintilian, in his

---

[77] This is set out in detail by A. Rumpf 'Die Entstehung des römischen Theaters' *MDAI(R)* 3 (1950) 40–50. Cf. Nicolet 1980: 363. For the association of theatre buildings with democratic meetings in the Greek world, see e.g. Athen. *Deipn.* 5.213d.

[78] The presiding magistrate decided who might speak in *contiones*. Nicolet suggests it was rare for anyone below the rank of a *praetor* to speak (1980: 286). [79] See Dupont 1985: 48.

[80] Though those who followed some other professions associated with public performance were also stigmatised. See Wiedemann (forthcoming) and Catharine Edwards 'Unspeakable professions: public performance and prostitution in ancient Rome' (forthcoming).

treatise on the education of the orator, repeatedly emphasises that the good orator should take care that his manner does not resemble that of an actor.[81] The orator Hortensius' skills were said to have been admired by the actor Roscius (Val. Max. 8.10.2).[82]

The theatre's importance as a political arena continued under the principate. Suetonius, in particular, records numerous incidents where a theatre audience expressed open disapproval of an emperor. Against so many what could an emperor do? Caligula wished the Roman people had only one head that it might the more easily be silenced (Suet. *Calig.* 30.2). On another occasion, an actor is alleged to have referred to the emperor Nero's murders of his step-father Claudius and mother Agrippina by making gestures of drinking and swimming to indicate the methods by which they had been dispatched, as he declaimed the lines: 'Goodbye father, goodbye mother!' (*Nero* 39.3).[83] Caligula was so disturbed by the power of the theatre that he had an outspoken playwright publicly burned (Suet. *Calig.* 27.4). The emperor was placed in an awkward position. By reacting violently to criticisms so ambiguously expressed he acknowledged his own guilt. Some chose to allow a degree of licence to the players and their audience or perhaps they enjoyed such intimations of their own notoriety.[84]

POPULAR THEATRE

The theatre in Rome was closely involved in mediating the relationship between government and people.[85] A passage from Ovid's *Fasti* suggests the significance of the theatre's political role (5.277–95). The narrator has asked the goddess Flora about the origin of the games performed in her honour. She replies that certain rich men had taken over some public land. Their case was tried before the people and the guilty were fined. The goddess received part of the proceeds. Those

[81] Quint. *Inst.* 1.8.3; 1.11.1–3; 6.3.29; 6.3.47. Cf. Cic. *De off.* 1.130.
[82] Though this story may well reflect a tradition hostile to Hortensius (cf. Gell. 1.5.2–3). For 'actor' as a term of abuse, cf. Cicero's attack on Clodius (*Pro Sest.* 116).
[83] For similar incidents, see e.g. Suet. *Aug.* 53, 68; *Tib.* 45; *Galba* 13; *Dom.* 10; Tac. *Ann.* 11.13.
[84] Cf. the story told about the emperor Domitian (Suet. *Dom.* 10.4). These anecdotes are discussed by Cameron (1976: 157–92). See too Ahl 1984.
[85] Cf. Hopkins on the mediatory role of the gladiatorial games (1983: 1–30). On the mediatory function of the games in general see Clavel-Levêque 1984: 15; Cameron 1976: 170–80; Yavetz 1969: 18–24.

who had defended the rights of the poor against the encroachments of the rich celebrated their successful suit by instituting new games. In the *Fasti*, then, the *Floralia* are presented as a symbol of the sharing of wealth among all citizens, of the defence of the rights of the poor against the selfishness of the rich.

Yet the idea of theatre as an entertainment which united the community was problematic for some of the *literati* of the late republic and early principate. While in Terence's day it seems that the theatre was seen as refined and sophisticated, appealing to a more select audience than other games, by the late republic some forms of theatrical entertainment were thought of as appealing principally to the 'lowest' elements in society.[86] Cicero emphasises that he attended some mimes only to please Julius Caesar who was providing them (*Ad fam.* 205.2); that sort of popular entertainment was not what he would watch by preference.[87] Similar sentiments are expressed by the younger Pliny (*Ep.* 9.6). Tacitus speaks of the lowest elements of Roman society as those among the poor who are not attached to any great house but spend their days at the theatre and circus (*Hist.* 1.4).

Such comments are often seen as evidence that popular theatre was becoming coarser. Certainly the educated elite often had different, more literary plays performed for their private entertainment; those with claims to literary talent sometimes wrote their own plays, modelled on earlier tragedies and comedies, for recitation to a select audience (Pliny *Ep.* 5.19; 9.36; 7.17; Martial 2.7). But private theatrical performances can be attested from an early date.[88] And aristocratic Roman notions of 'coarseness' should be treated with greater scrutiny than they generally receive. Signs of elite disdain for *ludi scaenici* should rather be related to an unwillingness to be seen as sharing popular pleasures.[89]

In particular, members of the Roman elite seem to have been uneasy about the laughter aroused in the theatre.[90] It is comedy of

---

[86] Terence *Hecyra* prologue. Cf. the distinction Horace draws between the taste of those in the equestrian rows and that of the rest of the audience, who would rather watch a bear or a boxing match than a play. This past situation is contrasted with the present where no-one in the audience cares for anything but spectacle (*Epist.* 2.1.182–207).

[87] For similar expressions of disdain, see *Ad fam.* 24.1; *Pro Mur.* 38–9. This material is discussed by André, who argues that the separation between public and private theatre became more marked in the late first and early second centuries CE (1973: 375–8).

[88] Sallust makes Marius allude to this practice (*BJ* 85.39).

[89] On this see chapter five below.

[90] E.g. Cic. *De off.* 1.103–4 (immoderate laughter is a sign of lack of self-control).

which Horace is most scornful in his attack on Roman drama (*Epist.* 2.1.168–76). Juvenal is horrified by the appearance of a Roman noble in a farce, where his antics will be a source of amusement to the common people (8.183–94). The elite marked themselves off by their manners as well as by their cultural preferences. We might want to argue that the kind of farces which seem to have dominated public theatre under the principate were not very suitable for adaption as vehicles of political protest. No doubt this suited the imperial regime and emperors must have exercised some control over the content of the plays they financed. But we should be wary of assuming that this 'depoliticisation' was the reason Rome's educated elite expressed disdain for the theatre.[91]

THEATRE AND CITY

Ambivalence regarding the building and location of permanent theatres should also be seen as a manifestation of anxieties aroused by the theatre's potential as a site for the contestation of social and political authority. Although plays were performed in Rome from at least the mid third century BCE, there was no permanent theatre until one was built by Pompey in 55 BCE. Anecdotes are told by historians and others relating to earlier attempts to build permanent theatres, in which the reluctance of Romans of earlier times to sanction such constructions is presented as a sign of their unimpeachable morals. Publius Scipio Nasica Corculum is said to have persuaded the senate that they should pull down a stone theatre constructed by order of the censors in 154 BCE.[92] Valerius Maximus attributes this measure to a desire to protect *virilitas propria Romanae gentis nota*, 'the famous virility particular to the Roman people' (2.4.2).

Tacitus remarks, in the context of his scornful discussion of Nero's interest in the theatre:

> quippe erant qui Gnaeum quoque Pompeium incusatum a senioribus ferrent, quod mansuram theatri sedem posuisset. nam antea subitariis gradibus et scaena in tempus structa ludos edi solitos, vel si vetustiora

---

[91] Though a passage from Pliny's *Panegyricus* (54.1) does seem to connect popular enthusiasm for 'low' theatre with the uncritical adulation of the 'bad' emperor Nero.

[92] Livy *epit.* 48; Val. Max. 2.4.2; Appian *Civil wars* 1.28; Tert. *De spect.* 10; Aug. *De civ. dei* 1.31.

repetas, stantem populum spectavisse, ne, si consideret theatro, dies totos ignavia continuaret.

Some remembered the reproaches made against Pompey by his elders for building a permanent theatre, when previously performances had been held using an improvised stage and auditorium or (in the remoter past) spectators had stood, since it was feared that seats would keep them idle for days on end.

(Tac. *Ann.* 14.20)

By the middle of the third century BCE, most Greek cities had their own theatres. Many Italian cities had permanent theatres long before Rome.[93] Romans of the middle and late republic had adopted many features of the Greek city.[94] But the theatre was not so easily accommodated.

The location of permanent theatres, when these were eventually built in Rome, was very different from that of the theatre in Athens and many other Greek cities. In Athens, the theatre was situated on the slopes of the Acropolis, within the precinct of the god Dionysus, in the heart of the city. When Pompey's theatre was built in Rome, it was constructed in the Campus Martius, that is, outside the city of Rome.[95] The theatres of Marcellus and Balbus, both constructed under the emperor Augustus, were also built outside the *pomerium*, the religious boundary of the city.[96] It is not always easy to determine exactly where the *pomerium* ran but, traditionally, the Campus Martius, where the Roman army gathered, was outside it, for the

---

[93] The theatre in Pompeii is one of the earliest. On the development of the theatre in Italy, see Rawson 1985b.

[94] On the Roman adoption of Greek types of building and town-planning, see Axel Boethius *The golden house of Nero* (Ann Arbor 1960) 77.

[95] Pompey's theatre was thus a free-standing theatre in the tradition of the theatre at Mytilene on the island of Lesbos, according to Plutarch (*Pomp.* 42.2), though the design of the temporary theatres of the late republic was no doubt also an influence. The architecture of Pompey's theatre is discussed by F. Coarelli 'Il complesso pompeiano del Campo Marzio e la sua decorazione scultorea' *RPAA* 44 (1972) 99–122. For a comprehensive discussion of the evolution of theatre architecture in Rome, see E. Frézouls 'Aspects de l'histoire architectural du théâtre romain' *ANRW* II 12.1 (Berlin 1982) 343–441. On the architectural differences between Greek and Roman theatres, see Vitruvius, *De arch.* 5.6, 5.7 (discussed by Bieber 1961 chs. 13 and 14).

[96] Julius Caesar allegedly contemplated building a theatre on the south-east slope of the Capitol (Suet. *Jul.* 44.1), which would have been firmly inside the *pomerium* and closely parallel to the situation of the theatre of Dionysus in Athens. However, this project was never carried out. The nature of the *pomerium* as a religious boundary was reinforced by Augustus' ban in 28 BCE on the celebration of Egyptian rites within it (Dio 53.2.4).

pomerium was the dividing line between the civil and the military spheres.[97] It may be significant that the theatres referred to by the emperor Constantius in an edict quoted above are described as 'outside the walls'. Perhaps the only space available in Rome which could accommodate a theatre (particularly one with an attached complex of monumental buildings) was the Campus Martius.[98] But there is surely a connection between unwillingness to build a theatre within the city itself and the tradition of righteous hostility to any permanent theatre.[99] Acting was physically as well as morally marginal in its relation to the city of Rome.

Actors, too, were relegated to a position outside the *pomerium* of full Roman citizenship. Many of those who performed in the theatre were slaves or non-citizen free.[100] But this does not explain the legal stigma attaching to those who were Roman citizens (many citizens worked alongside slaves as shopkeepers, craftsmen or agricultural workers without suffering any legal disabilities in consequence). The legal disabilities imposed on actors were severe, effectively assimilating them to slaves in important respects. Actors, in common with condemned criminals, soldiers dishonourably dismissed and those who followed a number of other professions, including gladiators and prostitutes, were *infames* – legally branded as disgraceful.[101]

Lists of professions branded as disgraceful in legal prescriptions do not always cohere with one another. Sometimes actors are subject to the same restrictions as, for instance, prostitutes and gladiators. In

---

[97] When the emperor Vespasian celebrated his triumph, the *porticus Octaviae*, where he awaited the senate's response before proceeding into the city, must still have been regarded as being outside the *pomerium* (this is significant because it is adjacent to the southernmost of the three theatres, that of Marcellus) (Josephus, *BJ* 7.5.4). Not long afterwards, however, the *pomerium* does seem to have been extended to include the southern half of the Campus Martius and thus all three theatres. For the details see Samuel B. Platner and Thomas Ashby *Topographical dictionary of Rome* (London 1929) 392–6.

[98] Cf. Hanson 1959: 48. Augustus in some of his other building projects certainly seems to have been ostentatiously scrupulous not to encroach on existing public buildings or the private property of those unwilling to sell (see e.g. Suet. *Aug.* 56).

[99] In the republic, however, games which included *ludi scaenici*, such as the Megalesia, had taken place in the vicinity of their associated temple, often within the *pomerium* (on the Megalesia, see Cic. *De har. resp.* 24). For the location of temporary theatres in general, see Hanson 1959: 9–28.

[100] Rawson argues that in the late republic groups of actors travelled all over Italy performing in different places. Many of the actors individually attested have names which suggest they were non-Romans or slaves (1985b).

[101] On *infamia* in general, see the monograph of Greenidge 1894. Less helpful is Max Kaser '*Infamia* und *ignominia* in den römischen Rechtsquellen' *ZSS* 73 (1956) 220–78. On the application of *infamia* to those following particular professions, see Edwards forthcoming b.

other cases they are treated separately. Some restrictions were imposed by the decision of magistrates, which became gradually systematised. The use of the term *famosus* ('disgraceful') in the praetor's edict (*Dig.* 3.2.2.5) indicates that actors had only limited rights of postulation for others, that is to say, the right to ask the praetor to grant an action on behalf of someone else (they are classed here with, among others, procurers, bigamists and soldiers who had been dishonourably dismissed). This restriction, though not particularly severe in itself, is an indication of the powerlessness of such persons in all legal situations where the value of one's word would be measured by the presiding magistrate (*Dig.* 22.5.3.*pr.* Callistratus). This disempowering of the actor's voice may be seen as another strategy for containing its subversive potential. Actors earned money by pretending to be what they were not. They lied for a living. Cicero remarks, in his discussion of the professions a man of honour may properly take up, that no action is more disgraceful than misrepresentation, *vanitas* (*De off.* 1.150). The speech of actors was paradigmatically false. Their words were not to be trusted in any context.[102]

The law did not accord actors (or other *infames*) the same physical protection as other citizens.[103] Protection from corporal punishment was one of the hallmarks of Roman citizenship. This protection marked off Roman citizens from non-citizens and, in particular, it marked them off from slaves. Liability to corporal punishment was one of the most vivid symbols of the distinction between free and slave in Rome.[104] Actors, even if Roman citizens, were assimilated to slaves in this respect. In the late republic, magistrates could flog actors at any time and in any place (Tac. *Ann.* 1.77; Suet. *Aug.* 45.3). Augustus restricted this power to the time of theatrical performances, but did not remove it.[105] Suetonius then describes how an actor was beaten with rods through the three theatres of Rome because of his

[102] Numerous anecdotes emphasise the untrustworthiness of actors, e.g. Livy 24.24.2–3, Tac. *Dial.* 10.5. This is suggestively though sometimes misleadingly discussed by Florence Dupont 'La scène juridique' *Communications* 26 (1977) 62–77. Cf. too Dupont 1985: 96–7.
[103] Those who followed infamous professions generally seem to have been left physically vulnerable by the law. Most prescriptions relating to this focus specifically on actors.
[104] On the significance of corporal punishment in Rome, see Richard Saller 'Corporal punishment, authority and obedience in the Roman household' in Beryl Rawson ed. *Marriage, divorce and children in ancient Rome* (Oxford 1991) 144–65, esp. 151–5.
[105] Later texts reiterate the right of magistrates to inflict corporal punishment on actors with impunity e.g. Paul, *Sententiae* 5.26. Even non-magistrates could assault the bodies of actors without fear of punishment. Cf. e.g. Cic. *Pro Plancio* 30–1.

liaison with a well-born Roman matron – a humiliation no doubt considered appropriately conspicuous for one who appeared in public by profession.

Other restrictions were imposed by legislation. The *lex Iulia iudiciorum* (the Julian law on the administration of justice) prevented the infamous from making accusations against others (*Dig.* 48.2.4). The *lex Iulia de vi publica* (the Julian law on public violence) classed them with persons to whom the magistrate could with impunity refuse the right of appeal (Paul, *Sent.* 5.26). Under the *lex Iulia de adulteriis* of 18 BCE (whose provisions were examined in chapter one), a husband, if he found his wife in bed with another man, was permitted to kill him, if and only if the latter were a slave, a condemned criminal, a gladiator or an actor (*Dig.* 48.5.25 pr.; Paul, *Sent.* 2.26) – the Roman association between acting and sexual 'immorality' will be discussed below. Under the *lex Iulia et Papia Poppaea*, those who followed infamous professions were banned from marrying freeborn Romans (that is to say, their marriages would have no legal consequences) (Ulpian, *frag.* 13).[106]

Actors were not permitted to be magistrates.[107] They were denied many of the privileges of ordinary citizens. They seem to have been specifically banned from the army by the mid republic. Livy remarks that only actors in Atellan plays were allowed to serve in the army 'as though they had no connection with the stage'.[108] The *Digest*, as was noted earlier, prescribed capital punishment for soldiers who appeared on stage (48.19.14; 49.16.4.1–9). Actors were not included in the tribes into which most Roman citizens were organised. Cicero observes of earlier Roman practice:

---

[106] Cf. J.E. Spruit *De juridische en sociale positie van de romeinse acteurs* (Assen 1966) 254. The argument that actors in the republic, at least, were not all of degraded legal status was put forward by Tenney Frank ('The status of actors at Rome' *CPh* 26 (1931) 11–20). This was convincingly refuted by W.M. Green 'The status of actors at Rome' *Phoenix* 28 (1933) 301–4.

[107] Livy 7.2.12. Tertullian *De spect.* 22 emphasises this. Julius Caesar's law on municipalities banned them from standing for local magistracies, along with others who followed shameful professions ('Tabula Heracleensis' *CIL* I 593, 108–34). On this question see Greenidge 1984: 34, 106–12.

[108] Cf. Val. Max. 2.4.4. E.J. Jory argues that it was a privilege to be relieved of the obligation of military service, accorded to actors because of their important role in the religious ceremonies of which the *ludi scaenici* were a part ('Associations of actors at Rome' *Hermes* 98 (1970) 224–53). The passage from Livy indicates that in the case of actors this was surely not counted a privilege.

cum artem ludicram scaenamque totam in probro ducerent, genus id
hominum non modo honore civium reliquorum carere, sed etiam tribu
moveri notatione censoria voluerunt.

*Since they considered acting and the theatre in general disgraceful, they
wished that all persons connected with these activities should not only lose
the privileges of citizenship but should even be removed from their tribes by
sentence of the censors.*

(Cic. *De rep.* 4.10 *ap.* Augustine *De civ.dei* 2.13)

Livy points to the exceptional position of performers in the Atellan
drama, who, unlike other actors, are not *tribu moti* (moved from their
tribes) (7.2.12). It is not quite clear what this entailed but, since
voting was organised by tribes, it seems likely that actors were denied
the right to vote. Although formalised restrictions became more
numerous under the principate, actors were subject to some legal
disabilities even in the republic.

Legal disabilities did not apply to all types of theatrical production.
The Atellan drama is described as an exception by Livy (7.2.12).
Those who performed in this form of drama, he claims, were the only
performers in *artes ludicrae* not to be subject to legal disability.
Atellan plays seem to have been viewed as a distinctively Roman kind
of theatre (Valerius Maximus describes Atellan drama as *severa*,
'stern' 2.4.4).[109] According to the grammarian Festus, the actors in
Atellan plays were the only ones permitted to keep their masks on
throughout their performance (p. 238 Lindsay). The extent and
significance of the wearing of masks by Roman actors is unclear.[110]
The implication of Festus' comment is that masks were seen as
protecting the performer's social status by concealing his identity.
This gives added significance to Livy's picture of Atellan actors as the
only theatrical performers who were permitted to be soldiers (though
by the late republic it seems that professionals had taken over from
amateurs in Atellan plays).

[109] Petronius makes the wealthy freedman Trimalchio insist that he will only have Atellan plays
performed in his house, as a mark of his Italian birth (*Sat.* 53).
[110] It is not clear whether actors in Plautus wore masks (Beare 1964 appendix 1; Pierre Grimal
'Le théâtre à Rome' *Association Guillaume Budé. Actes du IXᵉ congrès* (Paris 1975) 286–8).
The fourth-century grammarian Diomedes remarks that originally Roman actors wore wigs
rather than masks to differentiate the characters (489 ed. Keil) but doubt has been cast on
this claim. Later, the use of masks seems to have become common practice.

DRAMATIC LICENCE

Actors could be legally and socially marginalised but all eyes were focused on them. The theatre was a place where power and hierarchy were displayed; it was in the theatre that they could most easily be subverted. Actors could make new meanings for the words they spoke. They had no place in the social and political hierarchy, no *dignitas*, no honour. They had no status to lose. Paradoxically, this put them in a position of great power.

Actors were associated with licence. They were characterised as dangerous and disruptive.[111] Whenever there were problems with public order in Rome, plays were banned. Players were sometimes banished from the city.[112] New regulations imposed on the theatre were a conspicuous means of parading the assertion of law and order. Augustus is said to have taken measures to curb licence in the theatre (Suet. *Aug.* 44–5). Suetonius also mentions among the more acceptable acts of the emperor Nero that he banished the pantomime actors and their partisans from the city (*Nero* 16.2).[113] Domitian is reported to have banned actors from appearing on stage, although they were allowed to perform in private houses (Suet. *Dom.* 7.1). Trajan, in 100 CE, allegedly banished actors.[114]

Frequent attempts were made to suppress theatrical players. These players were already, by the nature of their profession, highly visible. The regulations which attempted to exclude and suppress them only made them more so. Actors were empowered by the laws which disenfranchised them. This paradox may go some way towards explaining the curious relationship between actors and those who wielded 'real' power in Rome – the political and social elite and, of course, the emperor himself.

Many actors led miserable and precarious lives. Seneca refers to the figure of the actor as a symbol for lack of worldly position (in ironic contrast with the roles of kings and magistrates actors temporarily put on), though the point of the observation is to emphasise the unreality

---

[111] Tac. *Ann.* 1.16 (the leader of a mutiny was experienced in formenting sedition at the theatres); 1.54 (disturbance at the games due to rivalry between actors); 1.77 (theatrical *licentia*). Suetonius describes how Nero enjoyed watching the brawls between actors (*Nero* 26).   [112] An instance of this is dated to 115 BCE by Cassiodorus (*ad ann.* 639 a.u.c.).   [113] From other sources on Nero's reign, it seems this ban was only temporary (Suet. *Nero* 26; Tac. *Ann.* 13.25).   [114] They seem to have reappeared a few years later (Dio 68.10.2).

of what is usually seen, in contrast to the fictive world of the theatre, as the real world (*Ep.* 76.31; 80.7).[115] But some actors made fortunes (Pliny, *NH* 7.129).[116] And successful actors often mixed socially with those who governed Rome. Cicero is said to have recognised the actors Roscius and Aesopus as his friends (Macrob. *Sat.* 3.14.11–14). But Cicero's discussion of Roscius' position, in his speech in the latter's defence, is more problematic than Macrobius (writing several centuries later) allows. Cicero repeatedly emphasises the eminent respectability of his client. But Roscius' honour is stressed by contrasting him with other actors (for instance, *Pro Rosc. com.* 17). In another speech, Cicero argues of Roscius:

> etenim cum artifex eius modi sit, ut solus dignus videatur esse, qui in scaena spectetur, tum vir eius modi est, ut solus dignus videatur, qui eo non accedat.
>
> *For just as he is such an artist that only he seems good enough to appear on stage, so he is such a man that only he seems too good to appear on it.*
>
> (Cic. *Pro Quinctio* 78)[117]

Roscius does seem to have been in some respects exceptional. He was given equestrian status by the dictator Sulla (Macrob. *Sat.* 3.14.13) and is alleged to have refused to accept payment for any of his subsequent performances.[118] Yet the paradoxical nature of the position of Roscius, whose virtues as a man give him a dignity which could only be compromised by his skills as an actor, is symptomatic of the ambiguous status of actors in Rome.

Actors exhibited their bodies for the pleasure of the public. They were often assimilated to prostitutes.[119] The desire aroused by the very sight of actors was another manifestation of their degraded status.[120] Yet it also suggested their power to fascinate. Actors were

---

[115] Cf. Vell. Pat. 2.28.3.

[116] On the vast fortune earned by Roscius, cf. Cic. *Pro Rosc. com.* 23; Macrob. *Sat.* 3.14.13. Though Roscius was exceptional, others too could earn substantial sums, Pliny implies.

[117] Cf. the boast of the actor Latinus (Mart. 9.28).

[118] Cicero observes 'He has never ceased to serve the Roman people, he long ago ceased to serve his own interest' (*Pro Rosc. com.* 23). On the relevance of pay, see Greenidge (1894: 124) and Green (1933: 301–4). Some jurists considered pay an important factor in assessing whether a public performer should be marked with *infamia* (*Dig.* 3.1.1.6, Ulpian).

[119] E.g. Tac. *Ann.* 1.72. Actors and prostitutes were subject to many of the same legal restrictions. On the parallels between acting and prostitution, see Edwards forthcoming b.

[120] Cf. Juv. 6.63–5. On female desire for actors, see also Juv. 6.60–75; Pet. *Sat.* 126.

associated with sexual as well as political licence. The emperor Tiberius expelled actors from Italy, Tacitus writes, on the grounds that:

> multa ab iis in publicum seditiose, foeda per domos temptari; Oscum quondam ludicrum, levissimae apud vulgum oblectationis, eo flagitiorum et virium venisse, ut auctoritate patrum coercendum sit.

> *They frequently fomented sedition against the state and stirred up debauchery in private houses; the old Oscan farce, once the light entertainment of the common people, had attained such extremes of immorality and power, that it had to be contained by the authority of the senate.*

(Tac. *Ann.* 4.14)

Here, as so often in Roman attacks on immorality, sexual and political licence are associated.[121]

The sexual allure of actors was proverbial. Some of the most elevated members of Roman society are alleged to have succumbed to their charms. The wives of the emperors Claudius and Domitian were reputed to have had affairs with actors.[122] Augustus imposed a violent and humiliating punishment on an actor who had allegedly been waited on by a matron with her hair cropped to look like a page-boy (Suet. *Aug.* 45.4). These stories should be seen in the context of an ideological tradition which represented the low sexual tastes of upper-class women as paradigmatic of threats to social order in general (discussed in chapter one above). But there are particular features in the case of actors which distinguish them from other low objects of desire, such as slaves and gladiators.

While gladiators represented a nakedly masculine sexuality, actors were regarded as effeminate.[123] The gestures used in theatrical performance were often described as feminine.[124] Male actors played

---

[121] Cf. Tac. *Ann.* 1.16; *Dial.* 40.1.

[122] Tac. *Ann.* 11.28; 11.36; Suet. *Dom.* 3.1; 10.

[123] On the sexual allure of gladiators, see Ville 1981: 303, 330–1; Hopkins 1983 ch. 1; Wiedemann forthcoming; Edwards forthcoming b.

[124] Pliny *Paneg.* 46.5 *effeminatas artes*, 'effeminate skills'; 54.1 *effeminatis vocibus modis gestibus*, 'with effeminate voices, movements, gestures'; Quint. *Inst.* 1.10.31 *effeminata et impudicis modis fracta*, 'effeminate and marred by its indecent style', of the music associated with the theatre; Tac. *Ann.* 15.1 *gestus modosque haud virilis*, 'unmanly gestures and movements'; Tertullian, *De spect.* 10 *de gestu et corporis flexu mollitiae*, 'effeminacy of gesture and posture'; Lactantius, *Divin. inst.* 6.20 *histrionum . . . enervata corpora*, 'the impotent bodies of actors'. For a discussion of some of this vocabulary, see chapter two above.

female roles.[125] The epitaph of an actor Vitalis celebrates his ability to imitate female gestures (*Anth. Lat.* 487a). Juvenal sneeringly remarks of a Greek actor that one might think he even had female genitals (3.95–7). Roman texts frequently associate effeminacy with an excessive interest in sex with both male and female partners.[126] Actors are represented as arousing homosexual as well as heterosexual desire. The dictator Sulla had a lengthy affair with an actor called Metrobius, according to the biographer Plutarch (*Sulla* 3.3). Augustus' associate Maecenas was allegedly in love with an actor (Tac. *Ann.* 1.54). The emperor Trajan was enamoured of an actor called Pylades, according to Dio (68.10.2). Tertullian devotes a great deal of space to invective against the titillation he associated with the theatre. He describes it as:

> ... privatum consistorium impudicitiae, ubi nihil probatur quam quod alibi non probatur. ita summa gratia eius de spurcitia plurimum concinnata est, quam Atellarius gesticulatur, quam mimus etiam per muliebres res repraesentat, sensum sexus et pudoris exterminans, ut facilius domi quam in scaena erubescant, quam denique pantomimus a pueritia patitur ex corpore ut artifex esse possit.

> ... the proper home of all unchastity, where nothing is admired unless it is elsewhere disapproved of. Its greatest charm is above all contrived by its lewdness – the lewd gestures of the actor of the farce, the lewd performance of the mime playing the woman, without a shred of sense of sex or shame, so that they blush more easily at home than on stage, and finally the obscene experiences of the pantomime actor, who must suffer sexual humiliation from his youth, if he is to become a performer.

> (Tert. *De spect.* 17)

So closely are deviant sexuality and the stage associated, for Tertullian, that he represents the experience of being penetrated as a necessary part of an actor's professional training. Seneca describes actors as able to feign every emotion but shame, for they cannot blush (*Ep.* 11.7). Labelling actors as effeminate was a way of emphasising their powerlessness, a strategy for containing their potential for transgression. To be excessively interested in sex was 'unmanly',

[125] This was true both of traditional tragedy and comedy, on the one hand, and of pantomime, on the other (where one performer often played all roles). In mime, however, it seems to have been usual for female parts to be played by women (though Tertullian complains about male mimes playing female roles, *De spect.* 17). [126] See chapter two above.

'unRoman'. Here again the actor was the inversion of the soldier–citizen, paradigmatically lacking in *virtus*. Yet this insistent denial of the power of actors could not help but betray a fear that served to reinforce the threat they posed.

POWER PLAY

Actors had no independent power base, no ancestry, no dignity, no *Romanitas*. If an actor became the emperor's favourite, his position was entirely a reflection of the emperor's power. Vitellius was said to have regulated the greater part of his (very brief) rule according to the caprice of the commonest of actors and chariot drivers (Suet. *Vit.* 12). Domitian was entertained at the end of each day by a recital of the day's gossip given by the mime actor, Latinus (Suet. *Dom.* 15.3). Even a 'good' emperor, such as Vespasian, might give generous gifts to actors and musicians (Suet. *Vesp.* 19). Conspicuous promotion of those of very low status was another way of humiliating those who believed they had an inherited right to advise the emperor. Anecdotes of this kind should be seen as expressions of more generalised resentment rather than reflections of the actual practice of any particular emperor. Favour shown to actors was part of a familiar pattern of tyrannical behaviour.[127]

The promotion of actors by emperors was mirrored by the degradation of members of the elite who appeared on stage. Julius Caesar (when dictator) is alleged to have humiliated the equestrian playwright Laberius whose work had been critical of Caesar, by forcing him to appear in one of his own mimes. Laberius is alleged to have protested at his humiliation in the prologue to his play:

> et enim ipsi di negare cui nihil potuerunt,
> hominem me denegare quis posset pati?
> ego bis tricenis annis actis sine nota
> eques Romanus <e> Lare egressus meo
> domum revertar mimus.

---

[127] The anecdotes told about, for instance, the dictator Sulla's liking for the company of actors should be seen in this context (Plut. *Sulla* 2.3–4; 36.1). The upstart Balbus is alleged to have given an actor a gold ring (the symbol of equestrian status) and invited him to sit in the fourteen rows, apparently in imitation of Sulla's treatment of Roscius (Pollio *ap.* Cic. *Ad fam.* 415). Cf. the stories told about Mark Antony, discussed in chapter five below.

*For who would let me a mere mortal refuse a request from him to whom the
gods grant all? Thus after more than sixty years of life without reproach, I,
who left my house a Roman knight, shall return home an actor.*

(Macrob. *Sat.* 2.7.3)[128]

Laberius' words emphasise the incompatibility of a position of
juridical honour with appearance on stage. Caesar's example was
followed by at least one of his successors. The emperor Nero is said to
have compelled many members of the elite to appear on stage (Tac.
Ann. 14.14–15; Suet. *Nero* 11).

Emperors were not the only Roman aristocrats to be fascinated by
actors. Tiberius banned senators from entering the lodgings of the
pantomimes, while equestrians were forbidden to associate with them
in public (Tac. *Ann.* 1.77).[129] But the fascination exercised by actors
went further. Some members of the elite were forced to appear on
stage, but there is also evidence to suggest that others chose to
perform as actors (also as gladiators).[130] Juvenal laments the appearance of members of elite families on stage *nullo cogente Nerone* – 'no
Nero forcing them' (8.193). No doubt they were at least partly
motivated by the desire for financial reward. But it seems unlikely
that members of the elite would have chosen to go on stage if they had
felt it to be utterly degrading.

Senatorial and equestrian actors are alleged to have appeared in the
games given by Augustus' son-in-law Marcellus in 23 BCE (Dio 53.31)
and also in games organised by a magistrate, Domitius Ahenobarbus
– the latter prefiguring the behaviour of his descendant, the emperor
Nero (Suet. *Nero* 4). In his account of games given in 2 BCE, Dio
mentions the appearance of equites and distinguished women on the
stage (55.10.11). Some emperors attempted to prevent members of
the senatorial and equestrian elite from embracing these forms of
conspicuous degradation. There are numerous references to legislation with this purpose passed during the first century of the principate.[131] A fragmentary inscription from Larinum in the south of Italy

---

[128] Cf. Suet. *Jul.* 39.1; Gell. 8.15.
[129] For elite interest in actors, see e.g. Sen. *Ep.* 47.17; Pliny, *NH* 29.9; Dio 77.21.2.
[130] On appearances in the arena by members of the elite, see Hopkins 1983 ch. 1; Carlin Barton
'The scandal of the arena' *Representations* 27 (1989) 1–36; Wiedemann forthcoming;
Edwards forthcoming b.
[131] For instance, in 22 BCE (Dio 54.2.5). Barbara Levick discusses in detail legislation against the
appearance of members of the elite on stage and in the arena ('The *senatus consultum* from
Larinum' *JRS* 73 (1983) 97–115).

preserves the text of a *senatus consultum* of 19 CE imposing severe penalties on senators and equestrians (and members of their families) who appear on stage or in the arena.[132] This legislation is also mentioned by Suetonius, who describes it as aimed at *ex iuventute utriusque ordinis profligatissimus quisque*, 'the most profligate young-sters of the senatorial and equestrian orders' (*Tib.* 35).

What was the appeal of the stage? There was slippage between the officially sanctioned socio-political hierarchy and other perceptions of where power might lie. I described above how official attempts to marginalise actors could be seen as a recognition, and consequently a reinforcement, of their power to disrupt. By becoming an actor (or a gladiator) a Roman senator or equestrian was questioning the value of the official hierarchy the emperor controlled, even questioning the emperor's authority to control it. Aristocrats perhaps envied the freedom brought by the total lack of *dignitas* of those who followed infamous professions, such as actors and gladiators.[133] Plutarch observes, in a discussion of the emotion of envy:

> *And, by Zeus, free men and aristocrats regard with wonder and admi-ration comedians who have made a hit in the theatre, and dancers and servants in the courts of rulers, and this causes them considerable anxiety and vexation.*

> (*Moralia* 473b, *On tranquillity of mind* 13)

The actor's licence to speak was a rare commodity, no longer shared by those who once monopolised authoritative speech, the honourable orders of senators and equestrians.

Several kinds of public performance offered the opportunity for members of the honorable *ordines* to parade their degradation.[134] The theatre offered something else, a public voice. Compelled by Caesar to appear on stage, Laberius got his revenge:

> in ipsa quoque actione subinde se, qua poterat, ulciscebatur, inducto habitu Syri, qui velut flagris caesus praeripientique se similis exclamabat:

---

[132] Levick gives the text, together with translation and extensive commentary (1983).

[133] Cf. Barton 1989: 6, 12–13.

[134] Cf. Hopkins 1983. Barton discusses the essential ambiguity of the aristocratic gladiator's position under the principate. Senators and equestrians by appearing as gladiators implictly condemn the 'slavery' of court life by preferring to it the slavery of the arena (1989: 9–11, 15–16, 19, 23).

porro Quirites libertatem perdimus;
et paulo post adiecit:
necesse est multos timeat quem multi timent.
quo dicto universitas populi ad solum Caesarem oculos et ora conver-
tit, notantes impotentiam eius hac dicacitate lapidatam.

And even when he appeared on stage, he would continually get his revenge
where he could. Dressed in the costume of Syrus, he played the part of a
man beaten with whips and making his escape, exclaiming:
'On, citizens of Rome, we are losing our liberty!'
and shortly afterwards came the following words:
'Many must he fear whom many fear.'
At these words, the whole audience turned their gaze towards Caesar, thus
fixing the meaning of this jibe as an attack on his excessive power.

(Macrob. *Sat.* 2.7.4–5)

For Caesar to have take action would have been to acknowledge the
accuracy of the charge. The ambiguities of lines spoken by actors,
even when spoken by persons with no claim to authority, could be
incendiary in their effect. How much more threatening must they
have seemed when spoken by one who had once enjoyed a position of
legitimate honour.

ACTING EMPEROR

Nero, besides compelling members of the elite to appear in public,
took to the stage himself. He appeared first in the city of Neapolis, a
Greek enough place for his transgression to be less obtrusive (Tac.
Ann. 15.33). But soon he even dared to appear as an actor in the city of
Rome. These stage appearances Tacitus presents as culminating in
disaster in the games of 65 CE, when many members of the crowd were
crushed to death (*Ann.* 16.4–5).[135]

When the emperor himself appeared on stage he demonstrated his
own power to transcend the social constraints that bound the rest of
society. But the emperor's stage appearances were deeply disruptive.

---

[135] Pliny, in his speech in praise of Trajan, speaks with horror of the *imperator scaenicus*, 'actor-
emperor', Nero (*Paneg.* 46.4). Juvenal sees elite actors and gladiators as almost excused by
the emperor's terrible example (8.198–9). For a more detailed discussion of Roman
representations of Nero as an actor, see Catharine Edwards 'Beware of imitations: acting and
the subversion of imperial identity' (forthcoming).

When the emperor became an actor, appearance was inextricably confused with reality.

> tragoedias quoque cantavit personatus heroum deorumque, item heroidum ac dearum, personis effectis ad similitudinem oris sui ac feminae, prout quamque diligeret,

> *He also wore a mask and sang tragedies in the character of gods and heroes and even of heroines and goddesses, having the masks made so that they resembled him or else whatever woman he was in love with at the time.*

(Suet. Nero 21.3)

If masks had originally been intended to protect the identity and honour of those wearing them, Nero inverted their function, using them to make a spectacle of his degradation. The mask represented the face behind it. The emperor acted himself. Suetonius goes on to relate that a young soldier in the audience was said to have been so confused that he failed to comprehend the dramatic conventions. He mistook illusion for reality and: 'seeing the emperor in rags and bound with chains, as the play [*The frenzy of Hercules*] required, rushed forward to render assistance.' There were some conventions even an emperor could not transcend.[136]

A soldier involved in the Pisonian conspiracy, when his complicity was discovered, confronted the emperor, saying that he had been loyal until the emperor was revealed as a parricide, matricide and actor (Tac. *Ann.* 15.67).[137] After the fire of Rome, Nero attempted to gain popularity by providing aid for those whose homes had been destroyed, claims Tacitus. As an attempt to win popular gratitude this was a failure, because, says Tacitus, 'A rumour had spread that, while the city was in flames, Nero had gone on his private stage and, comparing the disasters of his own day with those of antiquity, had

---

[136] Outrageous emperors are also represented as mixing the real and the fictive by ordering actions which would normally be feigned to happen for real as part of the dramatic performance. Elagabalus, for instance, allegedly had live sex shows take place in the theatre (SHA *Elag.* 25.4). Coleman discusses the staged killings of condemned criminals as episodes in plays (1990).

[137] Cf. the complaints attributed to the rebel Vindex by Dio. Nero is criticised as a character from a play (63.22.6). Juvenal makes a similar point (8.211–23). Tacitus presents the Pisonian conspiracy in terms of a failed dramatic performance – an ironically suitable attack on an actor-emperor (for an elegant exposition of this, see A.J. Woodman 'Amateur dramatics at the court of Nero: Tacitus *Annals* 15.48–74' in T.J. Luce and A.J. Woodman eds. *Tacitus and the Tacitean tradition* (Princeton forthcoming)).

135

sung of the destruction of Troy' (*Ann.* 15.39). Nero could only sing of action. He could not act to save his city. One of the most striking stories in Suetonius' life of Nero is that of the mock triumph celebrated by the emperor when he returned from his successes in the Olympic games (Suet. *Nero* 25.1–2).[138] Almost every detail of the triumphal procession was imitated, but in a distorted form – perverted. Nero was so concerned to do well in singing contests that, to spare his voice, he never addressed the Roman soldiers in person. He placed his relationship with his audience above his relationship with his troops. The emperor should have been the greatest Roman and the greatest soldier. Instead, he had revealed himself a dissembler, of uncertain gender, whose words could not be trusted, whose actions had no consequences, in sum, that antithesis of (Ro)manhood, an actor.

---

[138] Some benighted Spaniards, misled by all the celebration, are alleged to have mistaken the emperor's Olympic victories for military successes (Philostratus *Life of Apollonius of Tyana* 5.8).

CHAPTER FOUR

Structures of immorality:
Rhetoric, building and social hierarchy

The rhetoric of Roman moralising has often seemed alien to modern readers. This book, in linking together studies of apparently diverse topics, might be seen as appropriating a trope of Roman moralistic discourse, presenting arguments concerning different subjects as parallel so that they may serve to reinforce one another. A better understanding of this and similar literary devices, as they operate in Roman moralising texts, can help us to make sense of some features of those texts which modern readers have found puzzling. Let us begin with an apparently bizarre example of this kind of rhetoric (included in the book of rhetorical exercises put together by the elder Seneca):

> quin etiam montes silvasque in domibus marcidis et in umbra fumoque viridia aut maria amnesque imitantur. vix possum credere quemquam eorum vidisse silvas, virentisque gramine campos . . . quis enim tam pravis oblectare animum imitamentis possit si vera cognoverit? . . . ex hoc litoribus quoque moles iniungunt congestisque in alto terris exaggerant sinus; alii fossis inducunt mare: adeo nullis gaudere veris sciunt, sed adversum naturam alieno loco aut terra aut mare mentita aegris oblectamenta sunt. et miraris <si> fastidio rerum naturae laborantibus iam ne liberi quidem nisi alieni placent?

> *Men even imitate mountains and woods in their foul houses – green fields, seas and rivers amid the smoky darkness. I can hardly believe any of these people have ever set eyes on forests or plains of green grass . . . Who could take pleasure in such debased imitations, if he was familiar with the reality? . . . They pile up great buildings on the seashore and block off bays by filling the deep sea with earth; others divert the sea into ditches and artificial lakes. These people are incapable of enjoying what is real. Their minds are so twisted they obtain pleasure only from unnatural and misplaced imitations of land and sea. How can you be surprised that their*

137

contempt for nature leads them to dislike children – unless they are other people's?

(Papirius Fabianus *ap.* Sen. *Contr.* 2.1.13)

Perhaps not all Roman moralists would have perceived an immediate connection between a liking for landscape painting and a disinclination to have children. But this passage is a striking illustration of the tendency to draw parallels between the preservation of a 'natural' order in one area of people's lives – in this case, the decoration of their houses – and the preservation of supposedly natural values governing an area of behaviour which might seem to a modern reader totally distinct.

The practice of argument by analogy enabled moralists to articulate concerns about one subject by treating it as parallel to another, more obviously threatening. Attacks on luxurious building, the subject of this chapter, were a way for members of the Roman elite to air their anxieties about threats to the social hierarchy and their own places within it. In relation to the issue of social status, houses were especially 'good to think with'.[1] Houses in ancient Rome were the single most important manifestation of their owners' wealth. They played a crucial role in reflecting and reinforcing the images of themselves the elite – and would-be members of the elite – wished to put forward.[2]

Houses were also markers of the relationship between individual and community; they functioned as concrete representations of the divide between public and private (though Roman notions of public and private do not necessarily correspond with modern ones). House and state are often used in Roman texts as symbolically charged metaphors for one another. The house defined the area within which the *paterfamilias* exercised his power. Patrons' influence was at its

---

[1] Roman writers often use architecture as an analogy for literary style (cf. e.g. Sen. *Ep.* 100.5–6; Quint. *Inst.* 7 *pr.*). Michael Baxandall points out that in Latin literature there are many terms common to the technical languages of architecture and rhetoric (*Giotto and the orators* (Oxford 1971) 17–21). For discussions of houses as a means of organising thought in ancient Rome, see Frances Yates *The art of memory* (London 1966) ch. 1, and E. Rawson 'The introduction of logical organisation into Roman prose literature' *PBSR* 46 (1978) 12–34 (= Rawson 1991: 324–51).

[2] The places people live in have symbolic importance in every society. Anthropological work, as well as studies of more recent historical periods, has laid stress on the particularity of the associations of the dwelling in its cultural context (cf. e.g. Pierre Bourdieu 'The Berber house' in Mary Douglas ed. *Rules and meanings* (London 1975) 98–110; Norbert Elias *The court society* (Oxford 1983); Lawrence Stone *An open elite?* (Oxford 1984)).

most impressive within the houses where they received their clients.[3] The younger Seneca and the younger Pliny both write of their own households in terms which suggest parallels with states.[4] The emperor Nero was accused of turning all Rome into his own house and regarding its citizens as his guests (Tac. *Ann.* 15.37) – a favoured but vulnerable position for those who had, notionally at least, once been sovereign in their own city. This was a metaphorical extension of Nero's outrageously expansive building activity. Criticising the size and luxury of an emperor's house could constitute a resonant attack on the extent and arbitrariness of his power.

Complaints about luxurious building feature among the fragmentary writings of the elder Cato and continue to appear as a major preoccupation of moralising writing (poetry as well as prose) throughout the first centuries BCE and CE.[5] Several of Horace's Odes focus on this theme:

> iam pauca aratro iugera regiae
> moles relinquent, undique latius
>   extenta visentur Lucrino
>   stagna lacu, platanusque caelebs
>
> evincet ulmos.

It won't be long before our regal residences will leave only a few acres for the plough; on all sides our fishponds will be seen spreading wider than the Lucrine lake, and the barren plane will drive out the elm.

(*Carm.* 2.15.1–5)

---

[3] Cf. Vitruvius, *De arch.* 6.5.1–2, quoted below.

[4] Seneca, *Ep.* 47.14; Pliny, *Ep.* 8.16. Cf. Pet. *Sat.* 53 and the discussion by Paul Veyne, 'La vie de Trimalchion' *Annales ESC* 16.1 (1961) 213–47.

[5] Cato *ap.* Festus 282 ed. Lindsay (= 185 Malcovati). Other odes of Horace focusing on similar ideas include 2.16, 2.18, 3.1, 3.24. On the use of such images in the poetry of Horace, see L.T. Pearcy 'Horace's architectural imagery' *Latomus* 36 (1977) 772–81 and J.E.G. Whitehorne 'The ambitious builder' *AUMLA* 31 (1969) 28–39. Eleanor W. Leach sees some of these poems as celebrations of luxury, sensuously engaging with that which they appear to condemn (*The rhetoric of space* (Princeton 1988) 285–6). Other instances of texts attacking luxurious building, besides the texts specifically discussed below, include: Sallust, *Cat.* 12, 13, 20; Lucretius 2.20–36; Virg. *Aen.* 9.710–13; Hor. *Sat.* 2.3.308; Tib. 2.3.43–6; Ov. *Ars* 3.125–6; Pliny, *NH passim* esp. books 19, 33, 36; Sen. *Ep.* 89.21, 100.5–6, 114.9, 122.8, *De ira* 1.21; *Cons. ad Polyb.* 18.2; *NQ* 1. pr. 7–8; Pet. *Sat.* 120.79–83; Tac. *Ann.* 3.53; Mart. 9.46; Manilius, *Astr.* 4.263. Many of these texts focus specifically on houses built out into the sea. The luxurious garden or estate was represented by many moralists as a common and reprehensible feature of the villas of the wealthy. Some texts focus in particular on luxurious fishponds: Varro, *De re rust.* 3.7.9; 3.17.2–3; Cic. *Ad Att.* 18.6; 19.6; 20.3; 21.5; Val. Max. 9.1.1; Macrob. *Sat.* 3.15.6; Sen. *Thyestes* 465–6.

The country houses of the elite resemble palaces. Land is wastefully devoted to vain display rather than being put to productive use. Here, too, the aesthetic preferences of the luxurious are associated with a disinclination to have children (the plane tree is *caelebs*, 'unmarried'). The creation of vast fishponds in this poem is parallel to the construction of houses which extend into the sea in other texts: the rich tamper with the 'natural' boundary between land and water. The poem moves on to contrast the present state of affairs with the heroic past when men's private estates were small and they devoted them-selves and their resources to the public good. This cluster of ideas characterises many attacks on luxurious building.

The specific articulation of texts attacking luxurious building is intimately connected with their preoccupation with its socially dis-ruptive consequences. Moralising attacks on luxurious building focus on confusion, inversion and novelty as its foremost characteris-tics. Building was a major way of displaying the wealth vital to the achievement of social and political success in ancient Rome but there was no guarantee that money would come into the hands of the 'right' people. Moralising writers saw an improper distribution of wealth as the cause of disjunctions they perceived between the social hierarchy as it was and as it ought to be. Excessive building – one of the most spectacular ways of displaying wealth – they represented as itself entailing the confusion of social categories. The luxurious, accused of disrupting nature, are implicitly held responsible for a social disrup-tion at once characterised as undesirable by its alignment with the disordering of nature itself.

Discussions of Roman invective against luxurious building have tended to stress the influence of Greek diatribe. R.G.M. Nisbet and Margaret Hubbard, for instance, invoke this tradition in their discus-sion of Horace, *Odes* 2.18.[6] Oltramare traces the history of attacks on luxurious building as a theme in diatribe from the writings of Diogenes Laertius, through Plutarch, back to populist Cynic orators of the third century BCE.[7] Those who choose to highlight this tradition thereby imply that Roman orators and historians attacked extrava-

---

[6] R.G.M. Nisbet and M. Hubbard *A commentary on Horace Odes, book II* (Oxford 1978) 288. They observe of those writing in the diatribe tradition, 'their dominating interest is moral rather than literary, and this is sufficient to differentiate them from Horace'. It may not be so easy to differentiate the 'literary' from the 'moral' in the poetry of Horace, or indeed in much of the rest of Latin literature.

[7] André Oltramare *Les Origines de la diatribe romaine* (Geneva 1926).

gant houses largely because earlier Greek rhetoricians had done so. Attacks of this kind, then, are to be seen as 'rhetorical' and thus no reflection of the real concerns of their authors. But to label the themes and topoi of invective 'rhetorical' or 'conventional' is no justification for dismissing them as unworthy of further consideration. Roman criticism of luxurious building is often far more detailed and specific than its supposed Greek forerunners (though there is, of course, a difference between, for instance, Cicero's criticisms of the villa of his contemporary Lucullus and the declamatory exercises of the elder Seneca). Romans were under no obligation to adopt all the features of Greek diatribe. They appropriated those which suited their own purposes. 'Conventional' does not have to imply 'meaningless'.

Rhetoric was a fundamental part of the education of the Roman elite. The 'rhetorical' language educated men used formed their habits of thought. These rhetorical habits were an integral part of the way men like Pliny or Seneca saw the buildings around them. Michael Baxandall, in a discussion of early Renaissance attitudes to art, emphasises the 'linguistic component in visual taste' and argues that 'the grammar and rhetoric of language may substantially affect our manner of describing, and then of attending to, pictures and other visual experiences'.[8] Few detailed descriptions of houses survive from ancient Rome. But we should note the frequently moralising tone even of a supposedly 'technical' work such as Vitruvius' *De architectura*, written in the late first century BCE.[9] The moralising tone is not something we should edit out in an attempt to recover how Romans 'really' responded to what they saw. It was a fundamental part of those responses.

Most of the texts from the late republic and early principate which relate to the houses of the wealthy are concerned with the criticism of luxury. If a house is praised, the author emphasises that it was built with modesty and restraint – the proper limits were observed.[10]

---

[8] Baxandall 1971: vii. The preoccupation of the humanist scholars studied by Baxandall with their own writing practice has, not surprisingly, many similarities with that of the Roman writers whom the former so often took as models.

[9] In particular 6.5, quoted below, on houses appropriate to people of different social ranks and 7.5 on the 'immorality' of fantastical wall-painting. This is discussed by Lise Bek '*Antithesis*: a Roman attitude and its changes as reflected in the concept of architecture' in *Studia in honorem Petri Krarup septuagenarii* (Odense 1976) 154–66, esp. 159. Cf., too, Lise Bek *Towards paradise on earth* (Odense 1980) part 3.

[10] See e.g. Nepos' description of Atticus' house, *Atticus* 13.1–2, 5. He observes, *plus salis quam sumptus habebat*, 'it was elegant rather than luxurious' (13.2).

Similarly, Cicero seems concerned to make clear that the style of building he advocates for honourable men is not luxurious (*De off.* 1.138–9). But, in the later years of the first century CE, texts were produced, apparently for the first time, which praise the very luxury of palaces and villas.[11] Does this suggest a general change in attitudes to luxurious building? Some writers continued to disapprove of luxurious building projects. The idea of luxury was still problematic. But this new literary development is important and can perhaps be related to changes in the socio-political position of the elite with the advent of the principate.[12]

We might also want to see these texts as the first literary expression of the attitude of the luxurious builder who had hitherto only expressed himself (rarely herself) in the creation of landscape gardens and marble dining rooms. Statius praises the juxaposition of exotic marbles from different parts of the world (*Silvae* 2.2.83–97), celebrates man's capacity to level mountains (4.3.80) and admires a dining room built out into the sea (2.2.98–106). These were features of 'luxurious' building frequently focused on and condemned as 'unnatural' by moralists. Elsewhere, Statius, with approval, observes of the arrangement of a villa: *nec servat natura vices*, 'nature abandons her ways' (*Silvae* 1.2.156). Those who praised luxury used the same categories as those who condemned it. Indeed, those who derived pleasure from subverting moral rules were dependent on the continuing assertion of those rules by others. This apparently new literary development, while it may have reflected the tastes of some wealthy Romans, derived at least a part of its meaning (as indeed did those aesthetic preferences) from the more established literary tradition of invective against luxurious building.

The relationship between literary texts and buildings constructed during the period when they were written is hard to determine.[13]

[11] E.g. Statius, *Silvae* 1.2; 1.5; 2.2; 3.3; Mart. 6.42; 8.68. On this development, see Zoja Pavlovskis *Man in an artificial landscape* (Leiden 1973). Pavlovskis remarks that in Statius 'refinement is no longer regarded as sinful' and 'technology delights'. Statius appears to have influenced the younger Pliny who describes with pride 'luxurious' features of his own villas (*Ep.* 2.17; 5.6). Pliny has different rooms for use at different seasons, a dining room built out into the sea and a room decorated to give the impression of being in a garden. Pliny's description, however, focuses on their refinement rather than *luxuria*.

[12] As Charles Martindale points out to me, it might also be related back to the ekphrasis tradition (as exemplified by Catullus 64.50–264), though in Statius and Martial the exquisite structures described are Roman rather than being placed in an exotic or mythological setting.

[13] H. Drerup *Zum Ausstattungsluxus in der römischen Architektur* (Münster 1957), gives a general survey of texts and some sites. On the use of marble, see Raniero Gnoli *Marmora Romana* (Rome 1971) and R.M. Schneider *Bunte Barbaren* (Worms 1986) 139–60.

Nicholas Purcell provides an enlightening picture of parallels between literary texts and some archaeological remains, in particular, architectural features such as terracing and the arrangement of gardens.[14] There is extensive archaeological evidence for houses built out into the sea, one of recurrent objects of moralists' indignation.[15] It seems that writers were responding, to some extent at least, to the buildings they saw, or else that those who built were responding to the literature they read and heard – or most likely both.

RHETORICAL STRUCTURES

The elder Pliny maintained that the most expensive building ever erected in Rome was a temporary theatre built by Marcus Scaurus, when he was aedile in 58 BCE (*NH* 36.113–15).[16] Pliny remarks of Scaurus that his aedileship 'may perhaps have done more than anything else to undermine morality and . . . [his] powerful ascendancy may have been a more pernicious achievement on the part of his adoptive father Sulla than the deaths of so many thousands of people by proscription.' Nineteenth- and twentieth-century scholars have preferred not to reflect on alienating observations of this kind, dismissing them as 'rhetorical' (and therefore, implicitly, not important).[17] But this rhetorical approach, I suggested earlier, merits closer attention, for it constituted a major strand in the way members of Rome's educated elite thought. Roman descriptions of buildings (much to the frustration of modern scholars) generally work not so much to give a picture of the building's physical appearance, as to evoke certain emotional responses.[18] While descriptions of buildings may be morally charged in many cultures, this seems unusually true of the Roman texts examined here.

This feature, too, of Roman descriptions of buildings can be connected with the fondness for argument by analogy characteristic of so much Roman moralising. Baxandall refers to a passage from

---

[14] Nicholas Purcell 'Town in country and country in town' in E.B. MacDougall ed. *Ancient Roman villa gardens* (Dumbarton Oaks 1987) 187–203.

[15] See Xavier Lafon 'A propos des villas de la zone de Sperlonga' *MEFRA* 93.1 (1981) 297–353, and also J.H. D'Arms *Romans on the bay of Naples* (Cambridge, Mass. 1970).

[16] For a discussion of the magnificence of temporary theatre buildings in the late republic, see chapter three above.

[17] Though recent work has emphasised that Pliny's rhetorical habits are integral to his overall project. See e.g. H. Zehnacker 'Pline l'ancien et l'histoire de la monnaie romaine' *Ktèma* 4 (1979) 169–81; Wallace-Hadrill 1990.   [18] Cf. Bek 1976.

Quintilian which sets out two forms of argument: argument by ratiocination and argument by induction (*Inst.* 5.9).[19] The latter form of argument, essentially argument by comparison, is of particular relevance here. The antithetical and parallelising character of this mode of argumentation is a feature of Roman moralising texts. Parallels are regularly drawn between the transgression of socially desirable norms in one area of experience and transgression of a far less obviously antisocial nature in other areas. To illustrate this, various texts attacking luxurious building will be examined below. This section of my argument does not differentiate between the discourses of the late republic and those of the principate. No doubt the concerns of the Roman upper classes did shift somewhat (possible changes will be examined in a later section). But there is a striking continuity in the images and the vocabulary used by Roman moralists in attacks on luxurious building written throughout these periods.

Attacks on luxurious building projects frequently insist that the luxurious offend against nature by disrupting an ordering of space determined by nature itself. For Roman moralists (Stoics, in particular, but also others like Cicero), the idea of the 'natural' is highly charged. Cicero makes the character named Atticus in the *De legibus* draw a parallel between his professed taste in landscape and his belief in 'natural law':

> . . . magnificasque villas et pavimenta marmorea et laqueata tecta contemno; ductus vero aquarum, quos isti Nilos et Euripos vocant, quis non, cum haec videat, inriserit? itaque, ut tu paulo ante de lege et de iure disserens ad naturam referebas omnia, sic in his ipsis rebus, quae ad requietem animi delectationemque quaeruntur, natura dominatur.

> . . . *And I despise luxurious country houses, marble floors and panelled ceilings. Take those artificial streams which some of our friends call 'Niles' and 'Euripi' – how could anyone who had seen what we see before us now not laugh at them? And so, just as you, a moment ago in your discussion of law and justice, traced everything back to nature, in the same way nature reigns supreme in the things men seek to give rest to their souls.*

> (Cic. *De leg.* 2.2)

The problem of how the natural is to be defined is not addressed by Cicero. The lines of argument about law and about landscape are

---

[19] Baxandall 1971: 31.

mutually reinforcing. In numerous other texts, an appeal to 'nature' is used to give supposedly irrefutable validity to what the author of the text concerned considers to be right.[20]

For the younger Seneca, too, excess, perversion and artificiality characterised the building projects of the luxurious:

> omnia vitia contra naturam pugnant, omnia debitum ordinem deserunt. hoc est luxuriae propositum, gaudere perversis nec tantum discedere a recto, sed quam longissime abire, deinde etiam a contrario stare.

> *All vices rebel against nature; they all abandon the appointed order. Luxury's plan is always to enjoy what is perverted and not only to turn away from that which is right but to leave it as far behind as possible and finally even to take a stand in opposition to it.*

(Sen. Ep. 122.5)

The luxurious take their pleasure from embracing precisely what is designated unnatural.[21] They are parasitic on the normal. Seneca's reification of concepts less vividly invoked by other moralists usefully throws the mechanisms of Roman moralistic discourse into relief.

The jaded palates of the luxurious seek stimulation in unnatural arrangements for their houses. Seneca, ostensibly addressing the luxurious builder, writes:

> ubicumque in aliquem sinum litus curvabitur, vos protinus fundamenta iacietis nec continenti solo nisi quod manu feceritis, mare agetis introrsus.

> *Wherever the shore curves round into a bay, there will you at once lay foundations, and, dissatisfied with any land unless it is artificial, you will bring the sea within your boundaries.*

(Sen. Ep. 89.21)

Criticisms in this vein are also invoked in attacks on the luxury of specific individuals. Confusion of land and water, love for the artificial, the technologically challenging, are preoccupations in Plutarch's account of the building projects of Lucullus, who had become very wealthy as a result of his successful campaigns in the east, in the 60s BCE:

---

[20] Cf. e.g. Cic. *De leg.* 1.43–4; Vitr. *De arch.* 7.5; Hor. *Carm.* 1.3.24–5; Vell. Pat. 2.10; Sen. *Ep.* 89, 122.   [21] Purcell stresses the importance of *variatio* as a feature of luxury (1987).

Even nowadays, despite the constant escalation of luxury, the gardens of
Lucullus are considered among the most lavish of the imperial gardens. As
for his constructions along the coast and in the area around Neapolis,
where he suspended hills over enormous tunnels, circled his residences with
moats linked to the sea and with streams for the breeding of fish – when
Tubero the Stoic saw them, he called him Xerxes in a toga.

(Plut. *Luc.* 39.2–3)

Attempts to compete with nature itself by reordering the boundaries
between land and sea were especially associated with the figure of the
tyrant, as Plutarch's reference to Xerxes the king of Persia suggests.[22]
The emperor Caligula, who was likened to – and perhaps modelled
himself on – mythical eastern despots, naturally did not omit this
characteristic facet of tyrannical behaviour. Suetonius reports:

in extructionibus praetoriorum atque villarum omni ratione postha-
bita nihil tam efficere concupiscebat quam quod posse effici negaretur.
et iactae itaque moles infesto ac profundo mari et excisae rupes
durissimi silicis et campi montibus aggere aequati et complanata
fossuris montium iuga, incredibili quidem celeritate, cum morae culpa
capite lueretur.

He built lodges and villas with no consideration of expense, aiming above
all to do what people said was impossible. He built moles out into the deep
and stormy sea, tunnelled rocks of the hardest flint, built up plains to the
level of mountain peaks and razed mountains flat with the plain – and all
with unbelievable speed, for the penalty for delay was death.

(Suet. *Calig.* 37.2–3)

Caligula was especially drawn to compete with nature by attempting
what was said to be impossible. Like Lucullus, he flattened mountains, built up plains and tunnelled through rock. Not content with
rearranging the boundary between land and sea (by this time commonplace), he went one better:

---

[22] For the comparison between Lucullus and Xerxes, cf. Vell. Pat. 2.33.4; Pliny, *NH* 9.170.
Purcell discusses the history of the association between grand rulers and large-scale projects
for altering the landscape (1987: 190–2). On Lucullus' building projects in Campania, see V.
Jolivet '*Xerxes togatus*: Lucullus en Campanie' *MEFRA* 99 (1987) 823–46. Jolivet suggests
part of the reason for the hostility aroused by Lucullus' Campanian estates was that their
position enabled him to dominate the trade route between Rome and the eastern
Mediterranean.

fabricavit et deceris Liburnicas gemmatis puppibus, versicoloribus
velis, magna thermarum et porticuum et tricliniorum laxitate magna-
que etiam vitium et pomiferarum arborum varietate; quibus discum-
bens de die inter choros ac symphonias litora Campaniae peragraret.

*He also had built Liburnian vessels with ten banks of oars, their sterns set
with gems, parti-coloured sails, huge spacious baths, colonnades and
banquet halls and even a great variety of vines and fruit trees. His desire
was to lounge about on these all day long and coast along the shores of
Campania serenaded with songs and choruses.*

(Suet. *Calig.* 37.2)

These vessels included many of the features traditionally associated
with luxurious villas – baths, colonnades, banquet halls, even exotic
plantations. But Caligula's villa was not merely built out into the sea.
It was altogether detached from the land – which could be read as a
vivid metaphor for the unbridgeable gulf between this emperor and
those he ruled.[23]

Why should Roman moralists have felt this kind of luxury to be
particularly improper? After all, large country estates might involve
the dispossession of peasants, great town houses the eviction of
poorer citizens, but it is hard to see who suffers other than the fish
when a rich man builds part of his house out into the sea or constructs
a fishpond in which to keep his pet mullet. The division between land
and sea often appears in invective against luxury as one of the most
archetypally natural distinctions. The sea itself (especially in its
association with trade and travel) is frequently linked with a decline in
morality. In narratives of decadence, the transition from the golden
age to that of baser metal is marked by the first use of ships.[24] Sea-
faring is often associated with the quest for wealth and luxury and
with the taint of exposure to foreign cultures. Building materials

---

[23] Remains of two boats probably dating from the reign of Caligula have been found in Lake
Nemi, near Rome. They were both over seventy metres long and decorated with exotic
marbles, mosaics of glass paste and sculptures. It is not, however, clear whether they were
used for pleasure or for some religious purpose connected with the temple of Diana nearby.
These boats are described by G. Ucelli *Le navi di Nemi* (Rome 1940) and P.L. MacKendrick
The mute stones speak (London 1960). For a discussion of luxurious Hellenistic barges, see
Klaus Fittschen 'Zur Herkunft und Entstehung des 2. Stils' in Zanker 1975: 539–63, esp.
544. Cf. too Athenaeus 5.204e–6c.

[24] Cf. Catullus 64; Hor. *Carm.* 1.3; Ov. *Met.* 1.94–6; Sen. *Medea* 301–74, *Phaedra* 525–32. On
Seneca, see H. Fyfe 'Seneca's *Medea*' in A.J. Boyle ed. *Seneca tragicus* (Victoria 1983) 77–93.
I am grateful to Denis Feeney for these references.

imported from across the sea are represented by moralists as particularly luxurious.[25] Cicero's discussion of the character of seaside towns emphasises the risk to ancestral morals associated with engaging in foreign trade (*De rep.* 2.7–9).[26] He goes on to connect the decline of Greece with the maritime situation of so many of its towns.

Another concern in attacks on the rich man's property extending into the sea is perhaps the implied parallel between the boundary between land and sea and the boundary between adjoining estates. Nisbet and Hubbard, in their commentary on Horace, *Odes* 2.18, list ancient texts which emphasise the sanctity of boundaries between properties. The greedy rich are frequently portrayed as encroaching on their neighbours' property by moving the boundary markers. Both these kinds of boundaries are to be regarded as sacred.[27] But the preoccupation of invective against luxurious building with houses built out into the sea also illustrates the rhetorical force of the parallels through which Roman moralising is articulated.

Confusion of the respective forms and functions of town and country houses is another recurrent feature of invectives against luxury building.[28] These categories are essentially cultural ones but Roman moralists nevertheless treat them as if they had as much justification in nature as the conception of land and water as separate elements. Thus those who blur the distinctions between town and country houses are also portrayed as attacking the 'natural' order. Varro (in his treatise on agriculture) and others complain about those who insist on urbane comforts in their rural retreats and take no interest in agriculture (*De re rust.* 2 pr.).[29] One of the most shocking aspects of the emperor Nero's *domus aurea*, his Golden House, was precisely that it was perceived as a country house in the middle of

---

[25] E.g. Pliny, *NH* 36.1–4; Tibullus 2.3.35–48. On the importation of marble, see John Ward-Perkins 'The marble trade and its organisation: evidence from Nicomedia' *MAAR* 36 (1980) 325–38.

[26] Though adapted from Plato (*Laws* 704d–e), Cicero did select it for inclusion in his own work.

[27] Whitehorne discusses some legal texts which suggest jurists, too, were concerned with the problems raised by alterations in the boundary between land and sea (1969: 28). Cf. e.g. *Dig.* 1.8.10: 'Aristo says that, just as a building erected into the sea becomes private property, so, too, one which has been overrun by the sea becomes public.'

[28] On types of villas and their grounds, see Pierre Grimal *Les Jardins romains* (Paris 1943); D'Arms 1970; E. Rawson 'The Ciceronian aristocracy and its properties' in M.I. Finley ed. *Studies in Roman property* (Cambridge 1976) 85–102 (= Rawson 1991: 204–22); J.H. D'Arms 'Ville rustiche e ville di *otium*' in Fausto Zevi ed. *Pompeii 79* (Naples 1979) 65–86; Purcell 1987.   [29] Cf. Varro, *De re rust.* 1.2.10; Columella 1.4.8; Mart. 3.58.

Rome.[30] Caligula had transgressed the 'natural' division between land and water; Nero was transgressing the cultural boundary between country and city. Tacitus describes Nero's building activities after the fire which devastated Rome in 64 CE as follows:

> ceterum Nero usus est patriae ruinis exstruxitque domum, in qua haud proinde gemmae et aurum miraculo essent, solita pridem et luxu vulgata, quam arva et stagna et in modum solitudinem hinc silvae, inde aperta spatia et prospectus, magistris et machinatoribus Severo et Celere, quibus ingenium et audacia erat etiam, quae natura denegavisset, per artem temptare et viribus principis inludere.

> *Nero took advantage of the destruction of his fatherland by building a palace whose marvels were to consist not so much in gems and gold, materials long familiar and made common by luxury, as in fields and lakes and the air of solitude given by woodland alternating with open spaces and prospects. The architects and engineers were Severus and Celer, who had the ingenuity and arrogance to try through their art what nature had forbidden and to fritter away even the resources of an emperor.*

> (*Ann.* 15.42).[31]

Tacitus' ironic treatment underlines the perversity of luxury's unceasing quest for novelty.[32] Nero perhaps came closest to achieving the ideal of rustic peace in an urban setting but he was by no means the only Roman to aspire to it. The elder Pliny remarks: *iam quidem hortorum nomine in ipsa urbe delicias agros villasque possident*, 'Nowadays, people enjoy the luxury of regular fields and country houses, which go by the name of *horti*, actually within the city' (*NH* 19.50). Cato, Varro and Columella, in their treatises on agriculture (written in the second century BCE, first century BCE and first century CE respectively), describe rustic life as an ideal closely associated with the 'golden age' of the early republic. Varro emphasises the superiority of life in the country over life in the city (*De re rust.* 2.1.1–2). However, as is clear from the words of the elder Pliny, in the wrong place, rustic 'simplicity' and 'peace' become a luxury.

---

[30] Noted by Purcell who gives an excellent discussion of Roman distinctions between town and country (1987, esp. 187–203).

[31] Cf. Suet. *Nero* 31. Purcell explores the associations of the passage from Tacitus, emphasising particularly its highlighting of the luxury of *variatio* (1987: 199).

[32] M.P.O. Morford suggests that the poorer citizens of Rome may well have taken a very different view of the *domus aurea* ('The distortion of the *domus aurea* tradition' *Eranos* 66 (1968) 158–79).

HOUSE AS SYMBOL

The houses of the Roman elite were an integral part of the political stage, functioning both as a means of displaying status, wealth and taste and as a place in which much of the business of political life was transacted.[33] They were not 'private' places but played an essential role in public life. Vitruvius lists the parts of the house to which the 'uninvited' have access (*De arch.* 6.5.1). Archaeologists and historians have tended to deduce from this that Roman houses were strictly divided into 'public' and 'private' areas. Yvon Thébert argues that the privacy and openness of different parts of the house would rather have been a matter of degree.[34] Lowly visitors, the poorest *clientes*, might only have been allowed access to a side room, while more distinguished guests would have been admitted into the more intimate parts of the house (this is the implication of Vitruvius 6.5, quoted below).

In a sense, however, a leading Roman could count no part of his life as private. The good Roman behaved as though he was always in the public eye. He could not shirk the moral responsibility which was the inevitable accompaniment to preeminence. Velleius Paterculus tells an illuminating story about Livius Drusus (tribune of the *plebs* in 91 BCE):

> cum aedificaret domum in Palatio . . . promitteret . . . ei architectus, ita se eam aedificaturum, ut liber a conspectu immunisque ab omnibus arbitris esset neque quisquam in eam despicere posset. 'tu vero,' inquit, 'si quid in te artis est, ita compone domum meam, ut quidquid agam, ab omnibus perspici possit.'

> *When he was having a house on the Palatine built . . . the architect offered to construct it in such a way that he would be hidden from the public gaze,*

---

[33] There are several recent studies of Roman houses, focusing particularly on those of the elite: Richard Saller '*Familia, domus* and the Roman conception of the family' *Phoenix* 38 (1984) 336–55; T.P. Wiseman '*Conspicui postes tectaque digna deo*: the public image of aristocratic and imperial houses in the late republic and early principate' in *L'urbs: espace urbain et histoire. Collection de l'école française de Rome* 98 (1987) 393–413; Yvon Thébert 'Private life and domestic architecture' in Veyne ed. 1987: 313–409; A. Wallace-Hadrill 'The social structure of the Roman house' *PBSR* 43 (1988) 43–97.

[34] Thébert's discussion focuses on the archaeological remains of houses in North Africa (1987). However, much of what he says also applies to houses in other parts of the empire. Similar points about public and private space are made by Wiseman (1987: 393) and Wallace-Hadrill (1988: 46, 55–77, 84).

safe from all spying and that no-one would look down into it. Livius replied, 'If you have any ability, you must build my house in such a way that whatever I do shall be seen by everyone.'

(Vell. Pat. 2.14.2–4)

Livius Drusus' concern here is perhaps to be connected with his professed popular sympathies. We cannot know how the poorer citizens of Rome might have viewed the houses of the elite. Did they resent the splendid mansions of the rich or admire them? Were they, too, concerned that houses should exactly reflect the social status of their owners or was this rather a preoccupation of those who felt they were expected to compete?

The following passage from Cicero's *De officiis* suggests a splendid house might conjure up increased electoral support for its builder. Octavius, a man of relatively obscure ancestry, became consul for 165 BCE:

Cn. Octavio, qui primus ex illa familia consul factus est, honori fuisse accepimus, quod praeclaram aedificasset in Palatio et plenam dignitatis domum; quae cum vulgo viseretur, suffragata domino, novo homini, ad consulatum putabatur . . . ornanda . . . est dignitas domo, non ex domo quaerenda, nec domo dominus, sed domino domus honestanda est, et, ut in ceteris habenda ratio non sua solum, sed etiam aliorum sic in domo clari hominis, in quam et hospites multi recipiendi et admittenda hominum cuiusque modi multitudo, adhibenda cura est laxitatis.

We are told that Gnaeus Octavius, the first of his family to be elected consul, distinguished himself by building an attractive and imposing house on the Palatine hill. Everyone went to see it and it was thought to have gained votes for the owner, who was a new man, in his attempt to secure the consulship . . . A man's dignity may be enhanced by the house he lives in, but cannot be entirely secured by it; the owner should bring honour to the house rather than the house to the owner. And, as in everything else, a man must not consider himself alone, but others also, so care must be taken that the home of a distinguished man is spacious, for many guests must be entertained and crowds of all kinds of people received there.

(Cic. De off. 1.138–9)

This passage provides a good illustration of the public role of a politician's house. Cicero suggests it is the duty of a prominent citizen to have a large house so that his clients and friends may be properly accommodated.[35] Elsewhere, he attempted to justify his own purchase of a relatively expensive house on the prestigious Palatine in similar terms (*Ad Att.* 13.6).[36]

If a house could be seen as bringing added prestige to those who already 'deserved' political honour, it could also be viewed as a claim to undeserved *dignitas*.[37] A man's house was seen as reflecting his own perception of his social and political position.[38] Thus the size and splendour of someone's house was a barometer of his social and political ambitions. To accuse one's opponents of luxurious building was to imply that they were guilty of excessive ambition. Vitruvius stresses that a house must be appropriate to the position of its owner:

> igitur is, qui communi sunt fortuna, non necessaria magnifica vestibula nec tabulina neque atria, quod in aliis officia praestant ambiundo neque ab aliis ambiuntur . . . nobilibus vero, qui honores magistratusque gerundo praestare debent officia civibus, faciunda sunt vestibula regalia alta, atria et peristylia amplissima, silvae ambulationesque laxiores ad decorem maiestatis perfectae; praeterea bibliothecas, basilicas non dissimili modo quam publicorum operum magnificentia comparatas, quod in domibus eorum saepius et publica consilia et privata iudicia arbitriaque conficiuntur.

> *Magnificent vestibules, recesses and halls are not necessary to people of common standing because they pay their respects by visiting others, while others do not visit them . . . For people of high rank who hold offices and magistracies, and whose duty it is to serve the state, we must provide regal vestibules, high-ceilinged halls and very spacious peristyles, parks and*

---

[35] Cicero elsewhere complains that his house is so crowded he has no privacy (*Ad Att.* 18.1). Such a complaint served to demonstrate Cicero's own importance: if his house was crowded, it was with people who needed his services or sought to pay him their respects. On the political advantage of a central location, see also Plutarch *Marius* 32.1; *Cic.* 8.4.

[36] Cicero writes to Sestius that it is worth getting into debt to make the purchase, for the house greatly enhances his *bonum nomen*, 'good name' (*Ad fam.* 4.2). Saller suggests that Cicero's purchase was disapproved of because of his relatively humble origins (1984: 349). It is worth noting, however, that according to the elder Pliny, Crassus (whose ancestry was considerably grander) was criticised for buying a house on the Palatine which cost only slightly more than Cicero's (*NH* 17.2).

[37] Cf. Wallace-Hadrill 1988: 48. Norbert Elias, in his study of the French aristocracy in the time of Louis XIV, discusses 'the way court people arranged and experienced their houses in their own "image"' (1983: 55, 60). There are interesting similarities between Elias' picture of the 'meaning' of the house of a seventeenth-century nobleman and the 'meanings' Romans seem to have attributed to that of the late republican or early imperial aristocrat.

[38] Cicero, when it suits him, may emphasise the sanctity of a Roman citizen's house (*De dom.* 109) but the houses of the wealthy do not seem to have had strong family associations (see Rawson 1976: 85–90).

broad avenues in a majestic style; besides this, libraries and basilicas
arranged in a manner similar to the magnificence of public buildings,
because in palaces such as this, deliberations on public matters, as well as
private trials and judgements, are often transacted.

(Vitr. *De arch.* 6.5.1–2)

This passage, too, illustrates the point that the house of the Roman aristocrat was not a 'private' place. The splendour of the houses of the Roman aristocracy is justified by drawing attention to the public service in which they are employed. This is not private *luxuria*. And yet the vocabulary used by Vitruvius (*regalia, basilica* – words etymologically linked with the Latin and Greek terms for 'king') uncomfortably suggests that the aspirations of those who own such houses might be higher than the attainment of magistracies.

A letter of Cicero describes an exchange in court between himself and Clodius (*Ad Att.* 16.10). Clodius allegedly insinuated that Cicero was arrogating power to himself in a tyrannical way (the word *rex*, 'king', was used). Clodius seems to have brought up Cicero's recent purchase of a grand house in this context, at which Cicero became defensive. In his speech in defence of Sestius, Cicero alleges that Gabinius, when tribune of the *plebs*, had attempted to arouse public hostility to Lucullus by displaying a picture of his extravagant villa (*Pro Sest.* 93). Gabinius' own villa, Cicero asserts, made that of Lucullus look like a mere hut. Again we might wonder who was intended to be the most responsive audience to such claims, ordinary citizens or those who thought themselves the peers of Lucullus and his accuser?

Luxury is a problematic term. What might be perfectly proper for a consul could be seen as luxurious for one whose status was not authenticated by ancestry or public office. References to the luxurious homes of freedmen make it especially clear that whether a house was to be considered luxurious depended to a large extent on the social status of its owner. The elder Pliny in his discussion of the extraordinary growth in the scale of private wealth from the early first century BCE to his own time, relates anecdotes concerning the size of the triumvir Crassus' fortune. He continues:

atque ut memoriam quidem opum occupaverit . . . multos postea cognovimus servitute liberatos opulentiores, pariterque tres Claudii principatu paulo ante Callistum, Pallantem, Narcissum.

153

It was he who was the first to win a lasting reputation for wealth . . . but since that time many freedmen are known to have been richer – three at the same time, not long before our own days, in the reign of the emperor Claudius: Callistus, Pallas and Narcissus.

(Pliny, *NH* 33.134)

Pliny chose to point to Claudius' freedmen as examples not because they were the richest men in Rome, but because they were freedmen, whose wealth could not be justified by their ancestry or merit.[39] Their conspicuous wealth was offensive to those who resented their political power. Richard Saller cites a passage from Seneca in this connection (*Ep*. 47.9).[40] A master pays a morning visit to his own freedman, now Caligula's favourite. The formality of the *salutatio* exposes the ordering – and disordering – of the social hierarchy. It is in the freedman's house that 'proper' precedence can be most conspicuously overturned.

Seneca's attack on luxurious baths vividly betrays a concern with social status, a concern which characterises much of the invective against luxurious building examined in this chapter. Seneca has been describing the rather austere bathing arrangements in a villa in Campania said to have belonged to Scipio in the early second century BCE:

at nunc quis est, qui sic lavari sustineat? pauper sibi videtur ac sordidus, nisi parietes magnis et pretiosis orbibus refulserunt, nisi Alexandrina marmora Numidicis crustis distincta sunt . . . et adhuc plebeias fistulas loquor; quid, cum ad balnea libertinorum pervenero? quantum statuarum, quantum columnarum est nihil sustinentium, sed in ornamentum positarum inpensae causa! quantum aquarum per gradus cum fragore labentium! eo deliciarum pervenimus, ut nisi gemmas calcare nolimus.

But who nowadays could bear to bathe in this manner? We think ourselves poor and wretched if our walls do not gleam with large and expensive

---

[39] The scale of freedmen's fortunes is often remarked on. Cf. e.g. Cic. *Pro Rosc. Amer.* 133 (on the luxurious properties of Sulla's freedman Chrysogonus); Pliny, *NH* 18.7; 33.145; Sen. *Ep.* 27.5; Mart. 5.13; Juv. 1.109; Pliny, *Ep.* 7.29. Petronius (*Sat.* 71) makes the freedman Trimalchio boast that his fortune is 30,000,000 sesterces – considerably greater than the wealth of a relatively modest senator like the younger Pliny (according to the calculations of Duncan-Jones 1982 ch. 1).

[40] Saller emphasises the importance of the house as the location of the morning *salutatio* which 'was an open demonstration of a man's position in the social hierarchy' (1984a: 350). Cf. Wallace-Hadrill 1988: 84–5. The passage from Vitruvius quoted above also emphasises the importance of the *salutatio* in determining the scale of a man's house.

mirrors; if our Alexandrian marbles are not set off by Numidian stone . . .
So far I have been speaking of ordinary bathing establishments; what shall
I say about those of the freedmen? What an enormous number of statues, of
columns that support nothing, but are built for decoration, with the sole
purpose of spending money! and what masses of water that fall with a roar
from level to level! We have become so luxurious that we will have nothing
but precious stones to walk on.

(Sen. Ep. 86.6–7)

For Seneca, there was something 'wrong' and 'unnatural' about men
who had money but no real status, just as there was something
'wrong' and 'unnatural' about pillars which masqueraded as struc-
tural features.[41] No doubt such pillars were to be found in the houses
of men of free birth. Indeed, Seneca, in this very passage, slips back
from his attack on the luxurious building fashions which he implies
are peculiar to freedmen to a more generalised critique of the luxury
of his contemporaries. Still, this text is a good illustration of the
preoccupation of moralists with social status – an indication, if we
needed one, that criticisms of luxury were not just motivated by
perceptions that money might be better spent on public works, still
less that there was a significant link between the luxurious possessions
of some and the poverty experienced by others.[42]

One of the most evocative indications of the power of a house to
convey political aspirations is suggested by a series of incidents in
which houses were alleged to have been deliberately destroyed. The
best documented of these is the destruction of Cicero's house by his
enemy Clodius. When Cicero was exiled in 58 BCE for his role in the
execution of Catiline and his associates, his house was looted and
razed to the ground. While Cicero was in exile, Clodius put up a new
portico on the Palatine, in place of the old *Porticus Catuli*, which also
encroached on what had been the site of Cicero's house. Close by, he
built a shrine to the goddess Libertas, and, with the aid of a *pontifex*,
performed a ceremony of consecration with the apparent intention of
having Cicero permanently excluded on religious grounds from the
site. On his return, Cicero sought with eventual success to have the

---

[41] Cf. the elder Pliny's complaint about the luxurious pillars of a freedman (*NH* 36.59–60).
[42] Cf. Cicero, who refers to the villa of Lucius Lucullus to illustrate the importance of the
example set by the leading men in the state (*De leg.* 3.30–1). The flagrant extravagance of
Lucullus is harmful, argues Cicero, not so much in itself, but because of the example it sets.
Lucullus' extravagance is seen as a cause of the much more offensive luxury of his socially
inferior neighbours, an *eques* and a freedman.

consecration declared invalid and the site of his house returned to him.[43] His speech *De domo sua* of 57 BCE outlines his claim. Cicero draws attention to the symbolic significance of destroying a man's house: 'Spurius Maelius sought to become a tyrant [*regnum appetens*] and his house was torn down to the ground . . . For the same reason, Spurius Cassius' house was flattened and a temple to Earth put up on the site.' He goes on to tell how the same happened to the houses of Marcus Vaccus and Marcus Manlius, before continuing: 'And shall I meet with and suffer the very same penalty which our ancestors thought the most severe that could be enacted against criminal and sacrilegious citizens?' (*De domo sua* 101). Cicero's assertions that this is the severest possible punishment are, of course, to be treated with caution, but this passage does suggest the particular symbolic associations the destruction of a man's house might have.[44]

An anecdote from Plutarch's life of Publicola also illustrates the associations between tyrannous aspirations and this form of punishment – or in this case expiation – through the destruction of the would-be tyrant's house. Plutarch describes how, shortly after the overthrow of the kings of Rome, Brutus the regicide (a man conspicuous for his republican sentiments) accused Valerius Publicola of living in a house as splendid as the residence of the now banished kings:

> For . . . indeed, Valerius was living in a very grand house on what is called the Velia . . . When he heard from the accounts of his friends . . . that he was thought by the people to be putting on airs, he . . . quickly summoned a large crowd of workmen, and, while it was still night, had the house torn down and completely flattened. In the morning, then, the Romans saw what had happened and quickly gathered. They were moved to love and admiration by the man's public spirit.

(Plut. *Publ.* 10.2–4)

By deliberately destroying his suspiciously grand house, Publicola cleared himself of the charge of excessive political ambition by the most effective means at his disposal. This story may bear little relation to events in the early republic but its importance lies in its

---

[43] For the details, see R.G.M. Nisbet's edition of Cicero *De domo sua* (Oxford 1939) introduction and appendix 5.

[44] A similar list of men who lost their houses in the early republic is to be found in Valerius Maximus (6.3.1).

status as a myth preserved by later Romans.[45] Magnificent houses were associated with kings, with their excessive power and lack of concern for the public good.

In a passage from a speech defending the recently elected Murena on a charge of bribery, Cicero writes: *odit populus Romanus privatam luxuriam, publicam magnificentiam diligit*, 'The Roman people hate private luxury but love public magnificence' (*Pro Mur.* 76).[46] A recurring theme of invective against private luxury is the argument that it harms the interests of the community. But, as we have seen from Vitruvius, grand private houses might be justified by pointing to the public functions which occurred within them. And elite competition, as manifested in public building, did not, of course, have public benefit as its only end. Public buildings, too, could be blamed as a source of corruption, as the elder Pliny's comments on Scaurus' theatre reveal.[47] Cicero argued that some public buildings, such as aqueducts and walls, are more laudable than other more glamorous ones, such as new temples and theatres (*De off.* 2.60). Velleius Paterculus asserted that luxury from the east first infected Rome through public buildings.[48]

Nevertheless, the abstract opposition between 'public' and 'private' could, in the context of building, be negotiated in concrete terms. Criticism of luxurious building was an important means of asserting that the relationship between an individual (or a group of individuals) and the community was not as it should be. One of the elder Seneca's rhetorical exercises deals with a suit brought by a poor man against a rich neighbour, on the grounds that the latter had burnt down his house in an attempt to destroy a tree which was blocking his view. Much of the poor man's speech attacks luxurious building. He is made to ask:

[45] There seem to have been several versions of this story. Livy's version appears in several other authors, including Valerius Maximus. Stefan Weinstock comments on the various versions in his discussion of the *domus publica*, emphasising that it was well known in the time of Caesar (*Divus Iulius* (Oxford 1971) 276–81). The story is also discussed by Wiseman (1987: 393–4). Filippo Coarelli argues for the historical basis of the anecdote (*Il foro romano* (Rome 1983) 79–82).   [46] Cf. Cic. *Pro Flacco* 28.
[47] Pliny *NH* 33. 13–15, part of which is quoted earlier in this chapter. Cf. the other texts associating pernicious luxury with extravagant theatre buildings discussed in chapter three above.
[48] Vell. Pat. 1.11.3–5; 2.1.1–2. On eastern influences on public building in the mid republic, see Pierre Gros 'Les premières générations d'architectes hellénistiques à Rome' *Mélanges Huergon* (Rome 1976) 387–410.

infinitis porrectae spatiis ambulationes et urbium solo aedificatae
domus non nos prope a publico excludunt?

*Promenades stretching over vast distances, houses covering the space
occupied by whole cities, don't these effectively keep us out of public spaces?*

(Sen. *Contr.* 5.5)

The creation of vast houses and gardens in the middle of Rome
involved the demolition of other buildings (remarked on by Strabo in
the late first century BCE), which was bound to exacerbate the housing
shortage in an already crowded city or else to encroach on what had
previously been public space.[49] Certainly this consequence was one
stressed by critics.

Nero's *domus aurea* occupied a large part of the centre of the city of
Rome.[50] Suetonius lists the following among attacks on the emperor:

Roma domus fiet; Veios migrate, Quirites,
si non et Veios occupat ista domus.

*Rome is becoming one house; run off to Veii, citizens! Unless that house
takes over Veii, too.*

(*Nero* 39.2)

However, the idea of Nero's Golden House taking over the whole of
Rome (also remarked on by Pliny *NH* 36.111–12) is, I think, also
connected with another recurring theme in the critique of luxurious
houses. Perhaps the most succinct expression of this comes in a
passage from the works of the Greek historian Olympiodorus, writing
in the early fifth century CE, who describes the houses of wealthy
Romans as follows:

*Each of the great houses of Rome has within it, he says, what one would
generally find in a decent sized town: a hippodrome, fora, temples,
fountains and different sorts of baths.*

(Olympiodorus fr. 41 in R.C. Blockley ed. *FCHLRE* II)

---

[49] Strabo 5.3.7.
[50] Cf. Tac. *Ann.* 3.85; 15.42; Suet. *Nero* 31; Mart. *Spect.* 1.2.4 (*unaque iam tota stabat in urbe
domus*, 'in the whole city there stood but one house'). On the probable extent of Nero's *domus
aurea* see Miriam Griffin *Nero: the end of a dynasty* (London 1984) 126–9 and 133–42.

Other texts express disapproval of extensive villa complexes in similar terms.[51] Purcell, in his discussion of Roman taste in the layout and position of villas, refers to this blurring of the physical differences between house and town.[52] He cites archaeological examples – villas with imitation town walls around their grounds, or monumental gateways, complexes which included temples in semi-public use. The resemblance between an aristocrat's estate and a town, perceived by others as sinister, was self-consciously played on and exaggerated by some wealthy land-owners.

The conceit of villas resembling towns may be seen in terms of a play on and perversion of the ideal of the self-sufficiency of the villa, advocated by champions of the moral worth of agriculture, such as Cato, Varro and Columella.[53] These writers attacked those who had country villas without productive estates attached, thus necessitating the importation of supplies, sometimes even from the city.[54] The villa, for these moralists, should be able to supply its own needs. The *villa urbana* was a perverted paradox. Similarly, those whose estates were small towns in themselves had disrupted proper civic order, erecting baths, temples and basilicas for their own private use. Activities once enjoyed by all citizens together in public buildings were now enjoyed by the wealthy on their private estates from which all but those they chose might be excluded. Practices which in earlier days were shared and served as an indication that, in some sense at least, all citizens were equal were now another means by which the rich had set themselves apart. Emperors are a rather special case but Hadrian's villa at Tivoli might be seen as an extreme example of this manifestation of luxurious building. The names of provinces and famous places given to the various parts of the villa suggest it was seen as corresponding not so much to a Greek or Roman city but rather to the entire world (SHA *Hadr.* 26.5).[55] Were all these criticisms

---

[51] Cf. Sall. *Cat.* 12.3 *villas . . . in urbium modum exaedificatas*, 'villas built to resemble towns'; Sen. *De ben.* 7.10.5 *aedificia privata laxitatem urbium magnarum vincentia*, 'private buildings which outdo large towns in their extent'. Purcell suggests the term *villa urbana* might also have evoked the idea of the villa resembling a town (1987: 197).

[52] Purcell 1987: 197–200. Cf. Eugenio La Rocca 'Il lusso come espressione di potere' in *Le tranquille dimore degli dei* (Rome 1986) 3–35, esp. 15–16.

[53] And joked on by other writers, e.g. Pet. *Sat.* 38, 48; Mart. 7.31.

[54] Varro, *De re rust.* 1.59.1–2. Cf. Mart. 3.47.

[55] On Hadrian's villa, see E.S.P. Ricotti 'Villa Adriana nei suoi limiti e nella sua funzionalità' *Mem. Pont. Accad. Rom. Arch.* 14 (1982) 25–55. There were precedents for some of the terms used in Hadrian's villa (La Rocca 1986: 16).

expressions of sympathy for the dispossessed poor or rather of concern that other members of the elite might not be able to keep up?

BUILDING RUINS

Moralists criticised luxurious building in much the same terms from the second century BCE to the second century CE. We might well suppose, however, that buildings which aroused the righteous indignation of the elder Cato would have been thought respectably modest by the younger Seneca. Archaeological evidence contributes little to a nuanced picture of the development of elite housing over the period examined here, for we are able to identify the owners (and hence gauge their social status) only very rarely. The scraps of information we can elicit from literary texts are scarce and problematic. From the archaeological and literary evidence available it is very difficult to say how much members of the elite expected to spend on their houses and whether this changed over time, either as a proportion of their incomes or in absolute terms.[56] But there is some justification for hypothesising.

The expansion of the Roman empire entailed an enormous increase in the available wealth in late republican Rome. Individuals made vast fortunes (if they were lucky) from their positions as army commanders and provincial governors.[57] By the late second century BCE, the Roman elite was becoming increasingly competitive. Political careers which might (or might not) bring large financial rewards required substantial initial investment. Many individuals seem to have been ruined in the process.[58] Correspondingly, the prizes were greater and there were more opportunities for those whose families had not been part of the central Roman elite to permeate its membership.[59] Not all those who did well out of the empire were 'new men' but some were. A splendid residence must have been one of the clearest ways of announcing one's social 'arrival', of laying claim to

[56] The elder Pliny does quote some house prices but his numbers are not reliable and in any case he tends to record only the exceptional. Rawson stresses the difficulty of 'making useful remarks about prices' (1976: 95). Even in the case of Cicero or the younger Pliny, whose financial affairs are exceptionally well documented, it is not possible to calculate the cost of their villas (as distinct from their country estates) and town houses in relation to their incomes.

[57] On the social, economic and political consequences of empire, see Hopkins 1978: 1–98. On the size of senatorial fortunes, see Shatzman 1975: 9–109; Duncan-Jones 1982: 17–32.

[58] Hopkins 1983: 107–16. For a discussion of debt among the political elite, see chapter five below. [59] On the permeability of the Roman elite, see Hopkins 1983, esp. 45.

membership of the elite. For those who were made uneasy by changes to the social order associated with the increasingly important role of money, someone else's 'luxurious' house could seem the most resonant symbol of social disruption.

The enormous increase in wealth flooding into Rome in the late republic and early principate seems to have brought with it an increase in the scale of private building. The elder Pliny remarks on the increasing grandeur of houses in Rome, comparing the position in 78 BCE with that in his own day:

> M. Lepido Q. Catulo coss., ut constat inter diligentissimos auctores, domus pulchrior non fuit Romae quam Lepidi ipsius, at hercules, intra annos xxxv eadem centesimum locum non optinuit ... centum domus posteaque ab innumerabilibus aliis in hunc diem victas.

> *Our most conscientious authorities agree that, in the consulship of Marcus Lepidus and Quintus Catulus, Lepidus' own house was the finest in Rome, but, by god, within thirty-five years the same house was not among the first hundred ... [Those] houses ... have themselves been surpassed by countless others, and so it continues to this day.*

(Pliny, NH 36.109–10)

Pliny's assertion needs to be seen in context. His project in the *Naturalis historia* is, in part, to demonstrate the cumulative moral damage caused by wealth.[60] But there are reasons for supposing Pliny's claim that leading Romans spent increasingly large sums on their houses has some justification.

During the late republic and early principate, members of the senatorial elite and those who wished to attain senatorial positions seem to have been involved in competitive displays of wealth and taste on an ever more ruinous scale.[61] From the middle of the reign of

---

[60] Wallace-Hadrill 1990: 80–96.
[61] Tac. *Ann.* 3.55. Cf. Wallace-Hadrill 1988: 45. Houses did not only display the wealth of their owners. Houses in Rome seem to have been less closely associated with family history than has been the case among elite groups in some other cultures (Rawson 1976: 85–9). However, they do seem to have been important for the display of good taste and refinement. The elder Pliny laments that, while in the time of 'our ancestors' *imagines* were the only ornaments in the halls of the upper classes, in his own day people buy statues of strangers because they are valuable works of art (*NH* 35.6, discussed by Saller 1984: 349). Pliny complains that the elite now compete with one another in terms of wealth and 'good taste' rather than genealogy. The younger Pliny's descriptions of his own villas emphasise their role as reflections of his own 'good taste' (*Ep.* 2.17; 5.6). Cf. Cicero's comments on the philosophical air of his brother's elegantly equipped villa (*Ad Q. fr.* 21.5). For Roman notions of 'taste', see Giovanni Becatti *Arte e gusto negli scrittori latini* (Florence 1951) and the collection of sources edited by J.J. Pollitt, *The art of Rome* (Englewood Cliffs, N.J. 1966).

Augustus, there was virtually no public building by individual members of the elite in Rome, unless they were members of the imperial family.[62] Many members of the elite continued to sponsor public building projects outside the capital (the younger Pliny, for instance, was responsible for several buildings in towns near his country estates, in particular, in his native Comum).[63] Villas outside the capital gave scope for discreet ostentation, but in Rome itself private houses were the only available opportunity for impressive building.[64] The higher turnover in elite families under the principate must have been due, in part at least, to the increased costs of keeping up a senatorial lifestyle in Rome. A major item of expenditure for many families must surely have been their Roman residence.[65]

The ruinous spiral of conspicuous consumption in which the elite were engaged worked to the advantage of the emperor, dividing the elite against each other and making them more dependent on imperial favour. Few aristocrats owned enough land to finance a life of necessary luxury in Rome. Those who had exhausted their capital in the quest for social and political prestige were thrown on the emperor's mercy. The only way to recoup one's losses was to secure appointment to a lucrative provincial governorship, appointments which effectively lay in the gift of the emperor.[66] Emperors, who set a crippling example of extravagance for their courtiers, were not necessarily conscious of the connection between the extravagance of court life and the control they exercised over the more fashionable members of the elite.[67] Still, from some points of view, the intense and expensive competition between rival aristocrats did work to the emperor's advantage.

[62] Werner Eck 'Senatorial self-representation' in F. Millar and E. Segal eds. *Caesar Augustus: seven aspects* (Oxford 1984) 129–68.

[63] E.g. Pliny *Ep.* 1.8; 4.1; 10.8. On public building under the principate, see Veyne 1990: 361–6, 388–90.

[64] Though some emperors might have resented anyone who dared to approach them in splendour (some nobles were alleged to have come to a bad end because a member of the imperial family coveted their properties, e.g. Tac. *Ann.* 11.1 – Valerius Asiaticus is said to have been accused of treason at the instigation of Messalina because she had designs on the gardens of Lucullus of which he was at that time the owner).

[65] Cf. the crippling cost of 'appropriate' housing for the French nobility in the period studied by Elias. He quotes the Duc de Croy, who observed at the end of the *ancien régime*: 'Ce sont les maisons qui ont écrasé la plupart des grandes familles' (Elias 1983: 5).

[66] Cf. Hopkins 1983: 171–7, 196. Again there are parallels with the court society studied by Elias, where regal favour was crucial for those who needed to secure lucrative offices (1983: 70).

[67] And some experors, such as Vespasian and Trajan, seem to have set an example of frugality. It is notable that they seem to have been far more popular among the upper classes.

Another imperial strategy for controlling the elite was the promotion of freedmen. They were the emperor's creatures, embodied reminders of his power to raise individuals to positions of enormous power from the lowest ranks of the 'proper' social hierarchy (and, by implication, the power to cast others down as dramatically).[68] They gave the emperor advice and often controlled access to him. Emperors endowed favoured freedmen with vast fortunes – or fortunes which appeared vast to jaundiced members of the elite.[69] It was natural that freedmen should invest a substantial part of their fortunes in architectural demonstrations of their wealth and influence. These houses became a focus for elite resentment, as we have seen.

Not all discussions of luxurious building were critical. The private baths of Claudius Etruscus (himself the son of a wealthy freedman of the emperor Tiberius) are praised for their refinement by both Statius and Martial (whose poetry consistently flatters the reigning emperor Domitian). The wealth which financed these baths presumably came, in part at least, from Tiberius. Praise of Claudius Etruscus' baths might be seen as a way of taunting the freeborn elite with a freedman's magnificence, or perhaps of inciting them to emulate it. A new approach to luxury was now licensed as a literary possibility (though most continued to write within an older literary tradition). But, just as moralising criticism might provide inspiration for the luxurious builder, so praise of luxury might be read with disapproval by the severe – or even with amusement by those who found this ostentatious manifestation of a freedman's social pretensions inept.

IMPERIAL BUILDING

Roman aristocrats of the late republic and early principate expressed their sense of their own social position by building or buying houses of suitable grandeur. But what sort of residence was appropriate for an emperor? How could the house of the *princeps* convey the sense that he was at once *primus inter pares* – a citizen just like any other senator – and the son of a god, saviour of his country – and a dangerous enemy? Emperors negotiated this tension in a range of ways which will be examined briefly in this final section. There is

---

[68] Cf. the relationship between emperors and actors discussed in chapter three. For a discussion of role of freedmen, see K. Hopkins 'Elite mobility in the Roman empire' in M.I. Finley ed. *Studies in ancient society* (London 1974) 103–20.

[69] For references, see note 39 above.

considerable continuity between invective against building mania on the part of emperors and criticism of the luxurious building projects of late republican aristocrats. The symbolic vocabulary of republican moralistic discourse was taken over and adapted, as we have seen from some of the passages discussed above.

For emperors, building was one of the most dramatic ways of making one's mark on Rome, of setting out what kind of a ruler one aspired to be. At the same time, criticism of an emperor's residence was a vivid way of criticising the extent of his power and the way he exercised it. Several stories told about the emperor Augustus should be considered in the context of the associations considered earlier between luxurious houses and the tyrannous aspirations of their owners. Augustus represented himself as a 'censor' figure, attempting to revive the values and habits of the early republic when Romans lived simply.[70] He is alleged to have set an example of moderate behaviour himself, while at the same time attempting to control the excesses of others. An *eques*, Vedius Pollio, (son of a freedman and very wealthy) who was renowned for his excessive cruelty as well as his luxurious tastes, is said to have left a great deal of property to Augustus, with instructions that some public work should be erected there to commemorate himself (Dio 54.23.5–6).[71] Augustus had Pollio's house on the Palatine pulled down. The monument erected in its place celebrated not Pollio but Augustus' wife, Livia.[72]

Ovid's treatment of this story vividly suggests the significance of this:

> disce tamen, veniens aetas: ubi Livia nunc est
> porticus, immensae tecta fuere domus;
> urbis opus domus una fuit, spatiumque tenebat,
> quo brevius muris oppida multa tenent.

[70] Cf. his attempts to revive 'traditional' sexual morality and religious practices discussed in chapter one.
[71] On Pollio, see Ronald Syme 'Who was Vedius Pollio?' *JRS* 51 (1961) 23–30.
[72] On the specific strategies by which the architecture of the new building reproved the luxury of its predecessor (and also the luxury of the nearby Gardens of Maecenas), see M. Boudreau-Flory '*Sic exempla parantur*: Livia's shrine to Concordia and the *Porticus Liviae*' *Historia* 33 (1984) 309–30. Cf. Paul Zanker 'Drei Stadtbilder aus dem augusteischen Rom' in *L'urbs: espace urbain et histoire. Collection de l'école française de Rome* 98 (1987) 476–89 and Zanker 1988: 137–39. Zanker also draws attention to Augustus' treatment of the notoriously luxurious house of Scaurus (1988: 137). This building was torn down and the famous marble pillars (originally imported to decorate the temporary theatre built when Scaurus was aedile in 58 BCE) incorporated into the new theatre of Marcellus (for the reuse of the pillars in Scaurus' house, see Pliny *NH* 36.7, and in the theatre of Marcellus, Ascon. *In Scaur.* 45).

haec aequata solo est, nullo sub crimine regni,
    sed quia luxuria visa nocere sua.
sustinuit tantas operum subvertere moles
    totque suas heres perdere Caesar opes.
sic agitur censura et sic exempla parantur,
    cum vindex, alios quod monet, ipse facit.

*But learn, future age, that where Livia's colonnade now stands, there was
once a massive mansion. The single house was as much labour to construct
as a city and occupied as much space as the walls of a town sometimes
enclose. It was razed to the ground, not because its owner aspired to be king,
but because its luxury was thought harmful. Caesar suffered to bring down
this vast structure, destroying wealth to which he was the heir. That is the
act of a true censor, that is the way for examples to be set, when the judge
himself behaves according to his rules.*

(Ovid, *Fasti* 6.639–48)

Pollio's house is criticised for its vast size and for the immense labour
which went into its construction. We should note again the comparison between outsize house and city. And here too an excessive house
is associated with tyrannous aspirations (*crimine regni*).[73] Ovid
implies that Augustus might have objected to Pollio's house on those
grounds but his objection was rather that the luxury of such a
building set a bad example. Luxury rather than tyranny was the real
threat to Augustan Rome. But different readings of this passage are
possible. The idea of tyranny has been raised, even if only to be
dismissed. Augustus' apparent preoccupation with luxury is perhaps
presented as a diversionary tactic. The power to tear down buildings,
ignoring the prescriptions of the owner's will, was not one exercised
by republican censors.

Augustus himself, of course, could not be suspected of regal
pretensions, for his houses were of exemplary modesty:

habitavit primo iuxta Romanum Forum supra scalas anularias, in
domo quae Calvi oratoris fuerat; postea in Palatio, sed nihilo minus
aedibus modicis Hortensianis, et neque laxitate neque culto conspi-
cuis, ut in quibus porticus breves essent Albanarum columnarum et

[73] The phrase *crimine regni* suggests both treason and tyranny. We might note the recurrence of
cognate and related terms in some of the treatments of grand building discussed so far (cf.
Cic. *Ad Att.* 16.10 *rex*; Cic. *De dom.* 101 *regnum appetens*; Vitruvius *De arch.* 6.5.2 *regalia,
basilica*; Hor. *Carm.* 2.15.1–2 *regiae . . . moles*; Mart. *Spect.* 1.2. *atria regis*; while Plutarch
describes Publicola's descent from the Palatine as βασιλικόν, 'regal', *Publ.* 10.2).

sine marmore ullo aut insigni pavimento conclavia. ac per annos amplius quadraginta eodem cubiculo hieme et aestate mansit, quamvis parum salubrem valitudini suae urbem hieme experiretur assidueque in urbe hiemaret . . . ex secessibus praecipue frequentavit maritima insulasque Campaniae aut proxima urbi oppida . . . ampla et operosa praetoria gravabatur. et neptis quidem suae Iuliae, profuse ab ea exstructa, etiam diruit ad solum.

First he lived near the Forum Romanum, above the stairs of the Ringmakers in a house which had belonged to the orator Calvus; later on, on the Palatine, but in an equally modest house (which Hortensius used to live in) that was outstanding neither for size nor for elegance. It had only short colonnades with columns of Alban stone and its rooms had neither marble decorations nor handsome pavements. For more than forty years, too, he used the same bedroom in winter and summer; even though he found the city harmful to his health during the winter, he still continued to pass the winter months here . . . For retirement, he went most often to places by the sea and the islands of Campania, or to the towns near Rome . . . He did not like large and sumptuous country palaces and actually had demolished one which his granddaughter Julia had built on a grand scale.

(Suet. *Aug.* 72)

The destruction of Julia's house is especially striking in view of the stories of the destruction of houses discussed above. Even the emperor's family had to take care to avoid the kind of buildings associated with excessive power.[74] We should also note some significant features of Augustus' house, as Suetonius describes it. The pillars were not of exotic, imported marble but of local stone. The colonnades did not stretch for miles but were short. Augustus was not so luxurious as to have different rooms for use in different seasons. The emperor did not pursue novelty in his living arrangements but was content with the same ones for forty years. All this forms a marked contrast with descriptions of the luxurious architectural tastes of some of the aristocrats of the late republic – and with Suetonius' descriptions of the tastes of some later emperors.[75] Augus-

[74] Though perhaps Augustus' action is to be seen in the context of the punishment for his granddaughter for adultery and treason (for the elision of adultery and treason as crimes by female members of the imperial family, see Tac. *Ann.* 3.24).

[75] For moralists' criticisms of the use of luxurious marbles, see e.g. Cato ap. Festus 282 ed. Linsday (= 185 Malcovati); Sen. *Ep.* 86; Pliny *NH* 17.6, 36.1–7, 48–9; Juv. 14.86–95; extensive colonnades: Juv. 4.1–10; 7.178–83; Pliny *Ep.* 4.2; Mart. 12.50; rooms for use in different seasons: Columella *De re rust.* 1.6; Plut. *Luc.* 39.4.

tus' 'private' but well-advertised frugality also contrasted with the lavish building programme he boasted of in the *Res gestae* (especially appendices 2–3). Augustus spent his money on temples not palaces.[76]

Suetonius' description gives us some idea how Romans may have perceived Augustus' house.[77] This is one of the few instances where a description of a house may be compared with the remains of the house itself.[78] Excavations on the Palatine have revealed a building which must have been the main house in the complex owned by Augustus.[79] The smaller rooms to the west, the so-called private rooms, do appear to have been quite modest in their decoration. The floors, for instance, are paved with black and white mosaic rather than marble. There are marble floors in the larger rooms (sometimes referred to by archaeologists as the 'public' rooms – though these sets of rooms are designated as 'public' and 'private' solely on the basis of their decor). An upper chamber which is unlikely to have been a 'public' room (Carettoni believes it to have been Augustus' study, mentioned by Suetonius) contains the remains of some sophisticated and exotic wall-paintings and its ceiling seems to have been at least partially gilded.[80] Some parts of the house could lay claim to old-fashioned Roman simplicity more plausibly than others.

Although the entrance to Augustus' house faced towards the river Tiber and the Circus Maximus until the fire of 3 CE, afterwards it seems to have been reoriented towards the *forum Romanum*. Paul Zanker suggests that Augustus may be seen as appropriating the

---

[76] The contrast between private frugality and public magnificence is evoked by Horace, *Carm.* 2.15. Cf. e.g. Sall. *Cat.* 12.3–4; Cicero *Pro Mur.* 76 quoted above. For the symbolic associations of Augustus' public building projects see Gros 1976a and Zanker 1988.

[77] Though his Palatine residence may not have seemed so modest to his contemporaries as it did to Suetonius. Cicero remarks that Lentulus, consul in 49 BCE, had his eye on Hortensius' house as a prize in the event of a Pompeian victory (*Ad Att.* 217.6). Cf. Millar 1977: 20.

[78] Excavations in progress on the lower slopes of the Palatine towards the forum reveal what may have been the remains of Scaurus' house (described by the elder Pliny) but this identification is by no means secure. See Andrea Carandini *et al.* 'Pendici settentrionali del Palatino' *BCAR* 111 (1986) 429–38.

[79] For an extensive discussion of the remains of Augustus' house, see Gianfilippo Carettoni *Das Haus des Augustus auf dem Palatin* (Mainz 1983) and 'La decorazione pittorica della casa di Augusto sul Palatino' *MDAI(R)* 90 (1983) 373–419. Augustus' house is also discussed by Millar 1977: 19–22; T.P. Wiseman 'Cybele, Virgil and Augustus' in Tony Woodman and David West eds. *Poetry and politics in the age of Augustus* (Cambridge 1984) 117–28; Wiseman 1987: 398–406; Zanker 1988: 51, 93, 207.

[80] Wallace-Hadrill disputes Carettoni's interpretation of the passage in Suetonius (1988: 81). On the history of this style of exotic painting, see Mariette de Vos *L'egittomania in pitture e mosaici romano-campani della prima età imperiale* (Leiden 1980).

forum as his own dynastic monument.[81] The visitor would come through the forum before ascending the Palatine, to the house of the emperor, a walk which would take one past the houses of many of the most prominent aristocrats in Rome, thus setting the house of Augustus in the context of those of his peers – a visible statement of his position as *primus inter pares*, 'first among equals'. These other houses, too, were decorated with triumphal ornaments, but Augustus' house, with its laurels, crown of oak and inscription, outdid them all.[82] This shows Augustus' residence in a rather different light from that shed on it by Suetonius – but the emperor's dwelling was open to a range of readings.

Whatever the ambiguities of Augustus' Palatine house (and these will be looked at again below) it was by no means a palace (though Augustus, like some republican aristocrats before him, does seem to have expanded his house by buying up some of those adjoining it). It was long thought by modern scholars that Tiberius, Augustus' successor, was the first emperor to build a palace in Rome, for when Domitian built his new palace, the older building was referred to as the *domus Tiberiana*. Recent research into the complex remains on the north west corner of the Palatine has cast some doubt on the accuracy of this designation.[83] It is now clear that there was an original unitary plan for the palace (it did not just develop haphazardly) which was probably initiated by Caligula or Claudius. Literary sources do not attribute any major building projects in Rome to Claudius and, though Caligula might seem a more plausible candidate, Josephus' description of his assassination implies that at the time of his death the palace was composed of many buildings (*AJ* 19.114–17). It is possible, however, that Caligula had started work on a new palace, even if the brevity of his reign did not allow him to complete it. The new building must have had a tremendous impact, for it proclaimed the emperor to be not a republican aristocrat but a Hellenistic monarch.

Caligula is said to have built a bridge from the Palatine to the Capitol, thus proclaiming his personal relationship with Jupiter

---

[81] Paul Zanker *Forum Romanum: die Neugestalt durch Augustus* (Tübingen 1972).

[82] Wiseman brings out the significance of Ovid, *Met.* 1.168–76 and *Tristia* 3.1.27–70 as descriptions of the approach to Augustus' house (1984). On the approach to Augustus' house, see also Zanker 1988: 51, 67, 93.

[83] The remains are described in U. Bellwald *Domus Tiberiana: nuove ricerche* (Zurich 1985).

(Suet. *Calig.* 22.4). He also 'extended the Palatine to the forum'.[84] The elder Pliny criticised Caligula's ambitious building projects:

> bis vidimus urbem totam cingi domibus principum Gai et Neronis, huius quidem, ne quid deesset, aurea. nimirum sic habitaverant illi qui hoc imperium facere tantum, ad devincendas gentes triumphosque referendos ab aratro aut foco exeuntes, quorum agri quoque minorem modum optinuere quam sellaria istorum!

> *On two occasions we have seen imperial palaces encircle the whole city, the palaces of Caligula and Nero. Indeed, Nero's palace, to cap it all, was a House of Gold. That was the sort of house, was it, lived in by the men who made this empire great, who went directly from plough or hearth to conquer nations or win triumphs, whose lands occupied a smaller space than these emperors' parlours.*

> (Pliny, *NH* 36.111–12)

This contrast between the luxurious dwellings of contemporaries and the simple lives of the mythical heroes of the early republic, so persistent a theme in attacks on luxurious building, may seem a tired rhetorical cliché, but it needs to be appreciated as a central part of the way at least some educated Romans responded to the building projects of their rulers.

The building mania of 'bad' emperors takes on added significance in view of the connection so many Roman texts assert between 'excessive' or 'perverse' building and tyranny. Eugenio La Rocca, in his discussion of the remains of imperial properties in the Horti Lamiani, explores the idea of luxury as an expression of power.[85] Extravagant palaces were associated with oriental tyrants, autocrats who abused their authority.[86] Caligula and Nero were playing dangerous games, perhaps deliberately setting themselves up as whimsi-

---

[84] Bellwald *et al.* (1985) argue that this extension may have been nothing more than the restoration and renovation of existing republican houses in that area. Recent excavations around Santa Maria Antiqua, however, have revealed what might be interpreted as the monumental atrium of Caligula's palace (Henry Hurst 'Area di Santa Maria Antiqua' *BCAR* 111 (1986) 470–8). The siting of this structure was such that it may well have been possible for the temple of Castor to have been used as an entrance. This would cohere with Suetonius' claim that Caligula used the temple of Castor as his vestibule (Suet. *Calig.* 22.2, cf. Dio 59.28.5; on this, see Wiseman 1987: 407–9). For some of the ideological uses Augustus made of temples, see below.

[85] La Rocca 1986.

[86] Cf. Strabo's description of the royal quarter in Alexandria (17.1.8). H. Heinen discusses Roman perceptions of eastern τρυφή – 'Die Truphe des Ptolemaios VIII Euergetes II' in *Althistorische Studien: Fests. H. Bengtson* (Wiesbaden 1983) 116–30.

cal autocrats rather than 'republican' magistrates. By inscribing their ambitions on the face of the city, they were building a new and potent image of imperial power.

Suetonius remarks of Nero: *non in alia re tamen damnosior quam in aedificando*, 'There was nothing, however, in which he was more ruinously extravagant than in building' (Suet. *Nero* 31.1). Extravagance in building, Suetonius suggests, was one of the most outrageous aspects of Nero's behaviour. The *domus aurea*, in particular, served to embody all his other crimes.[87] Vespasian's reaction, as it appears in anecdotes, confirms the significance of Nero's building, suggesting that Vespasian consciously sought to distance himself from the excesses of his predecessors in his living arrangements. Dio emphasises his munificence in public works and contrasts this with his modest private expenses. He continues: 'He spent little time in the palace, passing most hours in the gardens of Sallust, where he received anybody who wished to see him, not only senators but ordinary people, too' (Dio 65.10.4). In rejecting the palace that had become a symbol of the transgressions of earlier emperors, Vespasian was making a clear declaration of his own intentions, displaying his openness and accessibility (though it is not clear when the *domus aurea* was demolished – Vespasian and even Titus may have lived in it).[88]

This pattern is repeated in the stories told about later emperors, too. Domitian, we are told, succumbed to the same building mania as previous 'bad' emperors (though Tacitus implies he was less culpable than Nero, *Ann.* 3.85).[89] His palace seems to have been architecturally innovative.[90] Martial lavishes praise on its magnificence (8.36). Domitian's *domus augustana* covered virtually all of the Palatine and remained the residence of the emperors in Rome until they abandoned the city altogether. After Domitian, emperors no longer felt the urge to build new palaces, their position was no longer subject to negotiation.

---

[87] On the significance of the *domus aurea* see Griffin (1984: 126–42), Wiseman (1987: 409) and Purcell (1987: 199).

[88] Some parts of the building were only taken down in 104 CE (Laura Fabbrini '*Domus aurea*: una nuova lettura planimetrica del palazzo sul colle Oppio' *ARID* suppl. 10 (1983) 169–85).

[89] Domitian's palace is criticised by Plutarch (*Publ.* 15.3) and Suetonius (*Dom.* 14.4). It is praised by Martial (7.55.56; 8.36.1–6) and by Statius (*Silvae* 3.4.47–9; 4.2.18–31) who, in the latter passage, links Domitian's divine status to the splendour of his residence.

[90] See Lise Bek '*Quaestiones conviviales*: the idea of the triclinium and the staging of convivial ceremony from Rome to Byzantium' *ARID* suppl. 12 (1983) 81–109. On the influence of Domitian's palace on Roman architectural trends in general, see Wallace-Hadrill 1988: 90.

As for Trajan, in his panegyric addressed to that emperor the younger Pliny includes the following words of praise:

> idem tam parcus in aedificando quam diligens in tuendo, itaque non ut ante immanium transvectione saxorum urbis tecta quatiuntur; stant securae domus nec iam templa nutantia . . . at quam magnificus in publicum es!

> *Your interest in preserving existing buildings is equalled by your restraint in undertaking new projects. The walls and roofs of our city no longer shake as they used to do whenever enormous blocks of stone were dragged by. Our houses stand safe and secure and the temples are no longer threatened with collapse . . . But when it comes to public building, you do it on the grand scale.*

> (Pliny, *Paneg.* 51)

Public munificence is again directly related to private parsimony. 'Good' emperors built for the public good and lived modestly. That might have been a republican ideal, but building for the public good in the city of Rome had become an imperial prerogative by the end of Augustus' reign.[91]

Emperors negotiated their own positions in terms of a continuing debate over the relationship between private frugality and public generosity. The simple decor of an emperor's dining rooms, the generosity with which he endowed temples, were eloquent expressions of the honourableness of his political intentions. As republican politicians had found, there were other benefits to be had from the generous funding of public buildings. Next to his house on the Palatine, Augustus built a splendid temple to Apollo.[92] Thus, while the house itself may have been modest, its position was extremely prestigious.[93] When he became *pontifex maximus*, not wishing to move into the *domus publica* (traditionally the dwelling of the *pontifex maximus*), he made part of his own house public and transferred the shrine of Vesta there.[94] Ovid, whose poem on the Roman calendar was

---

[91] See Eck 1984: 129–68 and above.

[92] Which Augustus sometimes used as a place to conduct public business in (cf. Josephus, *AJ* 17.301).

[93] For a full discussion of the relationship between Augustus' house and the temple of Apollo, see Zanker 1988: 49–53, 65–70. For some of the other associations of the site of Augustus' Palatine house, see Wiseman 1984; 1987: 400–3.

[94] Dio 54.27.3. On the incorporation of the shrine of Vesta, see Zanker 1988: 207. In 3 CE, when the entire house was destroyed by fire, it was rebuilt at public expense and Augustus made the entire house state property. See the discussion by Weinstock 1971: 276–81.

completed on the margins of the empire to which he had been banished by Augustus, wrote of the ruler's house:

> Phoebus habet partem, Vestae pars altera cessit;
> quod superest illis, tertius ipse tenet.
> state Palatinae laurus, praetextaque quercu
> stet domus: aeternos tres habet una deos.

Phoebus has one part of the house, another part belongs to Vesta. He himself occupies the rest. May the laurels of the Palatine flourish! May the house, decorated with oak, flourish! A single house holds three eternal gods.

(*Fasti* 4.951–4)

A celebration that might well be thought sinister, coming from the pen of one who had been struck with a thunderbolt mightier than Jupiter's own. Augustus was emphasising his devotion to the worship of the gods and the public good and at the same time blurring the distinction between his own status and that of his divine neighbour and guest.[95] The relationship between public and private was being renegotiated. So was the relationship between men and gods.

---

[95] Possible republican precedents for this kind of appropriation of temples may be found. Filippo Coarelli detects a resemblance between Lucullus' suburban villa and the temple of Fortuna at Praeneste, a town with which Lucullus' family seems to have had some connections ('Architettura sacra e architettura privata nella tarda repubblica' in *Architecture et société. Collection de l'école française de Rome* 66 (1983) 191–217), though recent excavations on the Pincio suggest that Pirro Ligorio's measurements of the remains of Lucullus' villa, on which Coarelli bases much of his argument, are incorrect (Henri Broise and Vincent Jolivet 'Recherches sur les jardins de Lucullus' in *L'urbs: espace urbain et histoire. Collection de l'école française de Rome* 98 (1987) 747–61). Clodius seems to have intended to make the Porticus of Libertas, referred to above, into a public part of a house he intended to build for himself (Birgitta Tamm *Auditorium and palatium* (Stockholm 1963) 37–43). Julius Caesar seems to have been involved in the addition of a pediment to the *domus publica*, when he lived there as *pontifex maximus*, an architectural feature previously only associated with temples (Weinstock 1971: 276–81 and Coarelli 1983b).

CHAPTER FIVE

Prodigal Pleasures

Pleasure was a problem for members of the Roman elite – or so moralists felt. In his treatise on the good life, Seneca stresses the insidious threat posed by the attractions of sensual pleasure, while asserting that only the subhuman will want to surrender themselves completely:

> nam quod ad voluptatem pertinet, licet circumfundatur undique et per omnis vias influat animumque blandimentis suis leniat aliaque ex aliis admoveat, quibus totos partesque nostri sollicitet, quis mortalium cui ullum superest hominis vestigium, per diem noctemque titillari velit et deserto animo corpori operam dare?

> *As far as regards sensual pleasure, though it flows around us on every side and seeps through every opening, though it softens the mind with its charms and leaves no avenue untried in its attempts to seduce us in whole or in part, what mortal who has any claim to be a member of the human race, would choose to have his senses aroused day and night, abandoning the spirit to devote all attention to the body?*

> (Sen. *De vita beata* 5.4)

Seneca's language presents pleasure as fluid, both engulfing and invading its hapless victims. His insistence on its seductive dangers could be read as betraying a certain fascination with pleasure.

He goes on to contrast with some vehemence the unwholesome allure of the life of pleasure with the noble glow of the life of virtue:

> altum quiddam est virtus, excelsum et regale, invictum, infatigabile; voluptas humile, servile, imbecillum, caducum, cuius statio ac domicilium fornices et popinae sunt. virtutem in templo convenies, in foro, in curia, pro muris stantem, pulverulentam, coloratam, callosas habentem manus; voluptatem latitantem saepius ac tenebras captantem circa balinea ac sudatoria ac loca aedilem metuentia, mollem, enervem, mero

atque unguento madentem, pallidam, aut fucatam et medicamentis pollinctam.

Virtue is something lofty, exalted and regal, unconquered, indefatigable, pleasure something low, servile, weak, unstable, whose station and dwelling place are the brothels and taverns. Virtue you will find in the temple, in the forum, in the senate house, defending the city walls, dusty and sunburnt, her hands rough; pleasure you will find most often lurking around the baths and sweating rooms, and places that fear the magistrates, in search of darkness, soft, effete, reeking of wine and perfume, pallid or else painted and made up like a corpse.

(Sen. *De vita beata* 7.3)

Virtue is noble, dry and hard – sunburnt, with roughened hands. Virtue is to be found in public places, pursuing the public good, winning public renown. Pleasure, on the other hand, is wet, soft (*mollis, enervis*) and characteristic of slaves. Pleasure lurks in places associated with sensual indulgence – places which are public but surreptitiously, guiltily so. The ultimate fate of pleasure is not fame, but disgrace and death. The discussion of *mollitia* in chapter two should have made clear some other associations of these attributes – virtue is presented as masculine, pleasure as feminine.[1]

Seneca focuses on unrefined and purchased physical pleasure – associated with the brothel, the tavern, the baths – a potent image, of a kind which plays a prominent role in both ancient and modern representations of Roman life.[2] Pleasure is like a prostitute in its sollicitations and blandishments – and, implicitly, in its venality. Pleasure, to reverse the liquid metaphor employed by Seneca, soaks up one's substance. The kinds of pleasure immediately evoked by Seneca's image were not the only ones to worry Roman moralists. Pleasures of many kinds were the focus of anxiety – somatic pleasures, both coarse and exquisite, and even the cerebral pleasures of litera-

---

[1] This antithesis has precedents in Roman literature and indeed in Greek. Cf. e.g. Cic. *De off.* 1.106; Terence, *Adelphoe* 863–71. On the parallel incompatibility of the life of pleasure and the life of intellectual achievement e.g. Cic. *Pro Cael.* 45–6; Sen. *Ep.* 95.23. A similar contrast is compromised by being placed in the mouth of the hypocrite Eumolpus by Petronius (*Sat.* 88). There seem to have been numerous Hellenistic philosophical treatises on luxury and pleasure (Griffin 1985: 37). In general see R. Joly *Le Thème philosophique des genres de vie dans l'antiquité classique* (Brussels 1956).

[2] Although under the principate entry to the baths was free, perfumes, oils and refreshments, which are often presented as integral parts of the experience of bathing, could be expensive (Janet DeLaine 'Recent research on Roman baths' *Journal of Roman Archaeology* 1 (1988) 11–32).

ture and philosophy (which will receive less attention here). This chapter looks at the rhetoric of denunciations of prodigal pleasures – extravagant pleasures whose ultimate consequence is represented as shame and ruin.

Seneca's pleasure is only implicitly venal. I shall argue that anxieties about money play a major part in the denunciations of pleasure made by Roman moralists. Rome in the late republic and early principate was a city of unparalleled wealth. Various forms of what might be termed conspicuous consumption served to display the riches of individuals, as we have seen in examining Roman anxieties about luxurious building. While buildings had some permanence, adding lustre to the family, expenditure on the ephemeral in the form of public spectacles, chapter three argued, was an even more dramatic display of the spender's wealth, destroyed in the act of exhibition. Yet some part of the benefit from this expenditure was felt to accrue to the community. This final chapter examines another manifestation of wealth – costly pleasures, sexual and sumptuary, which are represented as generating only private pleasure.

Roman moralists harp on the damage done by the descendants of noble families who squander the family fortune and run up vast debts, drinking, feasting, whoring and gambling. Ruin and shame fall on the individual and the family as a consequence. And this has implications for the Roman social hierarchy in general. Individuals, driven by the desire for sensual gratification, fritter away their substance, undermining the foundations of the Roman state.

Denunciations of prodigal pleasures are full of images of fluidity and flux – Seneca's *voluptas* is drenched with unmixed wine and perfume; the brothels, taverns and baths, in which his personification of pleasure lurks, are all associated with the uncontrolled flow of various liquids. The money of the voluptuaries who haunt these places also flows uncontrolled. *Effundo* and *profundo* – 'to pour out', 'to pour forth' – are the verbs habitually used of those who spend without limit on their own pleasures.[3] The Roman social order is itself washed away with the spilt wines, perfumes and bodily effusions – and, of course, the dissipated fortunes – of its incontinent upper classes.

---

[3] *Effundo* – e.g. Cic. *Pro Cael.* 42; *Pro Rosc. Amer.* 68. *Profundo* – e.g. Sall. *Cat.* 5.4; Cic. *In Cat.* 2.10; Tac. *Ann.* 3.55.

PRODIGAL PLEASURES

PRODIGALITY AND MORAL DECLINE

The irresistible attractions of luxury and sexual adventure were often held responsible for particular political crises and suspected of posing a general threat to Roman public life, in the writings of Roman moralists, as we have seen in earlier chapters. The contrast of past poverty and virtue with present wealth and decadence is generally dismissed by modern scholars as a tedious commonplace, whose literary history may be traced by the zealous but whose frequent recurrence requires no real explanation.[4] But this 'commonplace' is a preoccupation of countless Roman texts which we must surely see as reflecting the anxieties of those who wrote them.

Livy, in the preface to his history, laments the deleterious effects of Rome's increased prosperity on the morals of its citizens:

> adeo quanto rerum minus, tanto minus cupiditatis erat; nuper divitiae avaritiam et abundantes voluptates desiderium per luxum atque libidinem pereundi perdendique omnia invexere.

> *For it is true that when men had fewer possessions, they were correspondingly modest in their desires. Recently riches have brought avarice and abundant pleasures the longing to carry luxury and lust to the point of personal ruin and universal perdition.*

> *(pr. 11)*

Luxury and lust are agents of destruction both particular and general. Money, pleasure and ruin are inextricably linked.[5]

Livy speaks in general terms. Other texts focus on the particular manifestations of luxury and licence. Polybius, writing in the second century BCE, remarks on the virtue of Scipio in contrast to his peers:

> *For some young men indulged in affairs with boys, others in affairs with courtesans and many of them in music and drinking parties and all the expenses associated with such activities, for, during the time of the war with Perseus, they had rapidly taken over the licence of the Greeks in these*

---

[4] Cf. Friedländer 1964 II: 282 (= Eng.tr. II: 143) 'an exaggerated commonplace'; Edward Courtney *A commentary on the satires of Juvenal* (London 1980) 'the eternal commonplace of Roman moralising' (on 6.255).

[5] This is a preoccupation especially but not exclusively characteristic of the literature of Augustan Rome. Cf. e.g. Hor. *Carm.* 1.12; 2.15; 3.2; 3.6. Under Tiberius: Vell. Pat. 2.1.1; Val. Max. 4.4. and, later, Sen. *Ep.* 87.9–11. For a discussion of the relationship Romans perceived between luxury and decadence, see Veyne 1990: 471.

matters. So great was this eruption of self-indulgence among the young men that many paid a talent for a boy bought for sexual gratification and many paid three hundred drachmas for a jar of caviar. Marcus Cato was outraged by this and, in a speech to the people, complained that one might be quite convinced of the decline of the republic, when pretty boys cost more than fields and jars of caviar more than ploughmen.

(31.25.4–5)

Polybius, a Greek living in Rome, integrated some of the preoccupations of the Romans he mixed with into his history. Young Romans, infected with foreign habits, spend their money on sexual gratification, drinking, music and expensive delicacies.[6] Polybius' summary of the speech of Cato makes that vigilant guardian of antique Roman morality express some of the preoccupations that were to be most characteristic of later attacks on luxury and moral decline. Cato inveighs against young men who spend vast sums gratifying their lust and greed, thereby undermining the state. He makes his point by contrasting these illegitimate expenses with others which are entirely justifiable – on agricultural land and slaves to work it.[7] Expenditure on the latter enhances, rather than consumes, one's substance.

Ancient writers differed in their views of the point from which Roman moral decline might be dated. Livy favoured the return, in 187 BCE, of Manlius Vulso's forces from their successful campaign in Asia, bearing precious spoils – and the seeds of eastern vices, including an interest in exquisite foods (39.6.7). Polybius presented the war with Perseus in 168 BCE as the critical time (31.25). The annalist L. Calpurnius Piso favoured 154 BCE as the turning point – *a quo tempore pudicitiam subversam*, 'when chastity was subverted' (*ap.* Pliny *NH* 17.244 = Piso fr. 38 *HRR*). Sallust selects the destruction of Carthage in 146 BCE as the event which set loose among Romans the desire for money and the desire for power, two lesser evils, to be succeeded, in their turn, by the worse ills of luxury and lust, which

---

[6] On the 'Greekness' of the life of pleasure, see Griffin 1985: 5–14. But see chapters two and three above on the problematic significance of designating certain practices as 'foreign'.

[7] Cf. Pliny's complaint, centuries later, that, while in earlier times critics of luxury complained that a cook cost more than a horse, in his own day an unlimited price might be commanded for a cook with the skill to make his master bankrupt – *qui peritissime censum domini mergit* (*NH* 9.67). Livy, too, complains at the value accorded to cooks (39.6).

accompanied the dictator Sulla's army back from Asia (*Cat.* 10).[8] While they differ as to the precise point marking the beginning of the end of Roman virtue, Roman moralists generally agree on the nature of the changes which took place.[9] Prosperity and foreign influence stimulated appetites until they became insatiable and Rome consumed itself.

The link between luxury, licence and the financial ruin of individuals plays a vital role in Sallust's analysis of the breakdown of the republic.[10] The aristocrat Catiline's luxurious habits have undermined his finances to such an extent that revolution is the only remedy.[11] As Shaw observes, the career of Catiline, in Sallust's narrative, is a paradigmatic example of the terrible consequences of luxurious habits for young Romans. His spending, like his desires, was out of control – *alieni adpetens, sui profusus, ardens in cupiditatibus*, 'covetous of other people's property, reckless with his own, fearsome in his desires' (*Cat.* 5.4.). Catiline finds supporters among others of similar habits: *quicumque impudicus, ganeo, aleator, manu, ventre, pene bona patria laceraverat* . . ., 'whatever wanton, glutton or gambler had, by means of his hand, belly or penis, ravaged his ancestral fortune' (Sall. *Cat.* 14.2). The term *patria* evokes not only the fortune of one's father but also the fortune of one's fatherland – the Roman republic. We should note the blurring of notions of financial and moral damage – a recurrent feature of attacks on prodigality.

PLEASURE AND RUIN

The link between pleasure, extravagance, debt and ruin is insisted on in a great variety of modes of literature. Cicero's speech in defence of

---

[8] See Donald Earl *The political thought of Sallust* (Cambridge 1961) 41–59; Earl 1967: 17–19; A.W. Lintott 'Imperial expansion and moral decline in the Roman empire' *Historia* 31 (1972) 626–38. Cf. Juvenal on the frugality of early Rome – 11.77–119; 6.286–351 (though echoes of Ov. *Ars* 3. 105–28 suggest Juvenal too may be parodying moralising clichés).

[9] Though some writers do not subscribe to the view that all change has been for the worse, for instance Lucretius 5.1440–57. Seneca at times suggests that his contemporaries have, through philosophy, the opportunity to be better men than their rough ancestors e.g. *Ep.* 90.44–6 (though they lived innocent lives, early men were not acquainted with the wisdom which is a necessary part of true virtue). Elsewhere, he claims that human affairs should be seen as remaining on a level (*De ben.* 1.10).

[10] See Brent Shaw 'Debt in Sallust' *Latomus* 34 (1975) 187–96. There is a similar emphasis in Cic. *In Cat.* 1.8; 1.13–14.

[11] Cf. Velleius Paterculus' picture of Gaius Curio (2.48.3), discussed in chapter two above.

his younger friend Caelius (made in 56 BCE) is partly preoccupied with negotiating the limits of acceptable self-indulgence. He concedes that his client takes a young man's pleasure in love affairs but denies that he is a pursuer of prodigal pleasures. In him you will find, he argues, *nulla luxuries . . . nulli sumptus, nullum aes alienum, nulla conviviorum ac lustrorum libido: quod quidem vitium ventris ac gurgitis non modo non minuit aetas hominibus sed etiam auget*, 'no luxury, no extravagance, no debts, no craving for parties and low eating-houses: those vices of the stomach and gullet which increase rather than diminish, as a man grows older' (*Pro Cael.* 44). A connection is made here, as in countless other texts castigating the prodigal, between extravagance, debts, gluttony and low haunts. Sexual pleasures are placed in a slightly different category on this occasion, but Cicero has particular reasons for his attempt to distinguish between sex on the one hand and gluttony on the other in his defence of Caelius, whose affair with the wealthy widow Clodia was widely known (and part of Cicero's case depended on acknowledging it). Some allowance may be made for youthful licence, argues Cicero, but let a young man not squander his patrimony nor be crippled by usury (42).[12] For Cicero, the long-term damage caused by pleasure is measured, to a large degree, in financial terms.[13]

The seriously prodigal must look forward to poverty, debt and disgrace. Moralists dwell on their shame. Tacitus tells of those excluded from the senate because of their poverty (*Ann.* 2.48). The incorrigibly extravagant habits of the prodigal aristocrat even reduce him to earning his living as a gladiator. Juvenal writes: *et quadringentis nummis condire gulosum\fictile; sic veniunt ad miscellanea ludi*, 'Reduced to eating their 400 sesterces' worth of dinner off earthenware, they finally descend to eating the mash served in the gladiatorial school' (11.19–20).[14] Having squandered all their material resources, they squander their reputations, too. But just as some voluptuaries are represented as taking perverse pleasure in consuming their

---

[12] Also stressed at 28 and 48. The notion that a certain degree of licence is to be allowed aristocratic young men (before they settle down to a life of respectability and public service) is a common one. Cf. Juvenal 8.163–5; Sen. *Contr.* 2.6.

[13] Cf. Cic. *Pro Cael.* 17.

[14] Other examples of the ultimate poverty of the prodigal: Hor. *Sat.* 1.2.4–11; 2.2.94–9; Juv. 1.33 (*comesa nobilitate*, 'nobility consumed', gnomically conveys the cause of the aristocracy's decline); 1.59–62; 1.88–109; 11.1–55; Sen. *Ep.* 87.10; *De ben.* 1.10.2; Tac. *Ann.* 3.55.

fortunes, so others are presented as taking even more perverse pleasure in embracing positions of conspicuous degradation.[15]

Moralists lament prodigality – but it is an offence to be regretted in some far more than in others. No-one complains about freedmen ruining themselves through conspicuous consumption (though they certainly complain about their wealth and extravagance – and their ascent of the social scale).[16] Here, as in the case of luxurious building, what matters is not only what you spend your money on, but also who you are. The prodigal are children of the rich. They spend money which is regularly described as inherited.[17]

The prodigal pose a threat to society, in part because, by surrendering to the attractions of the life of pleasure, they call into question the desirability of the life of virtue. But they also disrupt the social order by causing money to flow outside its proper channels. Gambling – an activity regularly attributed to the profligate – was an emblem of the uncontrolled and pointless flow of money from their hands.[18] For moralists, money should stay within the family, allowing the sons to enjoy the same social position as their fathers, and contributing to the general stability of Roman society.

MAD EXTRAVAGANCE

The notion of prodigality is not only invoked by literary texts lamenting the moral decline of Rome or orators denouncing the vices of their opponents. One of the most curious features of Roman attitudes to extravagance – though one seldom remarked on – is the treatment of the prodigal under the law. The prodigal were taken account of in Roman law from a very early period. Later Roman jurists cited a provision in the Twelve Tables – the earliest Roman law code, formulated in the mid fifth century BCE:

---

[15] On the glamour which was also associated with appearance in the arena, see Hopkins 1983 ch. 1; Wiedemann forthcoming; Edwards forthcoming b.

[16] Cf. chapter four above.

[17] E.g. *bona patria laceraverat*, 'he had ravaged his ancestral fortune' (Sall. *Cat.* 14); *patrimoniis amissis*, 'their patrimonies lost' (37); *patrimonia sua effuderent*, 'they squandered their ancestral fortunes' (Cic. *In Cat.* 2.10); *consumptis patrimoniis*, 'patrimonies used up' (Cic. *De fin.* 2.23); *caret omni maiorum censu*, 'he lacks all his ancestral fortune' (Juv. 1.59–60); *aere paterno*, 'ancestral fortune' (Juv. 11.39); *foedissimum patrimoniorum exitum, culina*, 'the foulest end for ancestral wealth, the kitchen' (Sen. *De ben.* 1.10.2).

[18] Examples of gambling as a feature of the prodigal lifestyle include: Sall. *Cat.* 14.2; Cic. *Phil.* 2.56; Hor. *Carm.* 3.24; Juv. 1.87–93; 11.171–8. Gambling seems to have been illegal in Rome, except during the Saturnalia in December (*Dig.* 11.5.2, Paul, 3, Ulpian, 4, Paul).

lege duodecim tabularum prodigo interdicitur bonorum suorum administratio, quod moribus quidem ab initio introductum est. sed solent hodie praetores vel praesides, si talem hominem invenerint, qui neque tempus neque finem expensarum habet, sed bona sua dilacerando et dissipando profudit, curatorem ei dare exemplo furiosi.

The law of the Twelve Tables prevents a prodigal's dealing with his property and this was originally introduced by custom. Today, however, praetors and governors, if they encounter persons who have set neither time limit nor boundary to their expenditure, but squandered their substance by extravagance and dissipation are accustomed to appoint a curator for them on the analogy of a lunatic.

(*Digest* 27.10.1 pr. Ulpian)

These persons were not bankrupt. They might not even be in debt. Yet their alleged abuse of their own property – *bona sua* – was thought to be sufficient cause for depriving them of control over their finances. Being placed in the charge of a *curator* brought a range of other restrictions besides those on engaging in financial activities.[19] Numerous titles in the *Digest* lay down regulations governing the responsibilities of *curatores*.

The prodigal were, like the mad, not to be trusted to look after their own money.[20] One might compare the words used by the mother of prodigal sons in her appeal to the magistrate to stop them from squandering their resources. They may appear sane, she says, but, without intervention, they will meet the fate of the mad – *furiosum exitum* (*Dig.* 26.5.12.2, Ulpian). No doubt the magistrate's decision to appoint a curator was often (as apparently here) in response to a request from members of the prodigal's family, who felt they had an interest in the property in question. The interests of the family certainly seem to be a concern in the words used by the magistrate, quoted by the jurist Paul:

quando tibi bona paterna avitaque nequitia tua disperdis liberosque tuos ad egestatem perducis ob eam rem tibi aere commercioque interdico.

---

[19] The oath of a prodigal carries no weight (*Dig.* 12.2.35.1, Paul). A prodigal may not initiate an action for fraud (*Dig.* 4.3.11.1, Ulpian).

[20] Though note the distinction drawn by Alan Watson (*The law of the Twelve Tables* (Princeton 1975) 78) who observes that, unlike *furiosi*, *prodigi* were thought capable of forming an intention, so were subject to *interdictio*.

PRODIGAL PLEASURES

Since, by your wickedness you are squandering the property inherited from your father and grandfather, and thereby reducing your children to poverty, I forbid you to deal in money or exchange.

(Paul, *Sent.* 3.4a.7)

The offence is characterised as the abuse of a charge entrusted by one's progenitors on behalf of one's progeny. Yet this is still a dramatic intervention on the part of the state in the individual's right to dispose of property of which he or she is the legal owner.

The state had traditionally been seen as having an interest in the property of individual citizens which might justify such intervention. The elder Pliny, speaking of the early republic, remarks – *agrum male colere censorium probrum iudicabatur*, 'To neglect one's land was judged an offence meriting censorial reprimand' (Pliny, *NH* 18.11).[21] Claude Nicolet suggests that the censors' interest in punishing the neglect of land was not a moral penalty but a reflection of the fact that social status was dependent at least in part on property qualification.[22] Rather we should recognise that in Roman texts social status is a moral issue.[23] The censors' responsibilities for the moral and the economic are not easily distinguished. Censors reproved luxurious habits and noted down moral reprimands on the census. The legitimate intervention of the state in the affairs of the family was a distinctive feature of the Roman state, according to Dionysius of Halicarnassus, writing under Augustus (20.13.2–3).[24] Legal controls on the 'prodigal' were not only concerned with protecting money for the individual family. The state was felt to have an interest in the financial stability of individual families.

The complaints about the misuse of money which abound in the writings of Roman moralists might be taken to suggest they felt that money should not be a means of marking social status.[25] On the contrary, such complaints serve rather to validate the role of money as an agent of social distinction, so long as it operates in conjunction with other criteria. The implications of complaints about ruinous extravagance are not that money should not play a role in marking social status. The problem is rather that the wrong people have

---

[21] Cf. Gellius 4.12.1–3.   [22] Nicolet 1980: 79.   [23] Cf. Astin 1988: 22–3.
[24] Cf. introduction.   [25] E.g. Juv. 1.110; 2.135.

money, on the one hand, and that, on the other, those whose wealth is justifiable, because inherited, use it in the wrong way.

FAMILY FORTUNES AND SOCIAL HIERARCHY

The great expense involved in embarking on a political career in Rome, under both republic and principate, is a commonplace of modern scholarship.[26] To qualify for election to a senatorial post, it was necessary in the late republic to attain the census of 400,000 sesterces. All contestants were, therefore, prosperous men, but fortunes were generally tied up in land, whose sale might prove both inconvenient and embarrassing. Those who had little ready capital were unwilling to dispose of landed property to raise money for election expenses. Instead, the politically ambitious regularly borrowed vast sums of money from their peers to finance the attainment of influential positions, in the hope that, once successful, they would be in a position to discharge their debts.

There seems to have been almost no shame attached to indebtedness in itself. Borrowing and lending were manifestations of trust – *fides* – part of the social and moral cement that gave the Roman elite cohesion.[27] Seneca observes that *beneficia*, 'benefits', are what, above all, hold a society together (*De ben.* 1.4.2). The network of social obligations consequent on widespread borrowing was of particular importance in a political culture which emphasised personal connection rather than ideological programme as the source of allegiance.[28] Large-scale lending and borrowing appear to have been especially common in the late republic. Cicero's correspondence is full of the complex finances of his family and peers. Some, like Julius Caesar, did very well from this system. At one point during the 60s BCE, Caesar was said to have been in debt to the tune of 25 million sesterces.[29] Later, after the conquest of Gaul, he was one of the richest

---

[26] Cf. Hopkins 1983: 74–9; Shatzman 1975: 84–98, 143–76.

[27] Lenders were expected to scrutinise carefully the character of those they lent to. Seneca in the *De beneficiis* considers at length the question of who one should lend money to or borrow from. A jurist suggests the lender is himself to blame if he loses his money as a result of making a loan to a spendthrift (*Dig.* 17.1.12.11, Ulpian).

[28] M. Frederiksen 'Caesar, Cicero and the problem of debt' *JRS* 56 (1966) 128–41. Preoccupation with gifts and loans among the elite is particularly evident in Cic. *De off.* 2.78–85; Sen. *Ep.* 87.5–8; *De ben. passim.*   [29] Plut. *Jul.* 5.4; Dio 37.8.2.

men in Rome. Others, like Catiline and some of his adherents, who failed to attain the lucrative posts which would have enabled them to repay their campaigning debts, were ruined by this system – a material contribution to the breakdown of order in the first century BCE.[30] Moralising writers were, it seems, often themselves heavily implicated in these networks of borrowing and lending (Cicero and Seneca are obvious examples).[31] Their preoccupation with expenditure and debt is hardly surprising.

From the time of Tiberius, the popular assemblies ceased to have much real control over elections to higher magistracies. There was consequently far less incentive for those seeking election to provide lavish spectacles for the Roman people (the provision of games in the city of Rome was fast becoming a virtual prerogative of the emperor). But election was still expensive. Candidates were expected to entertain their peers and the emperor in the appropriate style. And 'favours' (in the form of gifts or loans) for potential supporters could also prove a major expense.[32] Even those who did not particularly desire political success but wished nevertheless to cut a dashing figure in Roman society might face very substantial outgoings.

The turnover rate of families boasting members in the senate was high in the republic and higher still in the principate. Political careers were very expensive and consequent impoverishment has been seen as a major factor behind the degree of mobility evident in the Roman upper classes.[33] Individual senatorial and equestrian families experienced apparently violent changes in their financial circumstances in the space of one or two generations. Yet despite all this, some Romans seem to have wanted to view the senate as largely hereditary in its membership.[34] Such continuity had to be underwritten by continuity of family fortune. This goes some way towards explaining the frequency with which anxieties about the impoverishment of aristocratic families are aired in moralising literature.

Emperors sometimes felt it was incumbent upon them to supple-

---

[30] The seriousness of debt among members of the elite towards the end of the republic is emphasised by Frederiksen 1966. Roman law on bankruptcy is clearly set out by J.A. Crook 'A study in decoction' *Latomus* 26 (1967) 361–76. The *lex Iulia de bonis cedendis* modified some of the asperities of earlier legislation on bankruptcy. In general, members of the elite seem to have been unwilling to invoke the law against their social equals (though cf. the case of Mark Antony's father, discussed by Frederiksen).

[31] On Cicero, see Frederiksen 1966: 131–2; on Seneca, see Griffin 1976: 289.

[32] See Richard Saller *Personal patronage under the early empire* (Cambridge 1982) ch. 4.

[33] Hopkins 1983: 31–200. Cf. chapter four above.   [34] Hopkins 1983: 31, 36–7.

ment the finances of aristocratic families who had fallen on hard times. In 4 CE, Augustus is said to have provided funds to enable eighty senators to reach the minimum census requirement for their order (Dio 55.13). Augustus' wife Livia gave money for dowries (Dio 58.2). Tiberius, too, helped some who appealed to him (Tac. *Ann.* 2.37). Others, characterised as poor through their own prodigality, were not felt to merit imperial charity, despite the nobility of their families.

> ceterum ut honestam innocentium paupertatem levavit, ita prodigos et ob flagitia egentis . . . movit senatu aut sponte cedere passus est.

> *However, while he was liberal to those who were poor through no fault of their own, he removed from the senate or allowed to drop out those who were prodigal and needy as a result of their own vices.*

> (Tac. *Ann.* 2.48)

Virtus – that quality which marked out the good Roman – consisted of a complex mixture of ancestry, wealth and personal merit. The distinction between those deserving help, who are said to be poor through no fault of their own, and those who are denied help, on the grounds that their poverty was caused by their own extravagance, is an important one.[35] Not all declines in fortune were seen to be the result of luxurious living.[36] But what exactly constituted inappropriate expenditure and for whom? Prodigality was not always easy to identify.

These stories are striking illustrations of fluctuations in the financial circumstances of Roman elite families. They also show the obligation that was felt to lie on emperors to repair the fortunes of those whose ancestry supposedly entitled them to a place in public life. There was considerable pressure in support of a vision of elite continuity. Emperors were able, too, to demonstrate their own power, by arresting the downward mobility of aristocratic families, such as the Varrones or the Cornelii Sullae. The Roman elite, most of whom enjoyed their position at least in part as a consequence of their

---

[35] Tacitus represents the reprehensible emperor Nero as ignoring this distinction and offering financial assistance even to the prodigal (*Ann.* 13.34).

[36] Similarly, one might compare the language Sallust uses to describe the financial circumstances of Julius Caesar at a time when he was deeply in debt (as a consequence of what are implied to be legitimate expenses) with the very different terms he uses to describe Catiline and his supporters (Shaw 1975: 193).

family prestige (to varying degrees, of course), had a significant investment in the notion of a stable and hereditary aristocracy. Those at the apex of the social hierarchy – the emperors – had a particular interest in its solidity. But the flow of money, also a major determinant of social status, out of the coffers of some and into the coffers of others, always threatened to subvert this illusion of stability.

THE EXPENSE OF PLEASURE

Roman moralists regularly stress the ruinous expenses incurred by those who live for the pursuit of pleasure. Pliny's *Naturalis historia* is full of enormous sums expended by luxurious Romans, for instance the 100 million sesterces a year spent by Romans on pearls and perfumes from the east (*NH* 12.84).[37] Attacks on luxury often focus on food, which perhaps best symbolises the ephemeral nature of prodigal pleasures.[38] The elder Pliny exclaims with horror that some men are prepared to pay the price of three cooks for a fish (*NH* 9.67). Juvenal expresses outrage at the expenditure of 6,000 sesterces on a mullet.[39]

Insatiable greed for the novel and rare fuelled ever more exhaustive searches of the farthest corners of land and sea, according to the moralists' picture of the development of luxury. Delicacies from far-flung places were allegedly valued by voluptuaries, not only for the pleasure of their taste, but also for their rarity and expense. Sulla's army, according to Sallust, corrupted by their stay in Asia, scoured land and sea to gratify their palates (*Cat.* 13.3).[40] Seneca complains: 'Men eat to vomit and vomit to eat. Their dishes are brought from every corner of the earth – and yet they do not even bother to digest them' (*Ad Helviam* 10.3).[41]

Antony was sometimes held up as the most avid of Rome's gluttons, only outdone by Cleopatra herself:

---

[37] These numbers are totally unreliable. The textual problems associated with the transcription of numerals are notorious.

[38] Though attacks on luxury were not, of course, exclusively concerned with ephemeral products. Cf. chapter four on luxurious building. On the Roman passion for fine fabrics, exotic marbles, precious stones and other rarities, see Friedländer 1964 II.

[39] Juv. 4. Cf. the tirade against luxurious eating in Juv. 11.

[40] Cf. Juv. 5.92. Suet. *Vit.* 13; Gell. 6.16.6; Pliny, *NH* 19.52, 26.43; Sen. *Ep.* 89.22; Juv. 11.14 (and Mayor 1893 *ad loc.*). Friedländer 1964 II: 285–315 (= Eng. tr. II: 131–73) gives numerous references to ancient discussions of the expense of luxury foods.

[41] Seneca elsewhere compares over-refined food to vomit (*Ep.* 95.42).

nam cum Antonius quicquid mari aut terra aut etiam caelo gigneretur
ad satiandum ingluviem suam natum existimans, faucibus ac dentibus
suis subderet, eaque re captus de Romano imperio facere vellet
Aegyptium regnum, Cleopatra uxor, quae vinci a Romanis nec luxuria
dignaretur, sponsione provocavit insumere se posse in unam cenam
sestertium centies.

*Antony considered all that was produced on land, sea or even in the air
existed only to satisfy his maw and conquered it by chewing and swallow-
ing. Moreover it was because of his greed that he wished to subordinate the
kingdom of Egypt to Rome. But his wife Cleopatra could not bear to be
outdone in luxury by the Romans so she made a wager with him that she
could consume ten million sesterces in a single dinner.*

(Macrob. *Sat.* 3.17.15)

Antony agrees to the bet and looks on as Cleopatra wins by dissolving
a vast pearl in vinegar and then drinking it.[42] The substances
consumed by the luxurious came mainly from the east; luxurious
practices, too, were regularly alleged to have had their origin in
eastern lands.[43] Antony was drawn into a perverse battle of competitive consumption with an eastern female. Even here, he lost.

Luxurious food was not the only ephemeral pleasure Roman
voluptuaries were alleged to have squandered their money on.
Expensive, rare and evanescent, too, were the wines, perfumes and
flowers which were also characteristic features of the voluptuary's
convivium (evening party).[44] Seneca describes two notorious prodi-
gals, indulging every one of their senses:

aspice Nomentanum et Apicium, terrarum ac maris, ut isti vocant,
bona concoquentis et super mensam recognoscentis omnium gentium
animalia; vide hos eosdem in suggestu rosae despectantis popinam
suam, aures vocum sono, spectaculis oculos, saporibus palatum suum
delectantes; mollibus lenibusque fomentis totum lacessitur eorum
corpus et, ne nares interim cessent, odoribus variis inficitur locus ipse,
in quo luxuriae parentatur.

*Look at Nomentanus and Apicius, as they digest what they term the
blessings of land and sea and view the products of every nation heaped on*

---

[42] Cf. Pliny *NH* 9.120–1.   [43] This association is discussed in chapter two above.

[44] Perfumes and roses as ingredients in the *convivium*: Lucretius 4.1131–3; Val. Max. 2.6.1;
Mart. 6.80 (roses from Egypt); Juv. 6.297, 303; 9.128–9; 11.121. See too descriptions of the
banquets of self-indulgent emperors: Suet. *Calig.* 37; Suet. *Nero* 27, 30; SHA *Elag.* 19, 21,
23, 24, 31; *Verus* 5. The elder Pliny describes the provenance and cost of rare wines (*NH* 14),
perfumes (*NH* 13), flowers (*NH* 21).

their table. See them, too, lying on a mass of roses surveying their buffet, delighting their ears with singing, their eyes with spectacles, their palates with flavours. Their bodies are aroused with soft and gentle stuffs and, so that their noses shall not be missed out, the chamber in which sacrifices are made to the god luxury, is suffused with a variety of perfumes.

(*De vita beata* 11.4)

The *convivium* is here, as often, represented as the characteristic setting for prodigal consumption. In Seneca's description, the overwhelming accumulation of sensual delights cloys, repels and fascinates.

Seneca's voluptuaries experience the simultaneous stimulation of all their senses – or almost all. Sexual pleasure, too, often appears in moralising descriptions of the luxurious *convivium*. The after-dinner entertainers and the beautiful slave boys who serve the food and wine are often represented as providers of sexual gratification.[45] This, also, was a costly pleasure. The vast sums spent on beautiful slave boys are often mentioned by moralists.[46] Entertainers were part of the expense of the perfect party and were often themselves imported luxuries from exotic regions.[47] Sometimes prostitutes are explicitly listed as part of the after-dinner entertainment.[48] Often singers, dancers and mimes are themselves viewed as sexually available.[49]

Some attacks on prodigality mention the sums spent by the prodigal on engaging the services of prostitutes, others refer to brothels.[50] However, many texts imply that sex is expensive not only

[45] Sexual pleasure as an expected sequel to a banquet: Cic. *Phil.* 2.104–5; *De fin.* 2.23; Sen. *Ep.* 47.7; 95.23. On slaves as attendants at *convivia*, see J.H. D'Arms 'Slaves at Roman *convivia*' in W.J. Slater ed. *Dining in a classical context* (Ann Arbor 1991) 171–83.
[46] Polyb. 31.25.4–5; Hor. *Sat.* 2.8.10; Sen. *Ep.* 27.5; Pliny, *NH* 7.56; Juv. 5.55–6; 11.147–8; Mart. 1.58; 3.62.1; 9.23.11–12; 9.60.3–6; 9.74.6; 11.56.11–12; Suet. *Jul.*47. Slaves of both sexes seem to have been expected to provide sexual services for their masters (see M.I. Finley *Ancient slavery and modern ideology* (London 1980) 95–6; K.R. Bradley *Slaves and masters in the Roman world: a study in social control* (Brussels 1984) 115–37).
[47] For examples of singers, see: Gell. 19.9; Macrob. *Sat.* 2.4.28; players: Pliny, *Ep.* 7.24; Pet. *Sat.* 53; Macrob. *Sat.* 2.7.17; 3.14.4; dancers: Pliny, *Ep.* 9.17; Hor. *Sat.* 1.2.1; Mart. 5.78.26–8; 6.71; 14.210; Juv. 11.162–70; Macrob. *Sat.* 3.14.4. On entertainment at *convivia*, see C.P. Jones 'Dinner-theater' in W.J. Slater ed. *Dining in a classical context* (Ann Arbor 1991) 185–98.　[48] E.g. Pliny, *Ep.* 9.17.
[49] E.g. Juv. 11.162–70; Cic. *Pro Mur.* 13. On the association, common in Roman texts, between the provision of entertainment and the provision of sexual gratification see Edwards forthcoming b.
[50] E.g. Polybius 37.25.4; Sen. *De vita beata* 7.3. Hans Herter (Die Soziologie der antiken Prostitution' *JbAC* 3 (1960) 70–111) gathers together a great deal of material on prostitutes. For a highly coloured evocation of prostitution in Rome, see Violaine Vonoyeke *La Prostitution en Grèce et à Rome* (Paris 1990). In some legal texts, spending money on prostitutes is a characteristic sign of a prodigal, e.g. *Dig.* 41.4.8, Julian.

with prostitutes but with any woman who is not one's wife (or any boy). The love poets regularly complain about the venality of their mistresses.[51] But the connection between extramarital sex and the loss of money is not a necessary one. Sexual pleasure costs the giver nothing, Ovid argues (*Ars* 3.83–100). One might trace in texts which harp on the cost of illicit sex an implicit concern for the fruitlessness of the expense of semen in pursuit of pleasure which does not aim at the engendering of legitimate children.[52]

Sometimes the extravagant are pictured as making money from sex –though only young men and women are in a position to take on a receptive role with profit). Sallust describes some of the female supporters of Catiline whose extravagance is on the same scale as that of his male supporters. In their youth, he claims, they were able to support such extravagance by prostitution – *primo ingentis sumptus stupro corporis toleraverant*. Later, the ravages of age closed off this avenue and their debts mounted, hence their support for revolution (Sall. *Cat.* 24.3).[53] One of the charges made by Cicero against Antony is that he prostituted himself as a young man to support his extravagant habits (Cic. *Phil.* 2.44–5).[54] Chastity (*pudicitia*) could itself be seen as a squandered resource. The place of the pursuit of sexual pleasure in the life of the prodigal is not as straightforward as it might at first seem. The link between luxury and lust can be seen as one of analogy, each offence being further blackened by its juxtaposition with the other.[55]

Pleasure, for the prodigal, is directly correlated with expense, in some moralising attacks. Juvenal observes: *magis illa iuvant quae pluris emuntur*, 'Those things bring most pleasure, whose price is highest' (11.16). By implication, the luxurious are mistaken in their attempt to measure pleasure in monetary terms. Roman satirists, in

[51] E.g. Prop. 2.23; Ov. *Ars* 1.419–20; 3.529.
[52] Artemidorus, in his book on dream interpretation (dating from the late second century CE), suggests that to dream of having sex with a prostitute is a bad thing for it portends fruitless expense (1.78, discussed by Foucault 1990, part 1). Heath (1982, ch. 1) discusses nineteenth-century analogies between the 'spending' of semen and money in the pursuit of unfruitful sexual pleasure with prostitutes. Cf. the discussion in chapter two above of the association in many Roman texts between sexual excess and effeminisation.
[53] Luxury and extravagance as feminine vices – cf. Juv. 6.352, 505–10 (luxury was often held to effeminise men – cf. chapter two above).
[54] Discussed in chapter two above. Cf. Cicero's attack on Gabinius (*Post red. in sen.* 11). In his attack on Clodia in the *Pro Caelio* Cicero perhaps implies that Clodia bought the sexual favours of the young men she consorted with (38).
[55] For examples of such juxtaposition, see e.g. Sall. *Cat.* 13.3–4; Cic. *In Verr.* 2.1.3; Sen. *Ep.* 99.13.

particular, do not condemn all pleasures in themselves but offer an alternative model of the life of pleasures (in moderation) which does not require ruinous expense.[56]

The prodigal are presented, in many of these attacks, as motivated as much by the desire for display as by the desire for pleasure. They are accused of seeking notoriety through their extravagance (for instance, Sen. *Ep.* 122.14; Mart. 12.41). Their goal, then, is not only the attainment of particularly delightful physical sensations, but also to exceed their peers in the lavishness of their hospitality and their capacity to consume.[57] Luxury is heavily implicated in the competitive negotiation of social status. Moralists castigate the luxurious for fomenting an inflationary spiral of conspicuous consumption which will bring ruin on themselves and on others who attempt to compete.

LOW PLEASURES

Expense is not the only concern in denunciations of the prodigal. In attacking the prodigal, moralists frequently associate sensual pleasure with 'lower' beings, such as the poor, slaves and animals. Brothels, taverns, gambling dens, baths – the public haunts of venal pleasure – are regularly presented as especially attractive to low persons – slaves, in particular. Low pleasures are described as a phenomenon of promiscuous urban life, in contrast to the virtuous simplicity of the countryside.[58] Columella denounces the pastimes of urban slaves (*De re rust.* 1.8.2). They are all given to *otiis, campo, circo, theatris, aleae, popinae, lupanaribus*, 'indolence, promenading, the circus, the theatres, gambling, the taverns, the brothels'.[59] In general, though, as was emphasised in the introduction, Roman moralists

---

[56] E.g. Hor. *Sat.* 2.2, 2.7; Juv. 11 and 14.

[57] Cf. the story of the bet between Antony and Cleopatra quoted above. Pliny (*NH* 19.67) tells with horror of an ex-consul in the time of the emperor Caligula who spent 8,000 sesterces on a mullet and challenged all *prodigi* to outdo him.

[58] Varr. *De agr.* 3.1.1–2 and 2.1.1–2. The city is associated with indolence, pleasure and foreign influence. Cf. Plautus, *Vid.* 20–55, *Most.* 1–83; Terence, *Adelphoe* 860–7 (though in comedy urban refinement tends to be presented rather more positively. For a discussion of representations of town and country in Roman comedy, see Hunter 1985 ch. 4).

[59] Cf. Hor. *Epist.* 1.14.14–22 – the pleasures of master and slave are contrasted: the master chooses the refined simplicity of country life, the slave *ludos et balnea . . . fornix et uncta popina*, 'the games and baths . . . the brothel and the greasy tavern'. One might compare the desires regularly attributed to slaves in Roman comedy (e.g. Plaut. *Curc.* 185; *Most.* 64; *Stichus* 689–772). Note, too, the sensual excesses of the freedman Trimalchio in Petronius, *Satyricon*.

show strikingly little interest in castigating the vices of the poor – except when these 'low' vices are allegedly taken up by the rich.

Cicero's attacks on Mark Antony (when Antony was attempting to appropriate the resources and position of Julius Caesar, after the latter's death) include passages of some of the most ferocious invective in surviving Latin literature. Cicero's Antony offends against virtually every rule of aristocratic propriety. Having obtained many of the rich possessions of Pompey (at a knock-down price), he manages to squander them in an astonishingly short space of time. Cicero exclaims at his voracious ability to consume Pompey's substance – 'whole wine-bins were given as presents to the vilest persons. Actors snatched some things, actresses others. The house was full of gamblers and drunks. Whole days were devoted to drinking, in every room in the house; on top of all this (for he doesn't always have luck on his side) were the frequent gambling losses . . . Such profligacy could devour, not just a single patrimony, however substantial, but whole cities and kingdoms' (*Phil.* 2.66–8). Cicero emphasises Antony's drinking and gambling. Another important strain in Cicero's criticism is the lowness of the company Antony keeps. He consorts with slaves, actors and pimps, sharing their pleasures (cf. *Phil.* 2.58; 2.101).

Antony consumes indiscriminately, on a superhuman scale. He has abandoned the bodily control required in one of his status:

loquamur potius de nequissimo genere levitatis. tu istis faucibus, istis lateribus, ista gladiatoria totius corpore firmitate, tantum vini in Hippiae nuptiis exhauseras, ut tibi necesse esset in populi Romani conspectu vomere postridie. o rem non modo visu foedam, sed etiam auditu! si inter cenam in istis tuis immanibus illis poculis hoc tibi accidisset, quis non turpe duceret? in coetu vero populi Romani negotium publicum gerens, magister equitum, cui ructare turpe esset, is vomens frustis esculentis vinum redolentibus gremium suum et totum tribunal inplevit!

Let us speak instead of the nastiest kind of vulgarity. You, with that gorge of yours, that stomach, that body as strong as a gladiator's, had consumed so vast a quantity of wine at the wedding of Hippias that you had to vomit in the sight of the assembled Roman people the following day – a scene disgusting to behold – even to hear about! If this had occurred while you were in the middle of one of your drinking bouts, even then, who would not consider it shameful? Yet in a gathering of the Roman people, while engaged in public business, the Master of the Horse – in whom belching would be most indecorous – vomited, spilling fragments of food, stinking of wine, into his own lap and over the whole of the tribunal.

(Cic. *Phil.* 2.63)

Going beyond the private excesses regularly attributed to Roman voluptuaries – at banquets characterised by the overflow of wine and bodily fluids — Antony's body erupts in public. We catch a glimpse here of the self-presentation expected of Rome's political leaders, who should feel ashamed even to belch in front of others.[60] Antony is criticised both for his lack of self-control and for his promiscuous mingling with low persons in the pursuit of sensual gratification.[61]

Juvenal's eighth satire takes as its subject the argument that true *virtus* – virtue – lies not in ancestry but in character. Among the rogues' gallery of vicious aristocrats is the consul Lateranus, who is a regular visitor to a low tavern run by a greasy Syrian landlord:

> invenies aliquo cum percussore iacentem,
> permixtum nautis et furibus ac fugitivis,
> inter carnifices et fabros sandapilarum,
> et resupinati cessanti tympana galli.
> aequa ibi libertas, communia pocula, lectus
> non alius cuiquam nec mensa remotior ulli.
> quid facias talem sortitus, Pontice, servum?
> nempe in Lucanos aut Tusca ergastula mittas.

You will find him lying next to some cut-throat, hugger-mugger with sailors, thieves and runaways, among the executioners and coffin-makers, with eunuch priests (their tambourines at rest). This is equal liberty indeed – they all share cups and couches, no-one's table is set apart. If you were landed with such a slave, Ponticus, he'd be despatched to the chaingangs in Lucania or Tuscany at once.

(8.173–80)

---

[60] Cf. Cic. *De off.* 1.130 (discussed in chapter two). Cicero puts forward the ideal of a 'classical body', implicitly one without orifices (cf. M.M. Bakhtin's distinction between the classical body on the one hand and the grotesque, erupting, carnival body on the other, discussed by Stallybras and White 1986: 21–2). Another colourful example of drunken officials disgracing themselves in public is given by Macrob. *Sat.* 3.16.15–16 (quoting C. Titius, a contemporary of Lucilius).

[61] For attacks made by Cicero in a similar vein on Piso and Gabinius (consuls in the year he was exiled) see *In Pis.* 13, 18, 22; *Post red. in sen.* 13; *Pro Sest.* 20.

The scene in the tavern is a parody of civic equality. To participate in it is totally inappropriate for a consul. Such a place is too 'low' even for the slaves of respectable men.

But such censorious descriptions at the same time betray their own fascination with low life – a fascination which seems to have been shared by some emperors.[62] Nero was said to have made a practice of frequenting taverns and brothels in disguise, taking pleasure in starting brawls (Suet. *Nero* 26.1; Tac. *Ann.* 13.25). Suetonius and Tacitus present his behaviour as an outrageous transgression of the codes of behaviour which an emperor should observe. Yet we may suspect that, in the eyes of some citizens, such escapades served to reinforce Nero's position. The emperor might draw attention to his own transcendence of social rules by temporarily embracing a conspicuously low role.[63] Nero could safely ignore social convention for there was no danger he would be confused with those who really were 'low' (though Tacitus calls the emperor's identity radically into question by introducing some false Neros at this point in his narrative).

Juvenal complains that licentious behaviour is thought fitting for Roman aristocrats, but disapproved of in the case of humbler persons:

> audiat ille
> testarum crepitus cum verbis, nudum olido stans
> fornice mancipium quibus abstinet, ille fruatur
> vocibus obscenis omnique libidinis arte,
> qui Lacedaemonium pytismate lubricat orbem;
> namque ibi fortunae veniam damus. alea turpis,
> turpe et adulterium mediocribus: haec eadem illi
> omnia cum faciunt, hilares nitidique vocantur.

The man who spits wine onto floors of Lacedaemonian marble may hear the clatter of castanets and the sort of lyrics that a naked prostitute, standing in a stinking archway, would be ashamed of. He may utter obscenities and enjoy every variety of lustful pleasure. Men of exalted fortune are indulged. Gambling and adultery are thought shameful for those of lower

---

[62] On elite fascination with the 'low', see Stallybras and White 1986: 103–4.
[63] Cf. the associations of Nero's appearances on stage discussed in chapter three.

*status but no matter how far those others go, we call them 'gay fellows' and
'splendid chaps'.*

(11.171–8)

The pointless extravagance and lack of bodily control of such persons
is here, too, symbolised by an image of effused liquid – wine spat onto
the marble floor. The rich and aristocratic can get away with low
behaviour – it even enhances their reputations. The satirist's dinner
party, by contrast, will be characterised by literary entertainment and
provisions of refined simplicity.[64]

Another aspect of the indulgence in 'low' pleasures on the part of
those of high status is the bond this established with the poor.
Emperors who paraded their enjoyment of popular pleasures seem to
have thereby won popular favour.[65] This could easily be taken too far,
from the point of view of elite writers, who were made uneasy by any
warmth in the relationship between the emperor and the common
people of Rome. Nero, Caligula, Commodus and Helagabalus were
also said by hostile elite historians to have consorted regularly with
low characters, such as actors and gladiators.[66] These same emperors
are the ones who are alleged to have marked themselves off from their
senatorial peers by the incredible scale of their feasting, drinking and
sexual gratification. This kind of gargantuan sensual indulgence is
presented, by Roman writers, as the ultimate aspiration of low
characters, in particular slaves.[67] The Stoic philosopher Epictetus is
said to have remarked: 'a man without self-control is like a slave on
holiday' (*Discourses* 4.1.58). True nobility should be revealed in
restraint.

Numerous texts reveal attempts on the part of the literary elite to
distance themselves from what were perceived to be the pleasures of
the common people (though it is hard to know how far this fastidious-
ness is representative of attitudes of the elite in general). The festival
in the Roman calendar most closely associated with the poor was the
Saturnalia – a time when social distinctions were, in theory, forgot-

---

[64] On the literary significance of such simple meals, see E.J. Gowers *The loaded table.
Representations of food in Roman literature* (Oxford 1992).

[65] E.g. Tac. *Ann.* 14.14; Suet. *Nero* 53. On this, see Yavetz 1969: 128.

[66] Suet. *Calig.* 11; *Nero* 26–7; SHA *Comm.* 2; SHA *Elag.* 32–3.

[67] Cf. Stallybras and White 1986 (esp. ch. 1) on early modern representations of the excessive
pleasures enjoyed by the eruptive carnival body.

ten, as masters and slaves ate and played games together.[68] But Horace retires to the quiet of his Sabine farm, to avoid the festivities (*Sat.* 2.3). Seneca advocates some participation but holds back from total involvement in Saturnalian pleasures (*Ep.* 18.4). The younger Pliny prefers not to participate at all. He expresses satisfaction that his study is far removed from the noise of slaves enjoying themselves (*Ep.* 2.17). The pleasure of watching the games, too, was particularly associated with the poor. Cicero, Horace, Seneca, Pliny and others attend because it is expected of them, but explain that their enjoyment is far from whole-hearted.[69] As we shall see shortly, the literary elite were also keen to emphasise their moderation in the pursuit of other sensual pleasures, here, again, marking themselves off from their social 'inferiors'.

Some Romans feared for the collapse of social hierarchy in an orgy of promiscuity, a perpetual Saturnalia, but their anxiety was not only aroused by the thought of mixing with low persons. Perhaps more significant was the thought that in pursuing sensual pleasures, members of the elite were indulging themselves in a way that low persons would do if only they had the resources. Sensual pleasure was seen as dangerous, at least in part because its power, its appeal, was universal. Susceptibility to such pleasures was associated with women, slaves and the poor – those who had to be controlled by others if they were not to fritter away their lives in self-indulgence. A display of self-control enabled the wealthy and powerful to justify their position by pointing to their moral superiority and natural distinction.

THE BODY'S SLAVE

One may sense, in a range of moralising and philosophical texts, an urge to represent all sensual pleasures as posing a threat to the identity of the elite male. These texts associate the experience of pleasure with the servile and animal. Seneca, for instance, in the passage from *De*

---

[68] On this festival and elite ambivalence to it, see Sarah Currie 'Romans at play: the Saturnalia and Roman identity' (forthcoming).

[69] Cicero *Ad fam.* 7.1; 205.2; Hor. *Epist.* 2.1.200–13; Pliny, *Ep.* 9.6.3; Sen. *Ep.* 7; Marcus Aurelius, *To himself* 6.46; Dio Chrysostom, *Or.* 32.45. See Wiedemann forthcoming and Edwards forthcoming b as well as chapter three above.

vita beata with which this chapter opened, describes pleasure as *servile*. Pleasure is something slaves pursue (compare the observation made by Epictetus, quoted above). But there is another sense in which pleasure is *servile*. To give way to the uncontrolled pursuit of pleasure is to enslave one's mind to one's body:

> sufficit ad id natura quod poscit. a natura luxuria descivit, quae cotidie se ipsa incitat et tot saeculis crescit et ingenio adiuvat vitia. primo supervacua coepit concupiscere, inde contraria, novissime animum corpori addixit et illius deservire libidini iussit.

> *Nature provides enough to satisfy natural wants. But luxury has turned away from nature, luxury who, each day, urges herself on further, who has grown stronger with each age, whose ingenuity is deployed in the promotion of vice. At first luxury began to covet what was, according to nature, superfluous, later what was in opposition to nature, and then she made the mind the servant of the body and ordered it to be a slave to pleasure.*

> (Sen. *Ep.* 90.19)

Seneca elsewhere asserts that there is nothing in pleasure worthy of the nobility of man. Pleasure is rather a base thing, produced by subservience to the parts of the body which are disgusting and vile, and which comes always to a filthy end (*De ben.* 7.2.2–3).[70] The distinction between 'low' and 'high' as regards the social hierarchy (here the distinction between slave and free) is negotiated in terms of the body.[71]

Pleasure even threatens to blur the distinction between human and animal. Cicero describes sensual pleasure as an experience humans share with animals (*De off.* 1.105–6).[72] Aulus Gellius refers approvingly to Aristotle's discussion of the shamefulness of sensual pleasures:

---

[70] Cf. Sen. *Ep.* 8.5; 14.1–2; 15.3; 80.4; 92.33; *De vita beata* 8.2; *Ad Helv.* 9.6. The luxurious are often described as enslaved to their passions, e.g. Hor. *Sat.* 2.7.110–11. The baseness of a life devoted to sensual pleasure is a recurrent theme of ancient philosophical literature. The evils of the life of sensual pleasure are emphasised in Plato's *Republic* (573a–d; 581e–3a). The contrast between the worth of a life devoted to pleasure and one devoted to action or to philosophical contemplation is also stressed by Aristotle (e.g. *Nic. eth.* 1095b14–24). On this see Joly 1956.   [71] Cf. Stallybras and White 1986: 2.

[72] Cf. the opening sentences of Sallust's *Catiline*, where a life in pursuit of virtue, worthy of man, is contrasted with a life in pursuit of sensual pleasure, characteristic of beasts. Sallust condemns those who pass their lives *veluti pecora, quae natura prona atque ventri oboedientia finxit*, 'like sheep whom nature has created to walk of all fours and be slaves to their bellies' (1.1).

ex his omnibus quae inmodice voluptas capitur, ea turpis atque improba existimatur. sed enim quae nimia ex gustu atque tactu est, ea voluptas, sicuti sapientes viri censuerunt, omnium rerum foedissima est, eosque maxime qui duabus istis beluinis voluptatibus sese dediderunt, gravissimi vitii vocabulis Graeci appellant vel ἀκρατεῖς vel ἀκολάστους, nos eos vel 'incontinentes' dicimus vel 'intemperantes' . . . istae . . . voluptates duae gustus atque tactus, id est libidines in cibos atque in Venerem prodigae, solae sunt hominibus communes cum beluis et idcirco in pecudum ferorumque animalium numero habetur, quisquis est his ferinis voluptatibus praevinctus; ceterae ex tribus aliis sensibus proficiscentes hominum esse tantum propriae videntur.

The enjoyment of excessive pleasure from any of these [the five senses] is seen as low and reprehensible. But immoderate pleasure in taste or touch is the vilest of all, in the opinion of philosophers, and those who have surrendered themselves to these animal pleasures the Greeks term either ἀκρατεῖς *or* ἀκόλαστοι. *We call them either* incontinentes *or* intemperantes . . . *The two pleasures of taste and touch, that is to say gluttony and lust, are the only ones which humans have in common with the lower animals, and so whoever is enslaved to these animal pleasures is counted as among the brute beasts. The other pleasures, those resulting from the other three senses, seem to be peculiar to human beings.*

(19.2).[73]

The pleasures of touch and taste recur in these discussions as the least human pleasures.[74] Men who give themselves up to such delights imperil their own humanity. Once again, one who pursues sensual pleasure is assimilated to a slave – *praevinctus*. These texts can be seen as attempts to dissuade one's fellows – and of course oneself – from the pursuit of pleasure, by emphasising the baseness of all somatic pleasures. The images invoked, the characterisations of sensual pleasure as animal or servile, take their force from and in turn serve to reinforce the social order. Some men, as their lack of self-control reveals, are naturally slaves. Others, in their disdain for the attractions of pleasure, show their natural superiority. Self-control legitimated the power of the elite in a way that wealth alone could never do.

[73] Gellius goes on to quote Aristotle *Problems* 949a–50a.
[74] Cf. Plut. *Mor.* 686c. Often, however, moralists can be found emphasising the baseness of e.g. visual pleasures, too, in particular those afforded by watching spectacles (e.g. Cic. *De off.* 2.56–7; Sen. *Ep.* 7.2–3; Augustine, *Conf.* 6.8). Cf. Seneca's condemnation of Apicius and Nomentanus, which does not differentiate between the senses (*De vita beata* 11.4, quoted above).

PRODIGAL PLEASURES

In ancient philosophical literature, the pleasures of the senses are commonly contrasted with the pleasures of the intellect.[75] We should not overlook the fact that for those with the intellectual capital, intellectual pursuits were also a means of displaying wealth, since the expensive commodities of education and leisure were prerequisites (as an added advantage, the display of leisure and education did not involve much further expense).[76] There was perhaps a problem in using the same vocabulary to talk about sensual pleasures, on the one hand, and intellectual and moral pleasures, on the other. Seneca, giving way once again to his taste for paradox, observes: *vera voluptas erit voluptatum contemptio*, 'real pleasure will be the spurning of pleasures' (*De vita beata* 4.2). The argument that voluptuaries are mistaken, not in pursuing pleasure at all but in pursuing the wrong kind of pleasure, is a difficult one for the moralist, since it implicitly justifies pursuit of the right kind of pleasure.

THE TWO SENSUALISTS

A large part of Cicero's philosophical treatise, *De finibus*, is concerned with attacking the tenets of Epicureanism, in particular the notion that human beings are motivated by the desire for pleasure.[77] The character in the dialogue who bears Cicero's own name is careful not to accuse the serious followers of Epicurus of advocating sensual indulgence (*De fin.* 1.25).[78] But even their assertion of the legitimacy of pursuing pleasure he finds threatening. The pursuit of pleasure,

---

[75] Some of the material is collected by B. Gibbs 'Higher and lower pleasures' *Philosophy* 61 (1986) 31–59. There is, however, a tension, evident in Plato's *Republic* as well as some Roman texts, between the attractions of the pursuit of knowledge, on the one hand, and the claims of public duty on the other.

[76] The social prestige of cultural knowledge (and the ridicule which might await those whose pretensions outdid their capabilities) is emphasised in Seneca's portrait of Calvisius Sabinus, a rich man who attempts to parade his command of culture by paying fabulous sums for slaves who know the works of Homer and Hesiod by heart (*Ep.* 27.5–6). Early Roman moralists seem to have disapproved fairly wholeheartedly of Greek philosophy (e.g. Plut. *Cat. mai.* 22.4). Cicero argues that public duty has a prior call on the time and energy of the intelligent gentleman (*De off.* 1.43, 71; *De rep.* 1.1–4; *De orat.* 3.56–7). Some of Cicero's writings appear to privilege the contemplative life but, as Joly points out (1956: 161–4), such passages are much briefer and more tangential. Seneca seems readier to see the life of contemplation as justifiable in itself (*De otio* 7).

[77] On Epicureanism in late republican Rome, see Rawson 1985a: 282–97 and Griffin 1989.

[78] Elsewhere Cicero does attribute low motives to some who profess Epicureanism (e.g. *Post red. in sen.* 14).

according to 'Cicero', is in itself blameworthy, regardless of whether it has bad consequences for other people (2.21–2).[79]

In the course of his argument, 'Cicero' refers to two sorts of voluptuaries:

> nolim enim mihi fingere asotos, ut soletis, qui in mensam vomant et qui de conviviis auferantur crudique postridie se rursus ingurgitent, qui solem, ut aiunt, nec occidentem umquam viderint nec orientem, qui consumptis patrimoniis egeant.

> *I have no wish to imagine, as you are accustomed to do, these men who are sick at table and have to be carried away from dinner parties, yet the next day stuff themselves again before they have even recovered from the night before, those who, as they say, see neither the setting nor the rising sun; men who consume their inheritance and sink into poverty.*

> *(De fin.* 2.23)

We might note, here, some of the elements most characteristic of representations of the prodigal who eats and drinks to excess, lives by night rather than by day, has no control over his body, squanders his family fortune and falls into poverty. No reasonable person, argues 'Cicero', would consider such a man to be happy.

But sensuality can have a more refined form, rather more problematic for 'Cicero's' argument:

> mundos, elegantes, optimis cocis, pistoribus, piscatu, aucupio, venatione, his omnibus exquisitis, vitantes cruditatem, quibus 'vinum defusum e pleno sit' . . . adhibentes ludos et quae sequuntur, illa quibus detractis clamat Epicurus se nescire quid sit bonum; adsint etiam formosi pueri qui ministrent; respondeat his vestis, argentum, Corinthium, locus ipse, aedificium.

> *. . . men of taste and refinement whose excellent chefs and confectioners serve up fish, birds, game, all of the finest quality, who enjoy 'wine decanted from the newly opened cask' . . . together with games and those matters which come afterwards – by which I mean that without which Epicurus said he could have no knowledge of the good. There are good-looking boys, too, to serve at table. And the linens, silverware, Corinthian bronze, indeed the setting itself and the house – all these are correspondingly fine.*

> *(ibid.)*

---

[79] Cf. *Pro Cael.* 40–1 – philosophers who champion pleasure are accused of making statements which are a disgrace to oratory, *turpitudo orationis.*

'Cicero' is coy about sexual pleasure, here as elsewhere, which he refers to as 'those matters which come afterwards'.[80] Here, too, sexual pleasure is an integral part of the *convivium*. Despite the refinement and moderation of their pleasures (these men never pursue pleasure to the point of making themselves ill), they do not live well – *bene* – either, argues 'Cicero'. Their pleasant life secures them neither virtue nor fame.[81]

Like Seneca in *De vita beata*, Cicero is keen to advocate the ideal of the life of public service. Pleasure, no matter how refined, gets in the way of one's commitment to virtue. The vast expense involved in the pursuit of sensual pleasures – whether as a consequence of the quantities consumed, as in the case of the coarse sensualist, or of the exquisiteness of the fare, in the case of the refined sensualist – is also a preoccupation of Cicero's argument. Both strands in attacks on voluptuaries, stressing the weakness of giving in to the attractions of pleasure, and the damage caused by spending money, are to be linked to the discourses concerned with negotiating what it is to be a Roman, discussed in earlier chapters. But differentiating between kinds of sensuality also reveals another aspect of the role of pleasures, the positive function they may have in marking social distinction through refinement. Pleasures which involve the display of knowledge and taste (as well as money), far from blurring the 'proper' distinctions between and within social groups, could serve to reinforce them.

REFINEMENT AND DISTINCTION

A similar distinction between coarse and refined pleasures is invoked in Cicero's attack on Piso. Piso is criticised for his pursuit of sensual pleasures (which Cicero links to his professed commitment to Epicureanism) but also for not spending enough on his dinner parties:

> luxuriem autem nolite in isto hanc cogitare: est enim quaedam, quamquam omnis et vitiosa atque turpis, tamen ingenuo ac libero dignior. nihil apud hunc lautum, nihil elegans, nihil exquisitum; laudabo inimicum, quin ne magno opere quidem quicquam praeter libidines sumptuosum. toreuma nullum, maximi calices, et ei, ne

---

[80] Cf. 2.68.

[81] At 2.63, 'Cicero' refers to a man who lived for pleasure, 'a certain Lucius Thorius of Lanuvium, whom you cannot remember'. At 2.67, he notes the impossibility of citing names of famous men who are champions of pleasure.

contemnere suos videatur Placentini; exstructa mensa non conchyliis aut piscibus, sed multa carne subrancida. servi sordidati ministrant, non nulli etiam senes; idem coquus, idem atriensis; pistor domi nullus, nulla cella; panis et vinum a propola et de cupa; Graeci stipati quini in lectulis, saepe plures; ipse solus; bibitur usque eo dum de dolio ministretur.

Don't attribute to him the sort of luxury which, though reprehensible and shameful, is yet more worthy of a free-born gentleman. For there is nothing about him which is remotely refined, elegant or exquisite. In this at least I shall praise my opponent – he is extravagant in nothing beyond his sexual appetites. No embossed ware on his table, rather, huge tankards – from Placentia, for Piso does not despise his own people. The board is piled high – not with shellfish or fish but with huge joints of putrescent meat. Slovenly slaves wait at table, some of them old men. The cook also serves as porter. There is no bread baker, no cellar in the house, but the bread comes from a bakery, the wine from a tavern. Greeks are packed five to a couch, sometimes more; he himself is alone on one, knocking back the wine till it's poured straight from the cask.

(*In Pis.* 67)

This enumeration of Piso's failings is in part ironical. Piso's dinner party is a parody of traditional Roman frugality. Piso eats rancid meat, just like the noble Romans of earlier days (cf. Hor. *Sat.* 2.2.89–93). His utensils are of earthenware – a hall-mark of antique austerity (for instance in Pliny, *NH* 33.142–3). He employs no specialist cooks – one of the traditional focuses of attacks on Roman luxury (for instance, Livy 39.6). He is waited on by old men, not pretty boys (the elder Cato's criticisms of those who spend vast sums of money on such slaves are discussed above).[82] Cicero speaks of the luxurious refinement Piso lacks as *vitiosa atque turpis*, 'vicious and shameful' (like all luxury) but yet it is *ingenuo ac libero dignior*, 'more worthy [than some kinds of luxury] of a free man and a gentleman'. Here, again, we see the distinction between free and slave invoked in the negotiation of acceptable kinds of pleasure.

Piso's hospitality has nothing about it which is *lautum, exquisitum, elegans* – 'fine, refined, elegant'. Though Cicero has been using them to characterise reprehensible luxury, these were by no means always pejorative terms. Cicero would, one suspects, not have been insulted to have these epithets applied to his own dinner parties. Elsewhere, he

---

[82] Cf. Mart. 10.98; Juv. 5.55.

writes of the proper standards of hospitality to be observed by those who entertain foreign guests (*De off.* 2.64). His letters set out in approving detail the dishes consumed in the houses of friends and acquaintances.[83] The distinction between prodigality and liberality was not always easy to draw.[84]

Competitive entertaining was a crucial part of the social and indeed the political life of the Roman elite. Evening parties might be diverse in their composition (women were often included). The conversation might not touch on political matters at all.[85] Yet, when Roman politicians made decisions as to whom they meant to support or oppose, they considered qualities such as liberality and refinement (which might most obviously manifest themselves in the informal setting of the *convivium*) as readily as political skills and opinions.[86] There are good grounds for supposing that the entertainment of one's peers became increasingly important under the principate, as, in practice, senior magistrates came to be chosen by their fellow senators and the emperor, rather than by assemblies of the Roman people.

Excessive frugality would have been a grave social error for a man who aspired to a distinguished political or social position. Attacks on avarice – not only the desire to acquire money but also the refusal to spend it – are frequent in the writings of moralists.[87] Spending could be a legitimate expression of distinction. The emperor Tiberius is made by Tacitus to list the objections even the morally severe are likely to make to a proposed sumptuary law: *splendidissimo cuique exitium parari, neminem criminis expertem clamitabunt*, 'They will complain that this is the end of distinction and all are made into criminals' (*Ann.* 3.54).[88] Tacitus concludes his narrative of this debate in the senate by describing how the luxury which prevailed under the Julio-Claudian emperors came to an end: *postquam caedibus saevitum et magnitudo famae exitio erat, ceteri ad sapientiora conver-*

---

[83] E.g. *Ad fam.* 191.3; 193; 197.
[84] Cf. Horace (*Sat.* 1.2.4–11) on prodigality as a consequence of not wishing to be thought mean, and Seneca (*Ep.* 120.8) on prodigality as close to liberality.
[85] Cicero discusses the proper material and manner for informal conversation (*De off.* 1.132–7).
[86] See Saller 1982 esp. chs. 1 and 4. Cicero suggests that Aelius Tubero failed to be elected praetor because the feast he gave in honour of his deceased uncle Scipio Aemilianus was considered too modest (*Pro Mur.* 75–6). I am grateful to John Patterson for this reference.
[87] E.g. Juv. 14.107–37; Hor. *Sat.* 2.3.107–28; Mart. 3.58.42–4.
[88] Cf. the arguments attributed to the tribune Valerius, who speaks on the winning side in the debate set in 195 BCE which ends in the repeal of the *lex Oppia* (a sumptuary law restricting women's expenditure) (Livy 34.5).

tere, 'After the reign of terror, when to have a great reputation was fatal, those who survived became more circumspect in their habits' (3.55). Preeminence in expenditure was one of the distinguishing characteristics of leading Romans. This account is no doubt ironic. Yet it seems reasonable to suppose that in the early principate, despite the profound ambivalence towards what were seen as manifestations of luxury on the part of many members of the elite, most of those involved in more elevated social circles felt compelled to spend large sums as pledges of a liberality which would always be open to redescription as luxury.

It was important to spend money but it was vital to know how to spend it in the proper way. The late republic saw a proliferation of systems of specialist knowledge in Rome, not only in areas such as philosophy and law but also in connoisseurship of the arts and of food and drink.[89] Cicero refers jokingly to Hirtius and Dolabella as his 'pupils in oratory but teachers in gastronomy' (*Ad fam.* 190.7). Different kinds of knowledge might be considered appropriate by different people. While an Apicius might seek to be celebrated for his familiarity with the origin and taste of countless exotic foodstuffs, others might aim to command respect for the philosophical simplicity of what they offered their guests.[90]

The increasing regulation of manners was a more effective way of excluding outsiders, or controlling access by them, than a spiral of increasing expenditure.[91] Even those without enormous wealth could parade their connoisseurship.[92] The freedman Trimalchio's dinner might be lavish but his refined guests still despised his ignorance of proper etiquette.[93] Moralists spoke nostalgically of the days when Romans lived simply and ran no risk of bankrupting themselves when they invited friends to dinner. Many expressed an anxiety that

[89] Charted by Rawson 1985a. Griffin discusses wine connoisseurship, 1985: 65–9.
[90] On the ideal of refinement, see E.S. Ramage *Urbanitas: ancient sophistication and refinement* (Oklahoma 1973).
[91] Cf. the development of court culture in early modern Europe examined by Norbert Elias, *The civilising process* (Oxford 1978).
[92] Cf. Horace's claim to be a connoisseur of wine and girls (Griffin 1985: 81). Expert knowledge is regularly presented in satire, particularly, as a more important quality in a host than vast wealth. On this, see Gowers 1992.
[93] See Veyne 1961. On the proper behaviour for hosts, see J.H. D'Arms 'The Roman *convivium* and the ideal of equality' in Oswyn Murray ed. *Sympotica: a symposium on the symposium* (Oxford 1990) 308–20; Nicola Hudson 'Food in Roman satire' in Susan Braund ed. *Satire and society* (Exeter 1989) 69–88.

refinement of manners should not consist in an excessive adoption of Greek manners, thus compromising Roman identity.[94] At the same time, there is an implicit recognition in a number of texts that refined pleasure, properly controlled, can have a legitimate function as one of the signs marking out an honourable Roman. If 'vulgar' pleasures undermine the social hierarchy, 'refined' pleasure can serve to reinforce it.

APPROPRIATING LUXURY

Some moralists were themselves implicated in evolving patterns of social behaviour which committed them to expending a considerable amount of money on what might be termed pleasures. This helps to explain the recurrent anxieties about the relationships between pleasure, expenditure and social status paraded in the moralising texts under consideration in this chapter. Yet the luxuriant severity with which moralists castigated the vices of others can be seen as themselves fuelling Roman preoccupation with luxury.

Pliny, Seneca and others wrote catalogues of sumptuary vices, charged with the suppressed fascination of their authors. Moralists needed vice. *Quando uberior vitiorum copia?* 'When was there ever such abundance of vices?' Juvenal asks in his first satire (1.96). The satirist's appetite for vice is insatiable. He, too, cannot contain all he consumes.[95] The vices are disgorged, a parade of the forbidden which perhaps provided inspiration and stimulus to the jaded palates of voluptuaries. Censure gave them a vocabulary, enhancing the attraction of luxurious pleasures in the act of proscribing them.

Voluptuaries sought to outdo one another in spectacular and extravagant acts of consumption, or so moralists assert. The elite ethos of competition was appropriated for a new arena. Some descriptions of voluptuaries present their behaviour in terms which suggest a parody of traditional practices. The gourmet Apicius is said to have killed himself when his fortune had dwindled to 10 million sesterces (ten times the census requirements for a Roman senator), for he felt he could no longer afford to eat in the style to which he was accustomed (Sen. *Ad Helv.* 10.10; Mart. 3.22) – a curious perversion of the traditionally Roman noble suicide.

---

[94] E.g. Mart. 10.68. Cf. chapter two above.
[95] On the complicity of the satirist, see Gowers 1992.

PRODIGAL PLEASURES

Tacitus describes the consular Petronius, a man of exquisite refinement, undeniably luxurious, who also committed suicide.[96]

de C. Petronio pauca supra repetenda sunt. nam illi dies per somnum, nox officiis et oblectamentis vitae transigebatur; utque alios industria, itaque hunc ignavia ad famam protulerat, habebaturque non ganeo et profligator, ut plerique sua haurientium, sed erudito luxu. ac dicta factaque eius quanto solutiora et quandam sui neglegentiam praeferentia, tanto gratius in speciem simplicitatis accipiebantur. proconsul tamen Bithyniae et mox consul vigentem se ac parem negotiis ostendit. dein revolutus ad vitia seu vitiorum imitatione inter paucos familiarium Neroni adsumptus est, elegantiae arbiter, dum nihil amoenum et molle adfluentia putat nisi quod ei Petronius adprobavisset. unde invidia Tigellini quasi adversus aemulum et scientia voluptatum potiorem.

I should say something first about Gaius Petronius. For he was a man who, throughout his life, spent his days in sleep, his nights engaged in business and pleasures. Just as industry has conferred fame on others, so laziness conferred fame on Petronius. But he was not, like most who squander their fortunes, believed to be a glutton or a profligate. Petronius' luxury was erudite. His doings and sayings, the more languid and unselfconscious they seemed, pleased people with their apparent simplicity. As governor of Bithynia and, shortly afterwards, as consul, he revealed himself to be energetic and quite up to the management of public affairs. Thereafter, he returned to his earlier vices – or at least seemed to do so – and was accepted as one of the select intimates of the emperor Nero, where he filled the role of arbiter of taste, so that, eventually, nothing amid the superfluity was deemed desirable or elegant, unless first approved by Petronius. And so he incurred the enmity of Tigellinus who resented him as a rival, more expert in the science of pleasures.

(Tac. *Ann.* 16.18)

The roles of public servant and sensualist (alleged by moralists to be mutually exclusive) are collapsed. Petronius, according to the custom of Roman voluptuaries, lived by night – but used the time for business as well as pleasure. The life of pleasure and indolence, which Cicero asserted could never bring fame, brought precisely that in the case of Petronius.

[96] Griffin (1985 ch. 2) discusses 'the man of action who lives for pleasure' in Hellenistic and Roman manifestations. Calvus, Cornificius and Helvius Cinna are republican examples cited by Griffin 1985: 19. There are numerous Tacitean characters in a similar mode (Griffin 1985: 36; Syme 1958 II: 538 n. 6). See also Veyne 1987: 205.

Is all this a measure of the extreme corruption of Neronian Rome, where traditional virtues are inverted, indeed exploded? Or is it rather another example of perspicacious Tacitean irony? The man who dies perhaps the noblest, and certainly the wittiest, death in that book of accumulating fatalities, the *Annals*, was quite probably himself one the most subversive parodists of Roman moralising, the author of the *Satyricon*. 'The authentic voice of Rome speaks',[97] characteristically elusive in its self-mocking irony.

[97] As Eduard Fraenkel remarks of Tacitus (*Neue Jahrbücher für Wissenschaft und Jugendbildung* 8 (1932) 218–33, at 218).

Bibliography

Abbott, F.F. (1907) 'The theatre as a factor in Roman politics under the republic' *TAPhA* 38, 49–56

Adams, J.N. (1982) *The latin sexual vocabulary* (London)

Ahl, Frederick (1984) 'The art of safe criticism in Greece and Rome' *AJPh* 105, 174–208

André, J.-M. (1966) *L'otium dans la vie morale et intellectuelle* (Paris)
  (1975) 'Les *ludi scaenici* et la politique des spectacles au début de l'ère antonine' in *Association Guillaume Budé. Actes du IXe congrès* (Paris), 468–79

Appadurai, Arjun (1986) 'Commodities and the politics of value' in Appadurai ed. *The social life of things* (Cambridge), 3–57

Arangio-Ruiz, V. (1938) 'La legislazione' in *Augustus: studi in occasione del bimillenario augusteo* (Rome), 101–46

Astin, A.E. (1978) *Cato the censor* (Oxford)
  (1988) '*Regimen morum*' *JRS* 78, 14–34

Badian, Ernst (1985) 'A phantom marriage law' *Philologus* 129, 82–98

Balsdon, J.P.V.D. (1962) *Roman women: their history and habits* (London)
  (1979) *Romans and aliens* (London)

Baltrusch, Ernst (1989) *Regimen morum: die Reglementierung des Privatlebens der Senatoren und Ritter in der römischen Republik und frühen Kaiserzeit* (Munich)

Barton, Carlin (1989) 'The scandal of the arena' *Representations* 27, 1–36

Barton, Tamsyn (forthcoming a) *Power and knowledge: astrology, physiognomics and medicine under the Roman empire*
  (forthcoming b) 'The *inventio* of Nero: Suetonius', in Elsner and Masters

Baudot, A. (1973) *Musiciens romains de l'antiquité* (Montreal)

Bauman, Richard (1968) 'Some remarks on the structure and survival of the *quaestio de adulteriis*' *Antichthon* 2, 68–93

Baxandall, Michael (1971) *Giotto and the orators* (Oxford)

Beard, Mary (1980) 'The sexual status of Vestal Virgins' *JRS* 70, 12–27

Beard, Mary and Crawford, Michael (1985) *Rome in the late republic* (London)

Beare, William (1964) *The Roman stage*, 3rd edn. (London)

Becatti, Giovanni (1951) *Arte e gusto negli scrittori latini* (Florence)

BIBLIOGRAPHY

Bek, Lise (1976) '*Antithesis*: a Roman attitude and its changes as reflected in the concept of architecture' in *Studia in honorem Petri Krarup septuagenarii* (Odense), 154–66

    (1980) *Towards paradise on earth* (Odense)

    (1983) '*Quaestiones conviviales*: the idea of the triclinium and the staging of convivial ceremony from Rome to Byzantium' *ARID* suppl. 12, 81–109

Bellwald, U. (1985) *Domus Tiberiana: nuove ricerche* (Zurich)

Bieber, Margarete (1961) *The history of the Greek and Roman theater* (Princeton)

Bloch, Maurice and Bloch, Jean H. (1980) 'Women and the dialectics of nature in eighteenth-century France' in C. MacCormack and M. Strathern eds. *Nature, culture and gender* (Cambridge), 25–41

Boethius, Axel (1960) *The golden house of Nero* (Ann Arbor)

duBois, Page (1991) *Torture and truth* (London)

Bollinger, Traugott (1969) *Theatralis licentia* (Winterthur)

Boswell, John (1980) *Christianity, social tolerance and homosexuality* (Chicago)

    (1988) *The kindness of strangers: the abandonment of children in western Europe from antiquity to the Renaissance* (New York)

    (1990) 'Concepts, experience and sexuality' *Differences: a journal of feminist cultural studies* 2.1, 67–88

Boudreau-Flory, M. (1984) '*Sic exempla parantur*: Livia's shrine to Concordia and the *Porticus Liviae*' *Historia* 33, 309–330

Bourdieu, Pierre (1975) 'The Berber house' in Mary Douglas ed. *Rules and meanings* (London), 98–110

    (1977) *Outline of a theory of practice*, tr. Richard Nice (Cambridge)

    (1984) *Distinction: a social critique of the judgement of taste*, tr. Richard Nice (London)

    (1990) *The logic of practice*, tr. Richard Nice (Oxford)

    and Passeron, Jean Claude (1977) *Reproduction in education society and culture*, tr. Richard Nice (London)

Bradley, K.R. (1984) *Slaves and masters in the Roman world: a study in social control* (Brussels)

Brandes, Stanley (1981) 'Like wounded stags: male sexual ideology in an Andalusian town' in Ortner and Whitehead, 216–39

Bremmer, Jan and Roodenburg, Herman eds. (1991) *A cultural history of gesture* (Oxford)

Bristol, Michael D. (1985) *Carnival and theater: plebeian culture and the structure of authority in Renaissance England* (New York)

Broise, Henri and Jolivet, Vincent (1987) 'Recherces sur les jardins de Lucullus' in *L'urbs: espace urbain et histoire. Collection de l'école française de Rome* 98, 747–61

Brown, Peter (1987) 'Late antiquity' in Veyne

    (1989) *The body and society* (London)

Brunt, P.A. (1969) 'The *equites* in the late republic' in R. Seager ed. *The crisis of the Roman republic: studies in political and social history* (Cambridge), 83–115 (= Brunt *The fall of the Roman republic* (Oxford 1988) 144–193)

(1980) 'Evidence given under torture' *ZSS* 97, 256–65

(1982) '*Nobilitas* and *novitas*' *JRS* 72, 1–17

(1983) '*Princeps* and *equites*' *JRS* 73, 42–75

Buckland, W.W. (1908) *The Roman law of slavery* (Cambridge)

Burke, Peter (1978) *Popular culture in early modern Europe* (London)

Cameron, Alan (1976) *Circus factions: blues and greens at Rome and Byzantium* (Oxford)

Cantarella, Eva (1972) 'Adulterio, omicidio legittimo e causa d'onore in diritto romano' in *Studi in onore di Gaetano Scherillo* (Milan) I, 243–74

(1988) *Secondo natura: la bisessualità nel mondo antico* (Rome)

Carandini, Andrea, Medri, M., Gualandi, M.L. and Papi, E. (1986) 'Pendici settentrionali del Palatino' *BCAR* 111, 429–38

Carettoni, Gianfilippo (1983a) *Das Haus des Augustus auf dem Palatin* (Mainz)

(1983b) 'La decorazione pittorica della casa di Augusto sul Palatino' *MDAI(R)* 90, 373–419

Carstairs, G. Morris (1957) *The twice born* (London)

Chambers, E.K. (1903) *The medieval stage* (Oxford)

(1923) *The Elizabethan stage* (Oxford)

Clavel-Levêque, Monique (1984) *L'Empire en jeux* (Paris)

Clemente, G. (1981) 'Le leggi sul lusso e la società romana tra III e II secolo A.C.' in Andrea Giardina and Aldo Schiavone eds. *Società romana e produzione schiavistica* (Rome) III, 1–14

Coarelli, Filippo (1972) 'Il complesso pompeiano del Campo Marzio e la sua decorazione scultorea' *RPAA* 44, 99–122

(1974) *Guida archeologica di Roma* (Rome)

(1983a) *Il foro romano* (Rome)

(1983b) 'Architettura sacra e architettura privata nella tarda repubblica' in *Architecture et société. Collection de l'école française de Rome* 66, 191–217

(1983c) 'Il commercio nelle opere d'arte in età tardo reppublicana' *DArch* 1, 45–53

Cohen, David (1987) 'Separation, seclusion and the status of women in classical Athens' *G&R* 36, 3–15

(1991) *Law, sexuality and society: the enforcement of morals in classical Athens* (Cambridge)

Coleman, Kathleen (1990) 'Fatal charades: Roman executions staged as mythological enactments' *JRS* 80, 44–73

Colin, J. (1955) 'Luxe oriental et parfums masculins dans la Rome alexandrine' *RBRh* 33, 5–19

Corbett, P.E. (1930) *The Roman law of marriage* (Oxford)

Cornell, Tim (1981) 'Some observations on the *crimen incesti*' in *Le Délit religieux dans la cité antique. Collection de l'école française de Rome* 48, 27–37

Courtney, Edward (1980) *A commentary on the satires of Juvenal* (London)

Crook, J.A. (1955) *Consilium principis* (Cambridge)

(1967) 'A study in decoction' *Latomus* 26, 361–76

Csillag, Pal (1976) *The Augustan laws on family relations* (Budapest)

Culham, Phyllis (1982) 'The *lex Oppia*' *Latomus* 41, 786–93
Currie, Sarah (forthcoming) 'Romans at play: the Saturnalia and Roman identity'
Daly, L.W. (1950) 'Roman study abroad' *AJPh* 71, 40–58
D'Arms, J.H. (1970) *Romans on the bay of Naples* (Cambridge, Mass.)
    (1979) 'Ville rustiche e ville di *otium*' 65–86 in Fausto Zevi ed. *Pompeii 79* (Naples)
    (1990) 'The Roman *convivium* and the ideal of equality' in Oswyn Murray ed. *Sympotica: a symposium on the symposium* (Oxford), 308–20
    (1991) 'Slaves at Roman *convivia*' in W.J. Slater ed. *Dining in a classical context* (Ann Arbor), 171–83
Daube, David (1969) *Aspects of Roman law* (Edinburgh)
    (1972) 'The *lex Iulia* concerning adultery' *The Irish Jurist* 7, 373–80
Davidson, A.I. (1987–8) 'Sex and the emergence of sexuality' *Critical Enquiry* 14, 16–48
DeLaine, Janet (1988) 'Recent research on Roman baths' *Journal of Roman Archaeology* 1, 11–32
Dixon, Suzanne (1987) *The Roman mother* (Sydney)
Douglas, Mary (1966) *Purity and danger* (London)
Dover, K.J. (1978) *Greek homosexuality* (London)
Drerup, H. (1957) *Zum Ausstattungsluxus in der römischen Architektur* (Münster)
Duncan-Jones, Richard (1982) *The economy of the Roman empire*, 2nd edn. (Cambridge)
Dunkle, J.R. (1971) 'The rhetorical tyrant in Roman historiography: Sallust, Livy and Tacitus' *CW* 65, 171–4
Dupont, Florence (1977) 'La scène juridique' *Communications* 26, 62–77
    (1985) *L'acteur-roi* (Paris)
    (1989) *La Vie quotidienne du citoyen romain* (Paris)
Earl, Donald (1961) *The political thought of Sallust* (Cambridge)
    (1967) *The moral and political tradition of Rome* (London)
Eck, Werner (1984) 'Senatorial self-representation' in Millar and Segal, 129–67
Edwards, Catharine (forthcoming a) 'Beware of imitations: acting and the subversion of imperial identity'
    (forthcoming b) 'Unspeakable professions: public performance and prostitution in ancient Rome'
Edwards, G.M. ed. (1875) *Horatius and other stories. Adapted from Livy with notes and vocabulary* (London)
Eisenhut, Werner (1973) *Virtus Romana: ihre Stellung im römischen Wertsystem* (Munich)
Elias, Norbert (1978) *The civilising process*, tr. Edmund Jephcott (Oxford)
    (1983) *The court society*, tr. Edmund Jephcott (Oxford)
Elsner, J. and Masters, J. eds. (forthcoming) *Reflections of Nero*
Fabbrini, Laura (1983) '*Domus aurea*: una nuova lettura planimetrica del palazzo sul colle Oppio' *ARID* suppl. 10, 169–85

BIBLIOGRAPHY

Favret-Saada, Jeanne (1980) *Deadly words: witchcraft in the Bocage*, tr. Catherine Cullen (Cambridge)

Feeley-Harnik, Gillian (1981) *The Lord's table: eucharist and passover in early Christianity* (Philadelphia)

Feeney, Denis (1992) '*Si licet et fas est:* Ovid's *Fasti* and the problem of free speech under the principate' in Anton Powell ed. *Roman poetry and propaganda in the age of Augustus* (Bristol)

Ferrill, Arther (1980) 'Augustus and his daughter: a modern myth' in Carl Deroux ed. *Studies in Latin literature and Roman history* (Brussels) II, 332–46

Finley, M.I. (1980) *Ancient slavery and modern ideology* (London)
(1983) *Politics in the ancient world* (Cambridge)

Fisher, N.R.E. (1976) 'Hybris and dishonour' *G&R* 23, 177–93

Fittschen, Klaus (1975) 'Zur Herkunft und Entstehung des 2. Stils' in Zanker, 939–63

Forbes, R.J. (1965) *Studies in ancient technology* III (Leiden)

Foucault, Michel (1979) *The history of sexuality* I: *An introduction*, tr. Robert Hurley (London)
(1986) *The history of sexuality* II: *The use of pleasure*, tr. Robert Hurley (London)
(1988) *The history of sexuality* III: *The care of the self*, tr. Robert Hurley (London)

Fraenkel, Eduard (1932) 'Tacitus' *Neue Jahrbücher für Wissenschaft und Jugendbilding* 8, 218–33

Frank, Tenney (1931) 'The status of actors at Rome' *CPh* 26, 11–20

Frederiksen, M. (1966) 'Caesar, Cicero and the problem of debt' *JRS* 56, 128–41

Frézouls, E. (1981) 'La construction du *theatrum lapideum* et son contexte politique' in *Théâtre et spectacles dans l'antiquité. Actes du colloque de Strasbourg* (Leiden), 193–214
(1982) 'Aspects de l'histoire architectural du théâtre romain' in H. Temporini ed. *ANRW* II 12.1 (Berlin), 343–441

Friedländer, Ludwig (1964) *Darstellungen aus der Sittengeschichte Roms: in der Zeit von Augustus bis zum Ausgang der Antonine*, ed. Georg Wissowa (Stuttgart; 1st edn. Königsberg 1862) (= *Roman life and manners under the early empire* tr. J.H Freese and Leonard A. Magnus (London 1908–28))

Fyfe, H. (1983) 'An analysis of Seneca's *Medea*' in A.J. Boyle ed. *Seneca tragicus* (Victoria), 77–93

Gagnon, John and Simon, William (1973) *Sexual conduct: the social sources of human development* (London)

Gallini, Clara (1973) 'Che cosa intendere per ellenizzazione' *DArch* 7.2–3, 175–91

Gardner, Jane (1986) *Women in Roman law and society* (London)

Garnsey, Peter (1967) 'Adultery trials and the survival of the *quaestiones* in the Severan age' *JRS* 57, 56–60

BIBLIOGRAPHY

Garnsey, Peter and Saller, Richard (1987) *The Roman empire, economy, society and culture* (London)

Gay, Peter (1984–6) *The bourgeois experience: Victoria to Freud* (Oxford)

Gaythorne-Hardy, Jonathan (1977) *The public school phenomenon* (London)

Gellner, Ernest (1973) *Cause and meaning in the social sciences* (London)

Gibbon, Edward (1909) *The history of the decline and fall of the Roman empire*, ed. J.B. Bury (London: first full octavo edition London 1788)

Gibbs, B. (1986) 'Higher and lower pleasures' *Philosophy* 61, 31–59

Gleason, Maud W. (1990) 'The semiotics of gender: physiognomy and self-fashioning' in Halperin, Winkler and Zeitlin, 389–415

Gnoli, Raniero (1971) *Marmora romana* (Rome)

Gold, Barbara (1987) *Literary patronage in Greece and Rome* (Chapel Hill)

Gonfroy, Françoise (1978) 'Homosexualité et l'idéologie esclavagiste chez Cicéron' *DHA* 4, 219–65

Gowers, E.J. (1992) *The loaded table. Representations of food in Roman literature* (Oxford)

Green, W.M. (1933) 'The status of actors at Rome' *Phoenix* 28, 301–4

Greenidge, A.H.J. (1894) *Infamia: its place in Roman public and private law* (Oxford)

Griffin, Jasper (1985) *Latin poets and Roman life* (London)

Griffin, Miriam (1976) *Seneca: a philosopher in politics* (Oxford)

(1984) *Nero: the end of a dynasty* (London)

(1989) 'Philosophy, politics and politicians at Rome' in Miriam Griffin and Jonathan Barnes eds. *Philosophia togata* (Oxford), 1–37

Grimal, Pierre (1943) *Les Jardins romains* (Paris)

(1975) 'Le théâtre à Rome' in *Association Guillaume Budé. Actes du IXe congrès* (Paris), 286–88

Gros, Pierre (1976a) *Aurea templa: recherches sur l'architecture religieuse de Rome à l'époque d'Auguste* (Rome)

(1976b) 'Les premières générations d'architectes hellénistiques à Rome' in *Mélanges Huergon* (Rome), 387–410

(1987) 'La fonction symbolique des édifices théâtraux dans le paysage de la Rome augustéene' in *L'urbs: espace urbain et histoire. Collection de l'école française de Rome* 98, 319–46

Gruen, E.S. (1990) *Studies in Greek culture and Roman policy* (Leiden)

Hallett, Judith P. (1977) '*Perusinae glandes* and the changing image of Augustus' *AJAH* 2, 151–71

(1989) 'Female homoeroticism and the denial of Roman reality in Latin literature' *Yale Journal of Criticism* 3.1, 209–27

Halperin, D.M. (1990) *One hundred years of homosexuality* (New York)

Halperin, D.M., Winkler, J.J. and Zeitlin F.I. eds. (1990) *Before sexuality: the construction of erotic experience in the ancient Greek world* (Princeton)

Hanson, John A. (1959) *Roman theater-temples* (Princeton)

Heath, Stephen (1982) *The sexual fix* (London)

Heider, Karl G. (1976) 'Dani sexuality: a low energy system' *Man* 2, 188–201

BIBLIOGRAPHY

Heinen, H. (1983) 'Die Truphe des Ptolemaios VIII Euergetes II' in *Althistorische Studien: Festschrift H. Bengtson* (Wiesbaden), 116–30

Hellegouarc'h, J. (1972) *Le Vocabulaire des relations et des partis politiques sous la république*, 2nd edn. (Paris)

Henderson, John (1988) 'Entertaining arguments: Terence *Adelphoe*' in Andrew Benjamin ed. *Post-structuralist classics* (London), 192–226

(1989) 'Satire writes "woman": Gendersong' *PCPhS* 35, 50–80

Herter, Hans (1960) 'Die Soziologie der antiken Prostitution' *JbAC* 3, 70–111

Hodge, A.T. (1981) 'Vitruvius, lead pipes and lead poisoning' *AJA* 85, 486–91

Hopkins, Keith (1965) 'Contraception in the Roman empire' *Comparative Studies in Society and History* 8, 124–51

(1974) 'Elite mobility in the Roman empire' in M.I. Finley ed. *Studies in ancient society* (London), 103–20

(1978) *Conquerors and slaves* (Cambridge)

(1983) *Death and renewal* (Cambridge)

Housman, A.E. (1931) '*Praefanda*' *Hermes* 66, 402–12 (= Housman, *Classical papers*, ed. J. Diggle and F.R.D. Goodyear (Cambridge 1972), 1175–84)

Hudson, Nicola (1989) 'Food in Roman satire' in Susan Braund ed. *Satire and society* (Exeter), 69–88

Humbert, Michel (1972) *Le Remariage à Rome* (Milan)

Hunter, R.L. (1985) *The New Comedy of Greece and Rome* (Cambridge)

Hurst, Henry (1986) 'Area di Santa Maria Antiqua' *BCAR* 111, 470–8

Isager, Signe and Hansen, Mogens Herman *Aspects of Athenian society in the fourth century B.C.* (Odense)

Jocelyn, H.D. (1980) 'On some unnecessarily indecent interpretations of Catullus 2 and 3' *AJP* 101, 421–41

Johnston, David (1988) *The Roman law of trusts* (Oxford)

Jolivet, V. (1987) '*Xerxes togatus*: Lucullus en Campanie' *MEFRA* 99, 823–46

Joly, R. (1956) *Le Thème philosophique des genres de vie dans l'antiquité classique* (Brussels)

Jones, A.H.M. (1960) *Studies in Roman government and law* (Oxford)

Jones, C.P. (1991) 'Dinner-theater' in W.J. Slater ed. *Dining in a classical context* (Ann Arbor), 185–98

Jory, E.J. (1970) 'Associations of actors at Rome' *Hermes* 98, 224–3

Kaser, Max (1956) '*Infamia* und *ignominia* in den römischen Rechtsquellen' *ZSS* 73, 220–78

Kennedy, Duncan (1993) *The arts of love* (Cambridge)

Kiefer, Otto (1933) *Kulturgeschichte Roms unter besonderer Berücksichtigung der römischen Sitten* (Berlin)

Kolendo, Jerzy (1981) 'La répartition des places aux spectacles et la stratification sociale dans l'empire romain: à propos des inscriptions sur les gradins des amphithéâtres et théâtres' *Ktèma* 6, 301–15

BIBLIOGRAPHY

Kroll, Wilhelm (1933) *Die Kultur der Ciceronischen Zeit* (Leipzig)

Kuhn, Thomas S. (1977) *The essential tension* (Chicago)

Lafon, Xavier (1981) 'A propos des villas de la zone de Sperlonga' *MEFRA* 93.1, 297–353

La Rocca, Eugenio (1986) 'Il lusso come espressione di potere' in *Le tranquille dimore degli dei* (Rome), 3–35

Leach, Eleanor W. (1988) *The rhetoric of space* (Princeton)

Lecky, William (1869) *A history of European morals from Augustus to Charlemagne* (London)

Le Goff, Jacques and Schmitt, Jean-Claude eds. (1981) *Le Charivari* (Paris)

Levick, Barbara (1983) 'The *senatus consultum* from Larinum' *JRS* 73, 97–115

(1990) *Claudius* (London)

Liebeschuetz, J.H.W.G. (1979) *Continuity and change in Roman religion* (Oxford)

Lilja, Saara (1982) *Homosexuality in republican and Augustan Rome* (Helsinki)

(1985) 'Seating problems in the Roman theatre and circus' *Arctos* 19, 67–74

Lintott, A.W. (1972) 'Imperial expansion and moral decline in the Roman empire' *Historia* 31, 626–38

Litchfield, Henry W. (1914) 'National *exempla virtutis* in Roman literature' *HSPh* 25, 1–71

Lutz, Cora (1947) 'Musonius Rufus, the Roman Socrates' *YClS* 10, 3–147

Lyne, R.O.A.M. (1980) *The Latin love poets* (Oxford)

MacKendrick, P.L. (1960) *The mute stones speak* (London)

McKeown, J.C. (1979) 'Augustan elegy and mime' *PCPhS* 25, 71–84

MacMullen, Ramsay (1982) 'Roman attitudes to Greek love' *Historia* 31, 484–502

Marshall, A.J. (1990) 'Women on trial before the Roman senate' *EMC* 34, 333–66

Maslakov, G. (1984) 'Valerius Maximus and Roman historiography: a study in the *exempla* tradition' in H. Temporini ed. *ANRW* (Berlin) II 32.1, 437–96

Mattingley, H.B. (1960) 'Naevius and the Metelli' *Historia* 9, 414–39

Maurin, Jean (1983) '*Labor matronalis*: aspects du travail feminin à Rome' in Edmond Lévy ed. *La Femme dans les sociétés antiques* (Strasbourg), 135–55

Mayor, J.E.B. ed. (1893) *Thirteen satires of Juvenal* (London)

Millar, Fergus (1973) 'Triumvirate and principate' *JRS* 63, 50–67

(1977) *The emperor in the Roman world* (London)

Millar, Fergus and Segal, Erich eds. (1984) *Caesar Augustus: seven aspects* (Oxford)

Mommsen, Theodor (1899) *Römisches Strafrecht* (Leipzig)

Morel, Jean-Pierre (1969) 'La *iuventus* et les origines du théâtre romain' *REL* 49, 208–52

Morford, M.P.O. (1968) 'The distortion of the *domus aurea* tradition' *Eranos* 66, 158–79

Nicolet, Claude (1966) *L'Ordre équestre à l'époque républicaine* (Paris)
(1980) *The world of the citizen in republican Rome*, tr. P.S. Falla (London)
(1987) 'Augustus, government and the propertied classes' in Millar and Segal, 89–128
(1991) *Space, geography and politics in the Roman empire*, tr. Hélène Leclerc (Ann Arbor)

Nisbet, R.G.M. ed. (1939) *Cicero de domo sua* (Oxford)
ed. (1961) *Cicero In Pisonem* (Oxford)
(1978) '*Felicitas* at Surrentum (Statius *Silvae* 2.2)' *JRS* 68, 1–11

Nisbet, R.G.M. and Hubbard, Margaret (1978) *A commentary on Horace Odes, book II* (Oxford)

North, John (1979) 'Religious toleration in republican Rome' *PCPhS* 25, 85–103

Oltramare, André (1926) *Les Origines de la diatribe romaine* (Geneva)

Ortner, Sherry B. (1972) 'Is female to male as nature is to culture?' *Feminist Studies* 1, 5–31 (= M.Z. Rosaldo and L. Lamphere eds. *Women, culture and society* (Stanford 1974), 67–88)

Ortner, Sherry B. and Harriet Whitehead (1981) *Sexual meanings: the cultural construction of gender and sexuality* (Cambridge)

Parry, E. St. J. (1862) '*Origines Romae*', or, *tales of early Rome . . . for the use of schools* (London)

Pavlovskis, Zoja (1973) *Man in an artificial landscape* (Leiden)

Pearcy, L.T. (1977) 'Horace's architectural imagery' *Latomus* 36, 772–81

Peristiany, J.G. ed. (1966) *Honour and shame: the values of Mediterranean society* (Chicago)

Petrochilos, Nicholas (1974) *Roman attitudes to the Greeks* (Athens)

Pickard-Cambridge, Arthur (1968) *The dramatic festivals of Athens*, 2nd edn. (Oxford)

Piganiol, André (1923) *Recherches sur les jeux romains* (Strasbourg)

Pitt-Rivers, Julian (1977) *The fate of Shechem* (Cambridge)

Platner, Samuel B. and Ashby, Thomas (1929) *Topographical dictionary of Rome* (London)

Plummer, Kenneth ed. (1981) *The making of the modern homosexual* (London)

Pocock, J.G.A. (1985) *Virtue, commerce and history* (Cambridge)

Pollitt, J.J. (1966) *The art of Rome* (Englewood Cliffs, N.J.)

Pomeroy, Sarah B. (1976) *Goddesses, wives, whores and slaves* (London)

Poster, Mark (1986) 'Foucault and the tyranny of Greece' in David Couzens Hoy ed. *Foucault: a critical reader* (Oxford), 205–20

Price, S.R.F. (1986) 'The future of dreams: from Freud to Artemidorus' *P&P* 113, 3–37

Purcell, Nicholas (1986) 'Livia and the womanhood of Rome' *PCPhS* 32, 78–105
(1987) 'Town in country and country in town' in E.B. MacDougall ed.

Ancient Roman villa gardens (Dumbarton Oaks), 187–203

Raditsa, L.F. (1980) 'Augustus' legislation concerning marriage, procreation, love-affairs and adultery' in H. Temporini ed. *ANRW* (Berlin) II 13, 278–339

Ramage, E.S. (1973) *Urbanitas: ancient sophistication and refinement* (Oklahoma)

Rawson, Beryl ed. (1986) *The family in ancient Rome* (London)

Rawson, Elizabeth (1975) *Cicero, a portrait* (London)

(1976) 'The Ciceronian aristocracy and its properties' in M.I. Finley ed. *Studies in Roman property* (Cambridge), 85–102 (= Rawson 1991: 204–22)

(1978) 'The introduction of logical organisation into Roman prose literature' *PBSR* 46, 12–34 (= Rawson 1991: 324–51)

(1985a) *Intellectual life in the late republic* (London)

(1985b) 'Theatrical life in republican Rome and Italy' *PBSR* 53, 97–113 (= Rawson 1991: 468–87)

(1987a) '*Discrimina ordinum*: the lex Iulia theatralis' *PBSR* 55, 83–114 (= Rawson 1991: 508–45)

(1987b) '*Speciosa locis morataque recte*' in Michael Whitby, Philip Hardie and Mary Whitby eds. *Homo viator: classical studies for John Bramble* (Bristol), 80–8 (= Rawson 1991: 570–81)

(1991) *Roman culture and society* (Oxford)

Reesor, M.E. (1951) *The political theory of the old and middle Stoa* (New York)

Reich, H. (1903) *Der Mimus* (Berlin)

Reynolds, R.W. (1946) 'The adultery mime' *CQ* 40, 77–84

Riccobono, S. (1945) *Acta divi Augusti* (Rome)

Richlin, Amy (1981) 'Some approaches to the sources on adultery at Rome' in Helene B. Foley ed. *Reflections of women in antiquity* (New York), 379–404

(1983) *The garden of Priapus: sexuality and aggression in Roman humour* (New Haven)

(forthcoming) 'Not before homosexuality: the materiality of the *cinaedus* and the Roman law against love between men'

Ricotti, E.S.P. (1982) 'Villa Adriana nei suoi limit e nella sua funzionalità' *Mem. Pont. Accad. Rom. Arch.* 14, 25–55

Rosenstein, Nathan S. (1990) *Imperatores victi: military defeat and aristocratic competition in the middle and late republic* (Berkeley)

Rotondi, G. (1912) *Leges publicae populi Romani* (Milan)

Rousselle, Aline (1983) 'Parole et inspiration: le travail de la voix dans le monde romain' *History and philosophy of the life sciences* 5, 129–57

Rumpf, A. (1950) 'Die Entstehung des römischen Theaters' *MDAI(R)* 3, 40–50

Sahlins, Marshall (1976) *Culture and practical reason* (Chicago)

Saller, Richard (1980) 'Anecdotes as historical evidence for the principate' *G&R* 27, 69–83

(1982) *Personal patronage under the early empire* (Cambridge)

(1984) '*Familia, domus* and the Roman conception of the family' *Phoenix* 38, 336–55

(1991) 'Corporal punishment, authority and obedience in the Roman household' in Beryl Rawson ed. *Marriage, divorce and children in ancient Rome* (Oxford), 144–65

Sauerwein, Ingo (1970) *Die leges sumptuariae als römische Massnahme gegen den Sittenverfall* (Hamburg)

Scheid, John (1981) 'Le délit religieux dans la Rome tardo-républicaine' in *Le Délit religieux dans la cité antique. Collection de l'école française à Rome* 48, 117–71

Schneider, R.M. (1986) *Bunte Barbaren* (Worms)

Schofield, Malcolm (1991) *The Stoic idea of the city* (Cambridge)

Schrijvers, P.H. (1985) *Eine medizinische Erklärung der männlichen Homosexualität* (Amsterdam)

Scott, Kenneth (1933) 'The political propaganda of 44–33 BC' *MAAR* 11, 7–49

Segal, Erich (1987) *Roman laughter*, 2nd edn. (Oxford)

Sekora, John (1977) *Luxury: the concept in western thought from Eden to Smollet* (London)

Seltman, Charles (1956) *Women in antiquity* (London)

Shatzman, Israel (1975) *Senatorial wealth and Roman politics* (Brussels)

Shaw, Brent (1975) 'Debt in Sallust' *Latomus* 34, 187–96

Sherwin-White, A.N. (1967) *Racial prejudice in imperial Rome* (Cambridge)

Sifakis, G.M. (1967) *Studies in the history of Hellenistic drama* (London)

Skutsch, Otto ed. (1985) *The Annals of Quintus Ennius* (Oxford)

Slater, Niall (1985) *Plautus in performance* (Princeton)

Smith, R.E. (1951) 'The law of libel at Rome' *CQ* 1, 169–79

Spruit, J.E. (1966) *De juridische en sociale positie van de romeinse acteurs* (Assen)

Stallybras, Peter and White, Allon (1986) *The politics and poetics of transgression* (London)

Stone, Lawrence (1977) *The family, sex and marriage* (London)

(1984) *An open elite?* (Oxford)

Süss, W. (1910) *Ethos* (Leipzig)

Syme, Ronald (1939) *The Roman revolution* (Oxford)

(1958) *Tacitus* (Oxford)

(1960) 'Bastards in the Roman aristocracy' *PAPhS* 104, 323–7 (= Syme, ed. E. Badian *Roman papers* II (Oxford 1979), 510–17)

(1961) 'Who was Vedius Pollio?' *JRS* 51, 23–30 (= Syme, ed. E. Badian *Roman papers* II (Oxford 1979), 518–29)

(1974) 'The crisis of 2 B.C.' *Bayerische Akademie der Wissenschaften* 7, 3–34 (= Syme, ed. A. Birley *Roman papers* III (Oxford 1984), 912–36)

(1978) *History in Ovid* (Oxford)

(1980) 'No son for Caesar?' *Historia* 29, 422–37 (= Syme, ed. A. Birley, *Roman papers* III (Oxford 1984), 1236–50)

Talbert, R.J.A. (1984) *The senate of imperial Rome* (Princeton)

Tamm, Birgitta (1963) *Auditorium and palatium* (Stockholm)

Tanner, Tony (1979) *Adultery in the novel* (Baltimore)

Tarrant, R.J. (1978) 'Senecan drama and its antecedents' *HSPh* 82, 213–61

Taylor, Lily Ross (1966) *Roman voting assemblies from the Hannibalic wars to the time of Caesar* (Ann Arbor)

Thébert, Yvon (1987) 'Private life and domestic architecture' in Veyne, 312–409

Thibault, J.C. (1964) *The mystery of Ovid's exile* (Berkeley)

Thomas, Keith (1959) 'The double standard' *Journal of the History of Ideas* 20.2, 195–216

Thompson, John B. (1984) *Studies in the theory of ideology* (Oxford)

Tracy, V.A. (1976a) 'The *leno-maritus*' *CJ* 72, 62–4

(1976b) 'Roman dandies and transvestites' *EMC* 20, 60–3

Treggiari, Susan (1969) *Roman freedmen during the late republic* (Oxford)

(1991) *Roman marriage: iusti coniuges from the time of Cicero to the time of Ulpian* (Oxford)

Turner, F.M. (1981) *The Greek heritage in Victorian Britain* (New Haven)

Ucelli, G. (1940) *Le navi di Nemi* (Rome)

Usener, Hermann (1901) 'Italische Volksiustiz' *RhM* 56, 1–28

Versnel, H. (1970) *Triumphus* (Leiden)

Verstraete, B.C. (1980) 'Slavery and the dynamics of male homosexual relationships in ancient Rome' *Journal of Homosexuality* 5.3, 227–36

Veyne, Paul (1961) 'La vie de Trimalchion' *Annales ESC* 16.1, 213–47 (= Veyne 1991: 13–56)

(1978) 'La famille et l'amour à Rome sous le haut-empire romain' *Annales ESC* 33.1 (= Veyne 1991: 88–130)

(1983) 'Le folklore à Rome et les droits de la conscience publique sur la conduite individuelle' *Latomus* 42, 3–30 (= Veyne 1991: 57–87)

(1985) 'Homosexuality in ancient Rome' in Philippe Ariès and André Béjin eds. *Western sexuality: practice and precept in past and present times* tr. Anthony Forster (Oxford), 26–35

(1987) 'The Roman empire' in Veyne ed. 1987, 5–233

(1989) *Roman erotic elegy: love, poetry and the west*, tr. David Pellauer (Chicago)

(1990) *Bread and circuses* tr. Brian Pierce, abridged (London)

(1991) *La Société romaine* (Paris)

Veyne, Paul ed. (1987) *A history of private life* 1: *From pagan Rome to Byzantium*, tr. Arthur Goldhammer (Cambridge, Mass.)

Vickers, Brian (1990) 'Leisure and idleness in the renaissance: the ambivlance of *otium*' part I *Renaissance Studies* 4.1, 1–37

Ville, Georges (1981) *La Gladiature en occident des origines à la mort de Domitien* (Rome)

Vonoyeke, Violaine (1990) *La Prostitution en Grèce et à Rome* (Paris)

de Vos, Mariette (1980) *L'egittomania in pitture e mosaici romano-campani della prima età imperiale* (Leiden)

Wade Richardson, T. (1984) 'Homosexuality in the *Satyricon*' *C&M* 25, 105–27

Wallace-Hadrill, A. (1981) 'Family and inheritance in the Roman marriage laws' *PCPhS* 27, 58–80

(1983) *Suetonius* (London)

(1985) 'Propaganda and dissent? Augustan moral legislation and the love poets' *Klio* 67, 180–4

(1988) 'The social structure of the Roman house' *PBSR* 43, 43–97

(1990) 'Pliny the elder and man's unnatural history' *G&R* 37, 80–96

Ward-Perkins, John (1980) 'The marble trade and its organisation: evidence from Nicomedia' *MAAR* 36, 325–38

Wardman, Alan (1976) *Rome's debt to Greece* (London)

(1982) *Religion and statecraft among the Romans* (London)

Waszink, J.H. (1948) 'Varro, Livy and Tertullian on the history of Roman dramatic art' *VChr* 2, 224–42

Watson, Alan (1975) *The law of the Twelve Tables* (Princeton)

Weeks, Jeffrey (1981) *Sex, politics and society* (London)

Weinstock, Stefan (1971) *Divus Iulius* (Oxford)

Whitehorne, J.E.G. (1969) 'The ambitious builder' *AUMLA* 31, 28–39

Whittaker, C.R. (1989) 'Il povero' in Andrea Giardina ed. *L'uomo romano* (Rome), 299–333

Wiedemann, Thomas (forthcoming 1992/3) *Emperors and gladiators* (London)

Williams, Gordon (1968) *Tradition and originality in Roman poetry* (Oxford)

Winkler, J.J. (1990) *The constraints of desire* (New York)

Wiseman, T.P. (1969) 'The census in the first century B.C.' *JRS* 59, 59–65

(1970) 'The definition of the *eques Romanus* in the late republic and early empire' *Historia* 19, 67–83

(1971) *New men in the Roman senate, 139 B.C. – A.D. 14* (Oxford)

(1979) *Clio's cosmetics: three studies in Greco-Roman literature* (Leicester)

(1983) '*Domi nobiles* and the Roman cultural elite' in *Les 'bourgeoisies' municipales italiennes aux IIe et I^e siècles av. J.C.* (Naples), 299–307

(1984) 'Cybele, Virgil and Augustus' in Tony Woodman and David West eds. *Poetry and politics in the age of Augustus* (Cambridge), 117–28

(1987) '*Conspicui postes tectaque digna deo:* the public image of aristocratic and imperial houses in the late republic and early principate' in *L'urbs: espace urbain et histoire. Collection de l'école française de Rome* 98, 393–413

(1989) 'Roman legend and oral tradition' *JRS* 79, 129–37

Woodman, A.J. (forthcoming) 'Amateur dramatics at the court of Nero: Tacitus *Annals* 15.48–74' in T.J. Luce and A.J. Woodman eds. *Tacitus and the Tacitean tradition* (Princeton)

Wyke, Maria (1989) 'Reading female flesh: *Amores* 3.1' in Averil Cameron ed. *History as text: the writing of ancient history* (London), 111–43

(forthcoming) 'Woman in the mirror: the rhetoric of adornment in the Roman world' in Léonie Archer, Susan Fischler and Maria Wyke eds.

BIBLIOGRAPHY

Illusions of the night: women in ancient societies

Yates, Frances (1966) *The art of memory* (London)

Yavetz, Zwi (1969) *Plebs and princeps* (Oxford)

(1984) 'The *Res gestae* and Augustus' public image' in Millar and Segal, 1-36

Zanker, Paul (1972) *Forum Romanum: die Neugestalt durch Augustus* (Tübingen)

(1987) 'Drei Stadtbilder aus dem augusteischen Rom' in *L'urbs: espace urbain et histoire. Collection de l'école française de Rome* 98, 476–9

(1988) *The Power of images in the age of Augustus*, tr. Alan Shapiro (Ann Arbor)

ed. (1975) *Hellenismus in Mittelitalien* (Göttingen)

Zehnacker, H. (1979) 'Pline l'ancien et l'histoire de la monnaie romaine' *Ktèma* 4, 169–81

(1981) 'Tragédie prétexte et spectacle romain' in *Théâtre et spectacles dans l'antiquité. Actes du colloque de Strasbourg* (Leiden), 31–48

Index locorum

INDEX LOCORUM

Index of subjects and proper names

Printed in Great Britain by
Amazon.co.uk, Ltd.,
Marston Gate.